14.50

D1216883

Imagery
and the Mind
of Stephen Dedalus

Imagery
and the Mind
of Stephen Dedalus

A Computer - Assisted Study
of Joyce's
A Portrait of the Artist as a Young
Man

JOHN B. SMITH

Lewisburg
Bucknell University Press
London and Toronto: Associated University Presses

© 1980 by Associated University Presses, Inc.

Associated University Presses, Inc.
Cranbury, New Jersey 08512

Associated University Presses
Magdalen House
136–148 Tooley Street
London SE1 2TT, England

Associated University Presses
Toronto M5E 1A7, Canada

Library of Congress Cataloging in Publication Data

Smith, John Bristow, 1940–
    Imagery and the mind of Stephen Dedalus.
    Bibliography: p.
    Includes index.
    1. Joyce, James, 1882–1941. A portrait of the artist as a young man. 2. Joyce, James, 1882–1941—Style.
I. Title. 67 / 980
PR6019.09P6486   823'.9'12   78-17505
ISBN 0-8387-1758-6

PRINTED IN THE UNITED STATES OF AMERICA

Contents

Acknowledgments

I wish to thank the following for permission to quote from published works:

The Executors of the James Joyce Estate, for permission to quote from *A Portrait of the Artist as a Young Man*. (Rights throughout the British Commonwealth & Empire, excluding Canada.)

The (British) Society of Authors as the literary representative of the Estate of James Joyce for permission to quote from *A Portrait of the Artist as a Young Man*. (English language rights.)

For my Family

Imagery
and the Mind
of Stephen Dedalus

1

Introduction

The reader of *A Portrait of the Artist as a Young Man* today is likely to find little in the way of subject matter or form that is startling or revolutionary. Such was not the case in 1916. When the novel was first published, many were taken aback by its frank treatment of an adolescent's world of fantasy and the intense concentration on the experiences of a single character consisting of a series of portraitlike scenes often separated in time by months and even years but presented, seemingly, without transitions. Also unusual in a work of prose was the poetic use of imagery to provide structural and thematic continuity. But with time and developments in literary awareness, the reader of today may find Joyce's last two works difficult but approachable and *Portrait*, on first reading, fairly conventional.

Part of the reason for this change in the reader's understanding of literature lies with the large number of critical essays that have sought to interpret such works. Since *Portrait* is concerned with the developing personality of "the artist," Stephen Dedalus, it is not surprising that many of these early critical studies of Joyce's novel concentrated on

Stephen's sensual awareness. By their number as well as their arguments they have shown the importance of imagery for an understanding of the novel. However, most of these early studies deal with general characteristics of particular thematic groups of images.[1] Since the entire novel is developed from the point of view of Stephen's experiences, images are highly interrelated and often change in their connotations as Stephen grows older. Studies of isolated clusters of images usually do not consider this interaction or take into account changes in implication as the novel progresses. Indeed, to do so would mean that a scholar would need access to each occurrence of every image and, second, be able to "visualize" how this mass of data is structured. Just the clerical work of such a venture has made it impractical; however, with the availability of the modern, high-speed computer to the literary critic, at least the clerical stumbling block has been removed. By using the computer I have tried to study the imagery of *Portrait* in a comprehensive manner that has been impractical before now. Since this approach to literary analysis is relatively new and perhaps alien to the discipline, I have stated as thoroughly as I can my literary assumptions at each step of the analysis. The remainder of this introductory chapter attempts to locate the context of this study within traditional literary criticism and to develop the thesis and point of view to be used.

The process of images changing in their associative links has been discussed briefly by William York Tindall in his *Reader's Guide to James Joyce,* under the term *recurrent image:*

Unobtrusive, escaping notice at first appearance and even at second or third, it gains power through reappearance. Bringing meaning from one place to another, it deposits some there and,

acquiring more, brings it along. . . . Rarely essential, this car-
rier of meaning helps other agents out, adding richness, depth,
and immediacy to what we get from character and plot. The
structural value of recurrent images is clear; for, in winding in
and out, they knit the whole together. Escaping the notice of
a casual reader, they affect him beneath the level of notice.
The alert reader, preferring to know what affects him, finds
pleasure in its discovery.[2]

Tindall illustrates his thesis of dynamic associative development by discussing several important image groups. *Water,*
he notes, which is fundamentally repulsive in the early
pages of *Portrait,* begins to expand and change in its implications with the image of water dripping into the "brimming bowl" at the end of Chapter I.

Although Tindall states that "these images are not signs
with one fixed meaning," he sometimes emphasizes a single
association to the extent that the assignment seems fixed or
static. For example, all other implications of the *rose* image
are inundated by the association he sees between it and
Dante's rose symbol:

Dante's rose, multifloriate but not overblown, unites rose and
woman. Incapable as yet of apprehending this union, Stephen
approaches it in *A Portrait* on hearing the servant singing
"Rosie O'Grady" in her kitchen:

For I love sweet Rosie O'Grady
And Rosie O'Grady loves me.

"There's real love," says Cranly. "Do you know what the words
mean?" "I want to see Rosie first," says Stephen; but, escaping
him, she remains to be seen until the end of *Ulysses.* There
Stephen approximates Dante's vision, but here, however
roseate, Stephen's vision is pathetic from one point of view,
comic from another. Overblown prose is his nearest equivalent
for the green rose of his child's garden. (Connolly, pp. 91–92)

Similarly, images of females are generalized to the extent that they, too, seem static and restricted:

> Since most of the girls in A Portrait approximate or suggest the Virgin in one way or another, she seems as central in the book as in the mind of Stephen, prefect of her sodality and private adorer. Mary is woman to him and woman is Mary, ideal, unattainable. Eileen of the cool, white hands, his first best girl . . . is unattainable because Protestant; but even she is the "Tower of Ivory" from the Virgin's litany. (Connolly, p. 92)

The concept of images as dynamic, accumulating connotations and complexities of meaning, suggests that they must be embedded in some mind, presumably that of the protagonist. Tindall does not develop this implied relation between patterns of images and the structure of mind; however, Hugh Kenner does in his discussion of Joyce's use of language in *Portrait*:

> Joyce as an artist is working in language, but his material is psychology. His linguistic symbols represent psychological experiences detached from their context and put in motion in the new context of the printed page.[3]

The context of words on the page is similar to the mental context of the protagonist, but the links among words or images that Kenner sees are static as indicated by the word *crystallize* in the following passage:

> These verbal leitmotivs are a technique for indicating simultaneously the alignment of ideas in the protagonist's mind and the motivation of such alignment; the emotions which Joyce's dramatic context attaches to the key-words combine, interact, and crystallize as the language indicates. (Connolly, p. 38)

This attitude results in comprehensive statements which,

while helpful and true in general, sometimes miss subtle changes in associations. For example, he associates *fire* simply with sin.[4] This is true in Chapter III of *Portrait*, but *fire* has a radically different set of associations in the first chapter.

I wish to develop a thesis, combining aspects of both Tindall's and Kenner's viewpoints, arguing that the dynamic patterns of associations among images on the page reflect the developing structure of Stephen's mind. Support for this position can be found in Stephen's aesthetic theory developed in Chapter V of the novel. His ideas are based on a sentence from Aquinas which he translates as follows: "Three things are needed for beauty, wholeness, harmony, and radiance." [5] Wholeness he identifies with *integritas:*

> An esthetic image is presented to us either in space or in time. What is audible is presented in time, what is visible is presented in space. But, temporal or spatial, the esthetic image is first luminously apprehended as self-bounded and self-contained upon the immeasurable background of space or time which is not it. You apprehend it as *one* thing. You see is as one whole. You apprehend its wholeness. That is *integritas.* (p. 212)

Several points may be noted concerning this passage. First, Stephen's "aesthetic image" is closely related to the act of apprehension itself. Second, there is a finely drawn distinction between the active and passive participation of the mind in the perceptual act. Stephen states that the image "is presented"; thus the mind receives the initial form of the image. However, the mind's active participation is indicated in the process of "bounding" or "distinguishing" the individual sense impression. That is, the aesthetic image can be distinguished from the sensory data that flood the mind only by paring away all that is not the image. By focusing itself upon the one particular cluster of sensory impressions that constitute the aesthetic image, the mind is both receptive to and dependent upon a reality external to itself, but it can know and comprehend that reality only through selectivity and delineation.

The second phase of Stephen's discussion of the aesthetic image concerns harmony or *consonantia:*

> —Then said Stephen, you pass from point to point, led by its formal lines; you apprehend it as balanced part against part within its limits; you feel the rhythm of its structure. In other words the synthesis of immediate perception is followed by the analysis of apprehension. Having first felt that it is *one* thing you feel now that it is a thing. You apprehend it as complex, multiple, divisible, separable, made up of its parts, the result of its parts and their sum, harmonious. That is *consonantia.* (p. 212)

As Stephen points out, this is the analytic stage of apprehension. The impression is divided into its parts, and the perceiver sets about discovering relationships: part to part, part to aggregate of parts, and part to the whole. The question arises, does this harmony exist in the physical world or does it exist only in the mind of the perceiver? If the latter is true, there is the further problem of discovering the relation between the "harmony" within subjective apprehension and that within the phenomenal world. If we argue that the harmony exists solely within the mind, solipsism raises its ugly head; if we assume that harmony exists in the physical world, we are led to the conclusion that we can have absolute knowledge of the physical object. Stephen does not solve the problem in this statement, but he hints at the solution by emphasizing the affective dimension of the experience with the verb *feel:* "Having first felt that it is one thing you now feel that it is a thing." That "thing" that is being analyzed is, of course, the datum of apprehension that has already become part of the subjective state through sensory experience. Thus analysis is a part of the internal, subjective world of experience. The relation between this experience and the physical world that saves the theory from solipsism is developed in the third discussion, concerning *claritas*.

The discussion of *claritas* contains two major parts. First, Stephen states what he does not mean by the term; then he gives a precise statement of what he does mean. The first half of this statement has been largely ignored, often with unfortunate results. For example, Frank Kermode extracts from Stephen's theory his own working definition of the romantic image; in discussing Stephen's conversation with Lynch, Kermode notes:

> The main topic is, in fact, that "esthetic image" explained in Thomist language by Stephen Dedalus in the *Portrait of the Artist as a Young Man:* it is for him that beauty which has the three attributes of integrity, consonance and clarity; which is "apprehended as one thing . . . self-abounded and self-contained upon the immeasurable background of space or time which is not it"; apprehended in its *quidditas* by the artist whose mind is arrested in "a luminous stasis of esthetic pleasure." [6]

Kermode rightly sees Joyce's *image* as growing out of the romantic tradition, but he goes too far when he states that Joyce's image is the equivalent of Pater's vision[7] and that the "symbol of the French is . . . the Romantic Image writ large and given more elaborate metaphysical and magical support." [8] This interpretation contradicts what Stephen says. If we take Arthur Symons's definitions of symbol and symbolism, as Joyce probably did and Kermode explicitly

does, we see a clearly idealistic emphasis. Symons borrows
Carlyle's definition of symbol:

> In the Symbol proper, what we can call a Symbol, there is
> ever more or less distinctly and directly, some embodiment
> and revelation of the Infinite; the Infinite is made to blend
> itself with the Finite, to stand visible, and as it were, attain-
> able there.[9]

By symbolism Symons means "a literature in which the
visible world is no longer a reality, and the unseen world no
longer a dream." [10] Pater in similar fashion denies the "fruits
of experience" in favor of an exaltation of experience itself:
"To burn always with this hard, gem-like flame, to maintain
this ecstasy, is success in life." [11] The result is a world view
in which literature becomes a universal, replacing religion:

> Some spend this interval in listlessness, some in high passions,
> the wisest, at least among "the children of this world," in
> art and song. For our one chance lies in expanding that in-
> terval, in getting as many pulsations as possible into the given
> time. Great passions may give us this quickened sense of life,
> ecstasy and sorrow of love, the various forms of enthusiastic
> activity, disinterested or otherwise, which comes naturally to
> many of us. Only be sure it is passion—that it does yield you
> this fruit of a quickened, multiplied consciousness. Of such
> wisdom, the poetic passion, the desire of beauty, the love of
> art for its own sake, has most. The art comes to you proposing
> frankly to give nothing but the highest quality to your
> moments as they pass, and simply for those moments' sake.[12]

Stephen rejects both of these views:

> It [Thomas's phrase] would lead you to believe that he had
> in mind symbolism or idealism, the supreme quality of beauty
> being a light from some other world, the idea of which the
> matter is but the shadow, the reality of which it is but the

symbol. I thought he might mean that *claritas* is the artistic discovery and representation of the divine purpose in anything or a force of generalization which would make the esthetic image a universal one, make it outshine its proper conditions. But that is literary talk. I understand it so. (p. 213)

The term *literary talk* in this context indicates that Stephen considers both of these interpretations of *claritas* insubstantial and invalid.

Having denied the restrictiveness of transcendental idealism on the one hand and the diffusiveness of a completely autonomous art on the other, Stephen defines what he does mean by the term: [13]

When you have apprehended that basket as one thing and have then analysed it according to its form and apprehended it as a thing you make the only synthesis which is logically and esthetically permissible. You see that it is that thing which it is and no other thing.. The radiance of which he speaks is the scholastic *quidditas*, the *whatness* of a thing. This supreme quality is felt by the artist when the esthetic image is first conceived in his imagination. The mind in that mysterious instant Shelley likened beautifully to a fading coal. The instant wherein that supreme quality of beauty, the clear radiance of the esthetic image, is apprehended luminously by the mind which has been arrested by its wholeness and fascinated by its harmony is the luminous silent stasis of esthetic pleasure, a spiritual state very like Galvani, using a phrase almost as beautiful as Shelley's, called the enchantment of the heart. (p. 213)

Before considering the meaning of the statement, I wish to look at several of the images present. *Radiance,* the *glow of the fading coal,* the *inchantment of heart* produced in the frog's heart by Galvani's electrical stimulus all imply transfer—transfer of light or energy—resulting in some emotional or physical stimulation in the receiver. Thus the terms of the statement emphasize that the image originates in the physical world and is transmitted to the individual perceiver. This point, implied in *Portrait,* is part of the actual definition of *claritas* found in *Stephen Hero:*

> When the relation of the parts is exquisite, when the parts are adjusted to the special point, we recognize that it is *that* thing which it is. Its soul, its whatness, leaps to us from the vestment of its appearance. The soul of the commonest object, the structure of which is so adjusted, seems to us radiant. The object achieves its epiphany.[14]

There, Stephen indicates that the thing itself achieves epiphany; in *Portrait,* the empathic projection of feeling or sensation is recognized as an aspect of the perceiver and the emotion involved in the experience is seen to be his: "This supreme quality is felt by the artist." Thus, a great part of the emotion present involves the affective union of perceiver and that which is perceived. As we would expect, this union is not physical, but psychological.

The key term in the passage from *Stephen Hero* is *synthesis.* Once the aesthetic image has been isolated from all that is not it—just as Stephen's definition of image is distinguished first from what it is not—and analyzed into components, it must be synthesized into some larger whole. The nature of that whole can be inferred from Stephen's qualified description of the process of synthesis: " the only synthesis which is logically and esthetically permissible." The context of the logical and aesthetic faculties is, of course, the mind of the perceiver. Thus, the parts of the experience must "fit" into a pattern or structure that exists within the mind and that is "natural" or pleasing to that mind—that is, the associative links among the components of the image are merged with the vastly broader and more complex associative structure of the mind. It is not necessary that this contextual structure of the mind already embody the links inherent within the image; in fact, those links may be formed in the epiphanic experience itself. What is important is the realization of the validity of the structure both internally (in the subjective context) and externally (in the object perceived). A. D. Hope uses an analogy for this experience that is most helpful:

> If we take the metaphor of the traveller pausing on the hill top and surveying the landscape before him with the help of a map it may be possible to give some idea of the nature of the conception that underlies Joyce's description of *claritas*. If we imagine the map as in the traveller's mind and as the work of his mind, such that instead of the formal signs of roads, houses, fields and hills the mind has constructed a map-picture, we shall have something like the phantasma, or in the case under discussion, the esthetic image. We can further imagine the map-picture to be a transparent one such that when it is held between the intellectual eye and the landscape the traveller not only perceives the landscape endowed with its formal meaning, he is also able to observe the exact correspondence of the details of the map with the details of the landscape before him. He becomes aware of the truth of his mental work.[15]

Although the map or model is within the mind of the perceiver, it is subject to confirmation. When it is seen to fit, there follows a sense that there exists in the physical world some embodiment of the perceiver's mental structure. In *Stephen Hero*, Stephen indicated that this breaking down of the barrier is actual—that the image itself has the epiphany —and the viewer somehow participates in the experience; in *Portrait*, such actual union is denied and the whole theory is stated in terms of the perceiver's psychology.

Stephen does not approach directly the problem of the relation between inner and outer, perceiver and perceived;

however, his statements strongly suggest the distinction that Whitehead makes between the subjective and objective modes of experience. Subject and object, Whitehead states, are relative terms:

> An occasion is a subject in respect to its special activity concerning an object; and anything is an object in respect to its provocation of some special activity within a subject.[16]

He continues:

> The process of experiencing is constituted by the reception of entities, whose being is antecedent to that process, into the complex fact which is that process itself. These antecedent entities, thus received as factors into the process of experiencing, are termed "objects" for that experiential occasion. Thus primarily the term "object" expresses the relation of the entity, thus denoted, to one or more occasions of experiencing.[17]

The object, then, is an object only by virtue of the fact that it is a datum apprehended by a subject. Knowledge is defined across an interface, but it is the phenomenal interface between "subjective experience" and "objective experience" —not the literal, physical interface between physical world and epidermis. Whitehead summarizes:

> All knowledge is conscious discrimination of objects experienced. But this conscious discrimination, which is knowledge, is nothing more than an additional factor in the subjective form of the interplay of subject and object.[18]

He goes on to discuss the term *experience:*

> The process of experiencing is constituted by the reception of objects into the unity of the complex occasion which is the process itself. The process creates itself, but it does not

create the objects which it receives as factors in its own nature.[19]

Thus, the subjective state is active relative to the objective datum, but the entire complex is dependent upon some ultimate external reference. Knowledge, which develops from the organic interplay of these two modes, is subject to development, augmentation, and correction within the flux of the individual's experience.

Whitehead's object corresponds to Stephen's image of sensory data. It is experienced by the perceiver (objective experience) and becomes part of the subjective context (subjective experience). When the image is complex and when the mind's associative patterns have many ramifications, Stephen suggests that there will be an apparent dissolution of the barrier between inner and outer. While not possible physically, dissolution is possible psychologically. In cases of extreme emotional arousal, the individual may *experience* a fusion of the objective and subjective components such that the interface disappears in the process. He *senses* a continuity between his experience of self and his experience of his environment. He seeks and finds an embodiment of himself in his experience of physical reality. But such union occurs between internal modes of perception, not across actual, physical distances. This interpretation, while not stated by Stephen, is consistent with both the general formulation of his aesthetic within terms of his model of perception and his denial of mystical union with physical reality.

Neither Stephen's discussion of *claritas* nor Hope's analogy includes the affective dimension of the experience. In the moment of affirmation, the individual senses or experiences a continuum between the thing perceived and himself. This continuum, as we have seen, exists across the interface between the subjective and objective levels of experience, but the experience carries with it the illusion of actual union. Clearly the emotional level will not be the same for all moments of apprehension. While all human perception necessarily involves an affective dimension, in many of our experiences this dimension goes almost unnoticed. However, when the "harmony" or structure of components is defined in a way that is radically different from previous patterns in the mind, the individual experiences what Joyce in *Stephen Hero* calls "epiphanal joy" distinguishing the aesthetic image at epiphanic moments from the image involved in all acts of apprehension. Seen in this way, the epiphany is not a revelation of truth from some external or ideal realm, nor is it simply the individual's impassioned projection of his hopes upon the external; it is a fusion of objective experience and subjective experience, generating a substantial realignment of the relations among the images within the perceiver's mind.[20] The latter are moments that Stephen called moments of "luminous, silent stasis," which are infused with "epiphanal joy." The former constitutes the absorption of sensory data at a level such that the individual may be hardly aware of the process. These two levels of experience, however, are not completely independent. The epiphanic image is merely more complex in its structure of associations: more diverse —perhaps opposite—strains are brought into a harmonious relationship. The epiphanic perceptual experience is different from everyday perception in degree, not kind. It contains a wider range of components held by the mind in a particular moment. Thus, there is a quantitative relation between aesthetic images of epiphanic intensity and the images of ordinary experience that flood the mind at all times. As the individual becomes more and more aware of objective experience, he becomes emotionally stimulated and hence more receptive; the process builds until the experience either subsides or culminates in epiphany. We would suspect that not all epiphanies carry the same intensity: some embody more facets of experience than others. But the most important implication is that there is a direct, quantitative relation between epiphanic image and the image of ordinary perception.

This last point has interesting implications for literary analysis as well as for aesthetic or psychological theory. There has long been disagreement among critics as to what constitutes an image within a work of literature. At one extreme, Frank Kermode takes as his definition of image Stephen's definition of aesthetic image of epiphanic intensity such that a novel like *Portrait* may contain only a few dozen "images" of this kind. At the other extreme, Caroline Spurgeon uses the term to refer to

> [a] kind of simile, as well as every kind of what is really every compressed metaphor . . . connoting any and every imaginative picture or other experience, drawn in every kind of way, which may have come to the poet, not only through any of his senses, but through his mind and emotions as well, and which he uses, in the forms of simile and metaphor in their widest sense, for analogy.[21]

This use of the term, denoting all sensory experiences, corresponds to the image of immediate, everyday perception discussed above. Just as differences between levels of psychological experiences were resolved quantitatively, so the differences between these two literary terms can be resolved quantitatively within the text. Before doing this and stating the major thesis, however, I wish to summarize the implications of the psychological theory developed so far stated as a model of mind and then show how this model relates to the text of the novel.

A clear distinction between objective and subjective modes of experience has been seen above. The idea of objective experience assumes an ultimate physical reality, but this reality cannot be approached directly: all knowledge of it must come through the sensory mechanisms. The stimuli from these mechanisms when they enter the mind constitute the objective experience. On the "other side" lies the subjective experience. It is composed of several different facets. There is a clearly conscious level of awareness that contains consciously known associations among experiences, the logical faculty, and certain language components. Below this lies the subconscious, which contains much more complex associative links between past experiences and current image. The border between these two subjective levels, however, is not distinct. For example, in the last two chapters of *Portrait* the image of sea, with strands of seaweed coming up from unseen depths into ever lighter levels of water, becomes a major image of mind with the strands of seaweed connoting associative patterns among images. Permeating all levels of the subjective, then, are strands of associations that exist *de facto* or from experience. The most closely analogous relation is that of the arbitrary cultural association between word and meaning. Thus, it is "language" that permeates this entire complex and that most vividly embodies and reveals its organization and structure.

The interface between objective experience and the subjective continuum is the phenomenal level of experience, and it is in this domain that the image exists. As the person becomes more and more aware of the image components existing at this interface, he directs more and more attention to the examination or analysis of the components of objective experience. The more this is done, the more aware he becomes. The process is helical: as more and more images—

facets of experience—are brought together into a single experience, they are seen to conform to a larger, more complex pattern. When the ultimate fusion takes place, there is a great emotional response—epiphanic joy—such that the individual senses a realization or embodiment of himself within his experience of the physical world. This produces a sense of continuity between himself and the physical universe. What is actually happening, we have seen, is that the objective and subjective modes of experience momentarily fuse. It is this important point that keeps Stephen's aesthetics from collapsing into suggesting mystical union with physical reality. In this moment the complex of associations existing within the phenomenal dimension of experience is seen to conform with the more comprehensive pattern of the subjective state. This fusion is often marked by stronger reinforcement of relations among images previously linked as "opposites" or by totally "new" linkings. The result is a marked change in the composition of the personality or mind. The personality is in a sense a "different," more aware, more comprehensive structure than before. Apparently qualitative changes in personality are produced by experiences that are actually quantitatively different from "ordinary" experiences.

So far, this discussion has concentrated on the psychological aspects of Stephen's definition of image. While Stephen emphasizes this dimension, he indicates that it is the image that links the artist with his audience: "The image, it is clear, must be set between the mind or senses of the artist himself and the mind or senses of others" (p. 213). In the case of an autobiographical novel such as *Portrait*, we can interject in front of the artist's mind the fictive mind of Stephen and thus expect the image to link Stephen's mind with that of the reader. Consequently, we would expect concentrations in the text of images of varying connotations to be strongly affective in two directions—that is, these passages should correspond to the moments of major development in Stephen's personality (as suggested by the psychological aspects of his theory) but these passages should also be important in the reader's response to the novel as a work of art. The latter effect may be termed the aesthetic use of imagery. Although to prove or argue the affective quality of a work is impossible, I shall point out passages that seem to display imagery used in this way. The other side of the proposition can be handled more formally. That is, there should be a clear relation between Stephen's epiphanies, those climactic moments of experience which mark a fundamental change in personality, and the concentrations in the text of images of sensory impression as defined by Caroline Spurgeon.

These propositions may be summarized in the following hypothesis. There is a quantitative relation between the number of sensory images present in a section of text and the epiphanic moments. Those moments of realignment of associations of experience will be accompanied by a build-up in the density of important images. Second, since the personality of Stephen is in a sense reshaped at those moments, we can trace the development of his mind by first establishing the patterns of associations among images and then noting how these alignments are altered at epiphanic moments. Since the entire narrative concerns either Stephen's thoughts or the action, events, or physical objects around him, we may infer that images presented close to one another in the narrative line are near one another in Stephen's experience. Thus, images that occur close together in a section of text are very likely associated in Stephen's mind.

In discussing Joyce's aesthetic use of imagery, I shall concentrate on its structural role in the novel. Often entire scenes are organized or held together by repetition of image groups. In other instances, continuity is provided between scenes by the imagery, while on a larger scale, Joyce modulates the entire density of imagery rhythmically in chapter-long sections of text.

Formally, I shall consider an image any word or phrase with a sensuous or thematic aspect.[22] Included are all references to colors, odors, tastes, etcetera. A statement given a distinctly auditory quality—by a descriptive verb such as *shouted*—would be considered an image. I regard the motif "soft, grey air" as being composed of three distinct images —*soft, grey,* and *air*—that happen to be combined in some instances for thematic purposes. Words such as *God, sacrament,* and *pure,* which have limited sensory value but are known to function thematically, will also be included in the list of images; however, most themes will be demonstrated, not assumed.

To make this analysis as comprehensive as possible I shall use a large high-speed computer. Major attention will be given to those images which cluster around the larger images or epiphanic moments. To determine the evolution of associations among these images, we must note the environments of large numbers of images in the novel. This the computer can facilitate. It is not to be assumed that the computer has just "spilled out" the results. The computer does "look-up" tasks, produces graphs and tables for reference and demonstration, and in general carries out exhaustively the instructions and procedures provided. Responsibility for the interpretation of this material must lie with the author.

Because of the inherent linearity of the approach, the

major portion of this discussion will consist of five chapters, one devoted to the development of imagery patterns for each chapter of *Portrait*. A final summary of the major findings of this study will be made in the conclusion. Following this are a series of appendixes. The first describes computer techniques and defines terms such as *richness of imagery, statistical importance of an image,* and *weighed volume of imagery* for a section of text. A number of lists, charts, and graphs referenced in the discussion follow Appendix A.

2
Richness of Imagery

To demonstrate that the moments of epiphanic change for Stephen are related directly to the richness of his sensual experience as reflected in the density of imagery in the text, I developed a model for what might be termed *richness of imagery*. The model, defined in detail in the appendix, assumes that richness of imagery in the text is based upon both the number of images in a passage and some measure of importance for the particular images present. I further assumed that *in general* images that occur more frequently in *Portrait* tend to carry more weight than less frequent ones. This assumption may not be justified in other works; for example, in *Moby Dick* the ubiquitous *sea* imagery might play havoc with this model. But for *Portrait* this seems a reasonable assumption.

When applied to the novel, the model produces a "value" indicative of richness of imagery for each five-hundred-word section of text (five hundred words amounts to a little over one page of text in the standard Viking edition). These values are plotted on the graphs that follow. The reader may visualize the novel as "beginning" on the left and running as a continuous string of words toward the right.

The pattern of richness of imagery will be examined in detail in the discussion of the individual chapters of *Portrait;* however, the episodes that reveal themselves as richest in important sensual detail are the following:

Chapter I. 1. Stephen's fevered dreams the night before and during his stay in the infirmary resulting from his fall in the ditch.
2. The pandybat episode.
II. 3. The scene with the prostitute.
III. 4. The sermon on Death.
5. Stephen's imaginative union with Emma and the Virgin Mary.
6. The sermons on Hell.
7. The scene in Stephen's room following the retreat and his nightmare of the goatish creature.
8. The confessional scene.
IV. 9. The scene on the beach.
V. 10. Stephen imagines the yellow ivy on the wall.
11. The dream and early stages of the composition of the villanelle.
12. The villanelle.
13. The scene in which Stephen sees the birds and speculates on augury and his future.
14. Stephen's imaginative reflection on the nature of language.

Clearly, these are the experiences that mark major changes in the development of Stephen's personality, as predicted by the consideration of the aesthetic theory in the preceding chapter. In the chapters that follow I shall try to point out the very rich structural and thematic use of imagery in the novel and the changing patterns of association within Stephen's mind that occur in these particular scenes. The second part of the thesis will be demonstrated in these extended discussions.

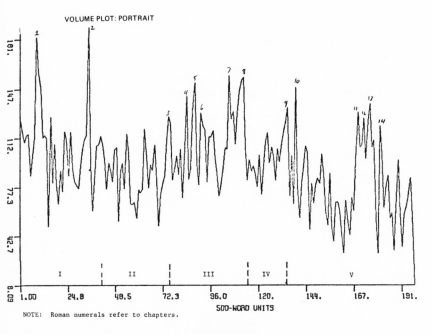

Figure 2.1

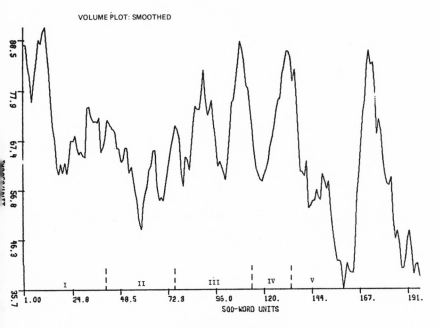

Figure 2. 2

CHAPTER I: POINTS OF INTEREST

A :   Stephen's illness at Clongowes
B :   Dialogue with Athy in infirmary
C :   Pandybat episode

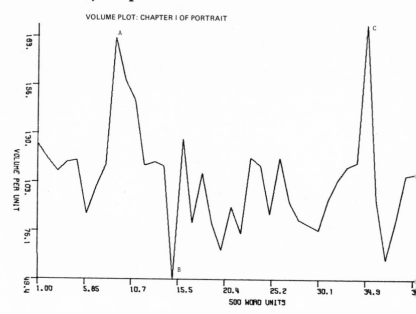

Figure 2.3

CHAPTER II: POINTS OF INTEREST

A : Stephen's explorations of Dublin
B : Stephen's attempt to write a poem for "E———C———"
C : Stephen leaves the school and goes to meet Heron
D : Stephen's defense of Byron
E : The train ride to Cork
F : His father's public denunciation of him
G : Scene with the prostitute

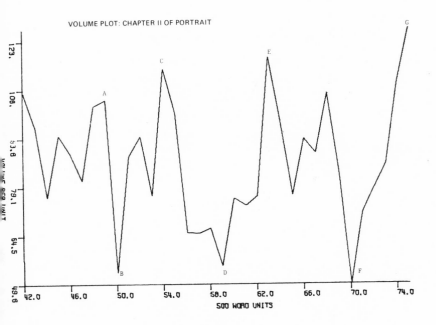

Figure 2.4

CHAPTER III: POINTS OF INTEREST

A: Outline of retreat
B: Sermon on Death
C: Sermon on Judgment, list of legal terms
D: Imaginative union with Emma and Virgin Mary
E: General remarks by preacher
F: Physical description of Hell
G: Language of tormentors in Hell
H: Stephen's reveries
I: Psychological description of Hell
J: Scene in Stephen's room, ensuing dream
K: Walk through streets
L: Confessional scene

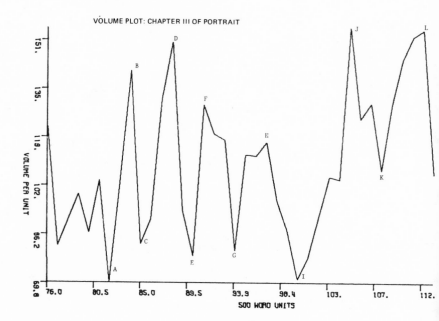

Figure 2.5

CHAPTER IV: POINTS OF INTEREST

A: Thoughts of Clongowes, small talk
B: Leaves priest, images of physical world
C: Indecision over joining Order
D: Phrase, "A day of dappled seaborne clouds"
E: Scene with girl on the beach

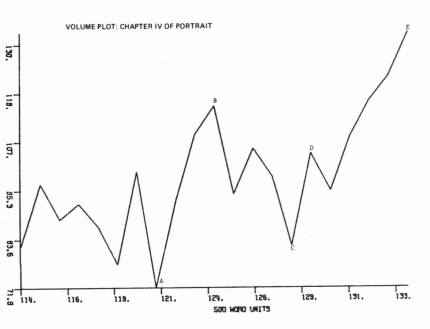

Figure 2.6

CHAPTER V: POINTS OF INTEREST

A: Yellow, whining ivy
B: Conversation and development of aesthetic
C: Villanelle
D: Stephen watches birds, thinks of vocation
E: Cranly called "ballocks"
F: Stephen's imagination
G: Walk with Cranly
H: Rosie O'Grady
I: Diary

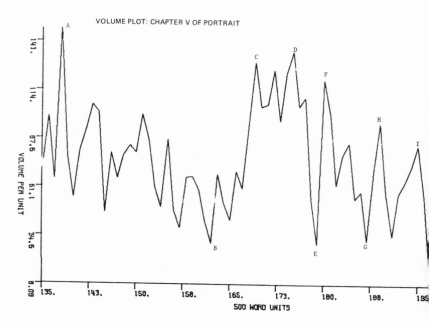

Figure 2.7

3
Analysis of Chapter I

Chapter I of *Portrait* consists of four major sections: a collection of earliest memories; Stephen's first months at Clongowes; his homecoming and the family dinner during Christmas break; and, finally, the events at Clongowes surrounding the pandybat episode. For convenience, I shall refer to these individual sections by number: 1.1—1.4. The discussion of imagery will generally move linearly through each of the four sections; however, individual images often demand comparative examinations of earlier and later occurrences. To show that the pandybat episode is one of the most important epiphanies of the novel, I shall pause between sections 1.3 and 1.4 to bring a number of image clusters up to date.

Section 1.1,, consisting of only slightly more than three hundred words, is by far the shortest section of Chapter I; but in many respects it is an introduction or overture to the chapter and the novel as a whole. On first examination the piece appears a rather disjointed set of Stephen's earliest memories. However, the images that appear in this section are among the most important ones in the chapter. Some of the major motifs introduced here are: *name, father, rose, green, red, water, warm, cold, bird,* and *eyes.* In fact, if a

comparison is made of the images of this very rich section—
some seventy-four images in only a few more than three
hundred words—with the list of the ten most frequent
images of the chapter, six of them appear:

Chapter I	Section 1.1
father	father
Dedalus	
hand	
eye	eye
face	face
prefect	
day	day
name	name
cold	cold[1]
God	

The imagery of section 1.1 is representative of the chapter
in ways other than these.

It is well known that Joyce gives greater attention to
the nonvisual senses than most writers. In this brief section
his imagery appeals to all five senses. The three *songs* and
the *clapping* of Uncle Charles and Dante are among the
auditory images present. The *wet bed* that is first warm and
then cold is tactile while Betty Beyrne's *lemon platt* and
the "cahou" are gustatory. The smell of the oil sheet and
the odors Stephen associates with his father are olfactory.
And, of course, there are numerous visual images: the *red*
and *green* brushes of Dante are two of the more obviously
important ones. Here, as well as in 1.2 and subsequent sections, Joyce leads the reader into a scene through groups of
images appealing to a variety of senses, thereby giving the
scene great immediacy.

This apparently unconnected set of remembrances is far
from structureless. In fact, the section divides into three

distinct groups of memories, approximately equal in length.
The first consists of the following passage :

> Once upon a time and a very good time it was there was
> a *moocow* coming down along the *road* and this *moocow* that
> was coming down along the *road* met a nicens little boy
> named *baby tuckoo.* . . .
>
> His *father* told him that *story:* his *father* looked at him
> through a *glass:* he had a *hairy face.*
>
> He was *baby tuckoo.* The *moocow* came down the *road*
> where Betty Byrne lived: she sold *lemon platt.*
>
>> O, the wild *rose blossoms*
>> On the little *green* place.
>
> He sang that *song.* That was his *song.*
>
>> O, the *green wothe botheth.*   (p. 7)

The italicized words are the words that I consider images
in the passage. The events within the narrative have no
clear temporal organization and one might be hard pressed
to justify the inclusion of these specific memories as opposed to a variety of others that might have been used.
However, the passage does have a definite structure carried
by the imagery. The individual images are presented in a
pattern such that we can trace exactly the associative links
between them. These links, most apparent to the reader in
terms of contiguity within the narrative line, represent patterns of associations within Stephen's mind. It is impossible
to explain them causally, but they do exist and can be
traced.

The chain of associations is relatively complex and cannot be developed all at once. For this reason, the narrative
often continues down one "path" of images for several steps
before going back to pick up a different association. This

process is obvious with regard to road, which Joyce traces through baby tuckoo and father, before finally establishing a link between the name *baby tuckoo* and Stephen's identity; he then goes back to road picking up the association with Betty Byrne and develops that "branch" of memories.

Another of the ways images are associated in Stephen's mind is evident in the matter of his song. Much has been made of the "green wothe." Barbara Seward takes the passage to be indicative of Stephen's "incipient creativity" and "by positing a green rose he is creating in his imagination that which does not exist elsewhere." But while the "green wothe" may

Figure 3.1

reflect the fundamental nature of his creativity, the act in this form is undeveloped. Stephen is not creating in his imagination that which does not exist elsewhere; he is merely rearranging what is already there in his subjective experience, for example, the words *wild, rose,* and *green.* He has merely reversed the order of them and elided wild rose (perhaps he couldn't pronounce an initial *r*), as is apparent in the diagram above (figure 3.1). There is no indication that this transposition has had any effect on Stephen or has even been noticed by him. The act of imagination, in the sense that Seward uses the expression, comes only in retrospect, only after the phrase or collection of images within the mind is scrutinized for meaning and implication. In this particular example, the phrase is made "imaginative" in section 1.2 where Stephen *remembers* the song and *then* speculates about the physical existence of its objects.

> White roses and red roses: those were beautiful colours to think of. And the cards for first place and second place and third place were beautiful colours too: pink and cream and lavender. Lavender and cream and pink roses were beautiful to think of. Perhaps a wild rose might be like those colours and he remembered the song about the wild rose blossoms on the little green place. But you could not have a green rose. But perhaps somewhere in the world you could. (p. 12)

The earlier act of verbal transposition is trivial, if not accidental; it becomes "creative" only in the imaginative recollection, after the transposed image is firmly embedded within the context of mind. That "somewhere" a green rose could, and does, exist is in the medium of language and images.

This argument gains support from the "creative'" pattern in the third song of section 1.1. There, his mother insists that

Stephen will apologize while Dante says that if he doesn't an eagle will come down and pull out his eyes. As before, Stephen's song consists of a rearrangement of the details of his objective experience, in this case the words *apologise* and *pull out his eyes*. The "creativity" involved is the transposition of what is already present, as can be seen in the following transpositions:

Pull out his eyes,— ─ ─ ─ ─ ─Apologise,
Apologise,─ ─ ─ ─ ─ ─ ─Pull out his eyes,
Apologise,— ─ ─ ─ ─ ─ Pull out his eyes,
Pull out his eyes,─ ─ ─ ─ ─Apologise,

Later, similar patterns of verbal or imagistic transposition supplemented by reflection are far from trivial, for this is Stephen's characteristic mode of creativity. Manipulating the symbol or word within its own physical context—the auditory dimension of language—before examining the referential implications has great potential for creativity: the exploration of relations among words and images suggested by their auditory quality and followed by examination of the semantic and associative implications leading to awareness of coherent relations that are new and startling sometimes transports Stephen to the highest level of Joycean epiphany.

The second portion of 1.1 begins with the bed-wetting image and concludes with the image *cachou;* the third part of the section begins with Eileen's family and terminates with the pull out his eyes/apologise refrain mentioned above. Again there are chains of associations from image to image: each portion has its own imagistic organization. However, all three portions are held together by recurring references to *father* and to *songs* (see figure 3.2). Of course, these images refer both

Figure 3.2

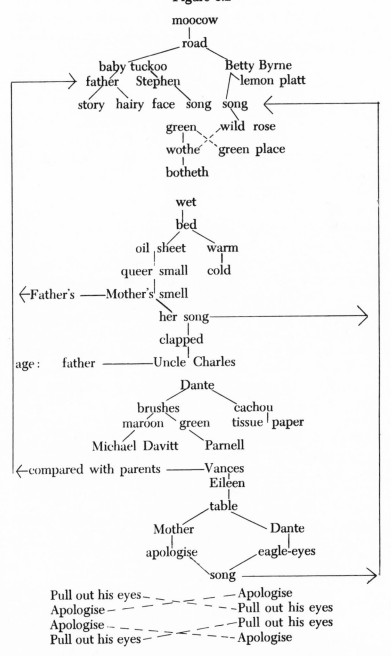

to Stephen's paternal father and to his Jesuit instructors; but both "fathers" are of immediate concern to him. Songs and the phenomenal or auditory dimension of language seen in the transformations already discussed emphasize the importance of this sense, which serves at times as Stephen's most important epistemic sense.

Thus, section 1.1 is in many respects an "overture." It introduces images that become major themes; it includes images of all five sense; and, finally, its organization can best be described as associational or thematic, not unlike a musical composition. Similar uses of imagery are found throughout the chapter and the novel.

Section 1.2, concerning Stephen's first few months at Clongowes, is dominated by three major clusters of images: the *bird/eye/fear* group already discussed; a related *water/cold/excrement* motif associated with Stephen's fall into the ditch; and a third group concerning *fire/warmth/home/security*. The narrative describes the fall into the ditch only in retrospect; but from the numerous recollections of that experience, we can infer its traumatic effect on Stephen. It is there that the first two groups of images are linked through the primary association between fear and the coldness of the water in the ditch. The scene actually developed that achieves epiphanic intensity concerns Stephen's fevered dreams resulting from his soaking in the ditch. There the third group, concerning *fire (warmth/home/security)*, rises in his imagination as the opposite of his present environment. The link between *fire* and *water* images that is only vaguely established in that scene is later galvanized in the even more traumatic pandybat experience at the end of the chapter.

The first section, it will be recalled, closed with the threat that an eagle would tear out Stephen's eyes if he didn't apologize for some pecadillo. Strongly implied is the fear that Stephen felt. It is characteristic of Stephen's developing psyche that these associations are linked with images, and it is characteristic of Joyce's writing that themes are carried from scene to scene linking the narrative through a closely knit and organically developing network of associations. Both patterns are apparent in the cluster of images that begins section 1.2. Stephen is on the playing field. The air is cool and the boys are playing football—all but Stephen. The ball flying through the air reminds him of a heavy bird in flight. Stephen does not play because he feels "small and weak" and because his eyes are "weak and watery." The associations of fear with birds and the feelings of weakness and vulnerability with his eyes implied in section 1.1 are much stronger here; on a structural level, the break in both time and narrative is bridged by the repetition of this group of images.

The association of fear and physical inadequacy with Stephen's eyes is carried throughout the section. Later, when Wells and some of the other boys tease Stephen about kissing his mother, their threat and his vulnerablity are focused in their respective eyes: "The other fellows stopped their game and turned round, laughing. Stephen blushed under their eyes" (p. 14). In the same scene:

> He tried to think of Wells's mother but he did not dare to raise his eyes to Wells's face. He did not like Wells's face. It was Wells who had shouldered him into the square ditch the day before because he would not swop his little snuffbox for Wells's seasoned hacking chestnut, the conqueror of forty. It was a mean thing to do; all the fellows said it was. And how cold and slimy the water had been! And a fellow had once seen a big rat jump plop into the scum. (p. 14)

The latter passage links Stephen's feelings of fear and vulnerability with another set of images: *cold, water, excre-*

ment, and *rats.* The implications of this last set of images are most important and will be discussed in detail below.

Another notable example of the association between *eyes* and *fear* occurs in the nightmare in which Stephen dreams of the castle ghosts: a black dog with eyes as big as carriage lamps and a marshall who stares at the servants out of "strange eyes." In both cases, the aspect of these ghosts that is most frightening and most threatening is their eyes. The cause of the nightmare is the fever Stephen has contracted as a result of getting soaked in the ditch. Since this is one of the richest sections in the novel in terms of imagery, it warrants close attention.

The scene begins with evening prayers. Joyce introduces for the first time two important new images: *sea* and *dark. Sea,* although a *water* image and associated with *cold,* seems to have connotations different from most of the other *water* images of the section, probably because of the association between *sea* and *home.* It is the sea "under the seawall beside his father's home" that Stephen is reminded of. Similarly, *darkness* is related to *cold* but with different connotations. *Darkness* is an immediate part of Stephen's experience. Thus the experiential association between this pair is much stronger than that between *cold* and *sea.* Another factor may be that *darkness,* occurring some sixteen times in this scene, is a much more frequent image than *sea.* During the service, Stephen's awareness of his physical environment is indicated by an olfactory image: "There was a cold night smell in the chapel" (p. 18). This smell reminds him of the typical Irish peasant at mass. The initial association is affirmative as he thinks of sleeping before a warm fire amid smells of air, rain, turf, and corduroy; however, this connotation is overpowered by the immediate image of darkness as he thinks of the dark road he will have to travel to get there.

The link between *darkness* and *fear* is further developed as Stephen offers a prayer in defense against the darkness outside the chapel: "He prayed it [the prayer] too against the dark outside under the trees" (p. 18). After the service when he is in bed, his experience of the darkened dormitory room is one of fear—in fact, his reaction is to "shiver" with fear, strengthening the link with coldness. It is in this context as he thinks of the tales of the castle ghosts that his fear becomes explicitly associated with death:

> O how cold and strange it was to think of that! All the dark was cold and strange. There were pale strange faces there, great eyes like carriagelamps. They were the ghosts of murderers, the figures of marshals who had received their deathwound on battlefields far away over the sea. What did they wish to say that their faces were so strange? (p. 19)

When Stephen finally goes to sleep, his dreams are in direct contrast to the cold fear he has experienced: he dreams of his homecoming. However, the two dreams and the events of the ensuing morning are linked by another image, *face*. As already noted, the fear Stephen associates with the ghosts was most strongly centered in the eyes and faces of the figures. During his dream of going home, he sees himself riding on a chocolate train with "cream facings." The implications of the pun are reinforced by repeated references to faces after he wakes. As he lies unmoving in his bed staring at the ceiling, he sees a number of masklike faces appear in his field of vision and then disappear. When the prefect comes, he checks Stephen's body temperature by feeling his forehead. Later, faces are portrayed as masklike, implying the basic nature of the individual. This development is particularly important in section 1.4 where Stephen questions whether his face reflects the fundamental character of a "schemer"; however, the question of Stephen's identity at this point is related much more strongly to a different set of images.

Following the *bird-and-eye* cluster of images at the very beginning of section 1.2, Stephen has an encounter concerning his name with another student, Nasty Roche, whom he describes as a "stink." As in section 1.1, the image of name is closely related to Stephen's sense of identity. When Nasty asks "What kind of a name is that?" and "Is he [Stephen's father] a magistrate?" Stephen is unable to reply. The next sentence gives the tone of the exchange. "He [Stephen] crept about from point to point on the fringe of his line, making little runs now and then. His hands were bluish with cold" (p. 9). Centered between two statements indicating Stephen's feelings of fear and inadequacy, the passage strongly implies that threats to his identity are just as real and just as disturbing as threats to his person.

This relation between name and identity is reinforced near the middle of section 1.2. During his geography lesson Stephen becomes fascinated by the names of different places. It is the auditory images or the sounds of the names that lead him to explore the relation between himself and the physical universe around him:

> Stephen Dedalus
> Class of Elements
> Clongowes Woods College
> Sallins
> County Kildare
> Ireland
> Europe
> The World
> The Universe   (p. 15)

In attempting to extend the limits of his conceptualizing, he
tries to imagine what lies beyond the physical limits of The
Universe. The only way he can approach this unknown is
through the name *God*. "God was God's name just as his
name was Stephen." He continued with a bit of wordplay,
thinking of the French word for God, *Dieu*. If someone
prayed using *Dieu*, then God would know that it was a
Frenchman. Stephen could extend this process into complete relativism, but he doesn't:

> Though there were different names for God in all the different
> languages in the world and God understood what all the
> people who prayed said in their different languages still God
> remained always the same God and God's real name was
> God.   (p. 16)

This type of wordplay may seem similar to the "creativity"
of 1.1; however, it is actually the reverse. There he was
merely playing with the auditory dimension of words; the
imaginative act of referential reassociation came later and
in retrospect. Here he is grappling with the concepts suggested by his wordplay. His inability to make an imaginative
synthesis negates any objective—word or name—transposition. For this reason God remains God.

   The final cluster of name images occurs while Stephen
is in the infirmary. There he meets a boy named Athy.
Unlike Nasty Roche, Athy accepts the name *Stephen Dedalus* even though it is a "queer" name. As in the preceding
scene, names establish the relationship between the individual and the physical world: "You have a queer name, Dedalus, and I have a queer name too, Athy. My name is the
name of a town. Your name is like Latin" (p. 25). Joyce goes
on to turn the relations back the other way—from the
physical world to the individual—by a pun: "Why is the

county Kildare like the leg of a fellow's breeches?" (p. 25).
Both contain "a thigh" (pronunciation of Athy).

Name   Physical World
(person)   (place)

As the passage indicates, it is much more difficult for
Stephen than for Athy to establish an exact correspondence
between his name and the phenomenal world: his is "like
Latin." The relationship for Athy exists within the phenomenal context of the name—the auditory; for Stephen,
the relation between his name and his identity is fundamental but on a substantive level. The full dimensions of this
relation with classical and Christian mythic traditions, however, are not developed until Chapter IV of the novel. That
his name is "like Latin" is interesting here because of the
motif of heroism associated with the Latin fathers of the
order suggested by the pictures hanging in the hallway outside of the prefect's office. It is noteworthy also that the prefect is one of the few characters in the chapter who know
Stephen's name and do not ask him to state it.

Following the name incident with Nasty Roche is a
passage containing one of the most important image clusters
in the chapter. Stephen thinks of the sentences in his spell-
ing book:

> Wolsey died in Leicester Abbey
> Where the abbots buried him.
> Canker is a disease of plants,
> Cancer one of animals.

It would be nice to lie on the hearthrug before the fire,
leaning his head upon his hands, and think on those sentences.
He shivered as if he had cold slimy water next to his skin.
That was mean of Wells to shoulder him into the square

ditch because he would not swap his little snuffbox for Wells's seasoned hacking chestnut, the conqueror of forty. How cold and slimy the water had been! A fellow had once seen a big rat jump into the scum. Mother was sitting at the fire with Dante waiting for Brigid to bring in the tea. She had her feet on the fender and her jewelly slippers were so hot and they had such a lovely warm smell!　　(p. 10)

Falling into the ditch or cesspool would seem to be prime material for a trauma, as indeed it was for Stephen. Even in retrospect, Stephen shivers as he remembers the cold water, for the association between the *ditch, water,* and *coldness* appears indelibly stamped into his psyche. Along with these images are those of *rats, slime,* and *scum,* implying excrement, The experience, which is always remembered in retrospect, contrasts sharply with thoughts of home symbolized by the literal warmth of the hearth fire. The pattern is usually an oscillation between *water/cold* and *fire/warmth* images. Closely linked, then, are images suggesting the imagined security of home and those epitomizing Stephen's most traumatic experiences at school. Although these images are worlds apart in explicit associations, their constant contiguity implies a developing, but as yet undefined, relationship between them.

This pattern of rapid oscillation is continued with Stephen's recollection of a trip with his father. He remembers the lavatory in the Wicklow Hotel:

To remember that [Simon Moonan's nickname, Suck] and the white look of the lavatory make him feel cold and then hot. There were two cocks that you turned and water came out: cold and hot. He felt cold and then a little hot: and he could see the names printed on the cocks. That was a very queer thing.　　(p. 11)

The passage also suggests a link between the *hot/cold* complex and the image *white,* which becomes important later. The pattern reoccurs twice within the next few pages. While working his sums, as the leader of the Yorkists, the white roses, Stephen first feels his face turn red when he thinks of losing the competition. Later he thinks his face must be white, since he feels quite cool. In the next paragraph he goes even further in his speculation concerning the relation between *white* and *cold:*

> He drank off the hot weak tea which the clumsy scullion, girt with a white apron, poured into his cup. He wondered whether the scullion's apron was damp too or whether all white things were cold and damp. (pp. 12–13)

After his failure to comprehend the nature of God and politics—the two most important abstractions that arise in his daily life at this time—Stephen turns his thoughts to something much more physical and immediately present:

> It would be lovely in bed after the sheets got a bit hot. First they were so cold to get into. He shivered to think how cold they were first. But then they got hot and then he could sleep. It was lovely to be tired. He yawned again. Night prayers and then bed: he shivered and wanted to yawn. It would be lovely in a few minutes. He felt a warm glow creeping up from the cold shivering sheets, warmer and warmer till he felt warm all over, ever so warm; ever so warm and yet he shivered a little and still wanted to yawn.   (p. 17)

Again the oscillation is between images that are fundamentally opposite: *cold* implying basically unpleasant associations (in this context the images offer contrast to heighten the pleasure associated with warmth) and *heat* implying security and comfort.

Even in the scenes when Stephen is sick from his fall into the ditch, the images of fevered heat are affirmative in comparison to images of cold:

> A pale sunlight showed the yellow curtains drawn back, the tossed beds. His bed was very hot and his face and body were very hot.
>
> He got up and sat on the side of his bed. He was weak. He tried to pull on his stockings. It had a horrid rough feel. The sunlight was queer and cold.   (p. 21)

Similarly,

> He felt the prefect's hand on his forehead; and he felt his forehead warm and damp against the prefect's cold damp hand. That was the way a rat felt, slimy and damp and cold. Every rat had two eyes to look out of. Sleek slimy coats, little little feet tucked up to jump, black shiny eyes to look out of.   (p. 22)

Looking back at the section, we can note among the various groups of images four clusters or complexes that are most important. Each group has its own internal structure but all, ultimately, are related to one another. A schematic representation of this structure is given in figure 3.3 in which the associative links among images are indicated by lines. As the figure and the discussion show, all four groups are highly interrelated, joined primarily through associations with *cold* and *fear*. From another point of view, however, it is the pattern of oscillation between the *water/cold* and *fire/heat* complexes that constitutes the major focus of the section.

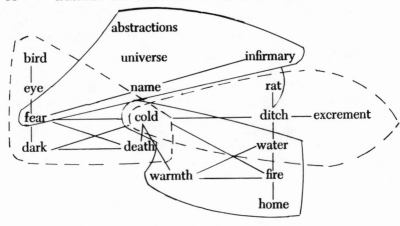

Figure 3.3

The pattern of tension between *hot/cold* and *fire/water* imagery runs throughout the section, serving as the axis around which most of the other image groups are related. Figure 3.4 shows the structural relations among this and the other cluster of images.[2] Groups of images usually appear not in isolation but in the context of other clusters. This can be seen in the close proximiity of pairs of the same image cluster. For example, at the very beginning there is the oscillating pattern between *hand* and *eye* groups. Similarly, between *hand* and *hot/cold; eyes* and *hot/cold; red/green* and *name; eyes* and *white;* and *eyes* and *hot/cold.* As one might expect, this pattern of using a particular image group, relating it to another group, and then returning to the original group often results in an almost symmetrical substructure embedded in the overall structure of the section and the novel as a whole. Note, for example, the pattern between *red/green* and *name* a little more than halfway through the section. This scene concerns the geography lesson. The original *red/green* group concerns the drawing of the green earth with maroon clouds. This picture stimulates Stephen to consider the relations among the physical universe, certain abstract principles, and himself. First he examines the abstraction *God;* then he relates this, through the *red/green* imagery of the picture, to *politics.* The relation between these two abstractions is more than he can comprehend at this time. His failure makes him feel "small and weak," and threatens him just as he felt threatened by the events associated with the earlier name image, that is, the Nasty Roche incident. Thus the scene is developed in terms of both substance and structure through image relations. Patterns similar to this can be found in a number of scenes in 1.2 but are most important in section 1.4.

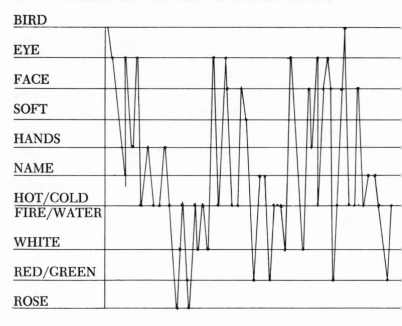

Figure 3.4

As can also be seen in figure 3.4, most clusters tend to appear at regular intervals. For example, the section begins with a *bird* image, and a *bird* image appears late in Stephen's stay in the infirmary; similarly, there are three important clusters of *eye* imagery: one near the beginning of the section, one near the middle, and one near the end. Images of whiteness occur about a third of the way through the section and again about two-thirds of the way through. However, the group that most obviously dominates the section is that associated with *fire : hot / water : cold*. This group, which occurs more than three times as often as any other cluster on the graph, is almost evenly distributed over the section and is directly related to just about every other group. One might term it the axis around which virtually all image clusters of the section are oriented. Structurally, it is the imagistic basis of the section. Since it is so consistently and fundamentally related to Stephen's fall into the ditch, this experience can be said to dominate his associations with virtually all experiences recounted in the section. As if to undescore the pattern of associations between Clongowes and *water / cold* images in contrast to associations of *fire* and *warmth* with *home,* Joyce ends the section with a *water* image and uses a *fire* image as the very first image of 1.3, Stephen's Christmas experiences at home.

Section 1.3 represents Stephen's homecoming at Christmas; however, the event actually depicted in the section is the Christmas meal itself. The scene centers around the hearth in which a great red fire is burning. Stephen is sitting between Dante and Uncle Charles while his father stands with his back to the fireplace warming himself. The tableau is one of security and unity among family and friends.

The scene later becomes emotionally charged for Stephen during the argument at the dinner table; however, since the section is developed almost entirely in dialogue, the reader does not have his usual direct and continuous insight into Stephen's responses. The pattern of associations among images, although not radically altered here, does contain several important transitions, preparing the way for the dramatic events of the following section.

One such group is the collection of *bird* images. The gustatory pleasures of the meal are brought to focus by the large turkey that Mr. Dedalus has purchased for a "guinea!" *Bird* images, even so apparently innocuous, carry a negative undertone associated with the earlier *bird* images linked with fear and apprehension for Stephen. This relation is apparent in Stephen's train of thought:

> Why did Mr. Barrett in Clongowes call his pandybat a turkey? But Clongowes was far away: and the warm heavy smell of turkey and ham and celery rose from the plates and dishes and the great fire was banked high and red in the grate and the green ivy and red holly made you feel so happy and when dinner was ended the big plumpudding would be carried in, studded with peeled almonds and sprigs of holly, with bluish fire running around it and a little green flag flying from the top.   (p. 30)

The association of *turkey* or *bird* with the *pandybat* as yet has little or no direct significance for Stephen: it is merely word association. In the section that follows, this link becomes very important; however, the immediacy of the present situation overpowers any distant, unpleasant association (just as earlier the immediacy of Clongowes had overpowered thoughts of home).

In the ensuing religious-political argument an important

development takes place with images of hot and cold. The following passages all occur within a page of one another:

> —We are all sinners and black sinners, said Mr. Casey coldly.
> —And very bad language if you ask me, said Mr. Dedalus cooly.
> —O, he'll remember all this when he grows up, said Dante hotly—the language he heard against God and religion and priests in his own home. (pp. 32–33)

Earlier, in section 1.2, this group of images was fundamentally tactile; they have now become auditory in their associations with language itself. This relation, here metaphoric, becomes synestheticly literal in section 1.4.

In the remainder of the scene, language dominates Stephen's experience. Although Stephen remains a silent observer, the reader is given access to his thoughts occasionally. Those occasions become very important from the standpoint of the patterns among images developing in his mind. This emphasis on language in 1.3 is reflected in the use of the word itself. Of the ten times that language is used in the chapter it occurs eight times in this short section. The other two occurrences are in the God/politics episode of 1.2, already seen to be closely associated thematically and imagistically with this scene. Language has always reflected the values and conflicts of Catholic Ireland; however, Stephen's reaction to the heated exchange is much more fundamentally related to the auditory and literal dimension of language. For example, in one of the glimpses given of Stephen's thoughts during the dinner, we see an interesting chain of associations. His thoughts move from Mr. Casey's face, to Dante, to Eileen, to the Protestant taunts "Tower of Ivory" and "House of Gold." There is a momentary flashback to Clongowes and the dark waters he associates with the death of Parnell. Then his thoughts settle on Eileen:

> Eileen had long white hands. One evening when playing tag she had put her hands over his eyes: long and white and thin and cold and soft. That was ivery: a cold white thing. That was the meaning of *Tower of Ivory*.   (p. 36)

The transfer has been made from the word *Ivory* to the referential *Eileen*. The association carries the properties of ivory-cold, white, and soft—to the other image, *Eileen*. One might expect the connotations to be negative because of the earlier association between *white* and *cold,* but the obviously affirmative tone of the passage seems to come from the image *soft* and the theme of protectiveness. It was Stephen's eyes, it will be recalled, that earlier represented his weakness and vulnerability. Thus the protective note suggested by Eileen's soft hands over his eyes is quite strong.

The association of fear and apprehension with eyes, however, returns in Mr. Casey's story and the ensuing confrontation with Dante. Mr. Casey, in defending the names of Parnell and Kitty O'Shea, gives the following account:

> —Phth! says I to her like that, right into her eye. He clapped a hand to his eye and gave a hoarse scream of pain.
> —O Jesus, Mary and Joseph! says she. I'm blinded! I'm blinded and drownded! (p. 37)

The woman's response, "I'm blinded and drownded!" probably revives memories of Stephen's two largest sources of fear: his eyes and his experience of the ditch. At the height of the argument,

> Mr. Casey struggled up from his chair and bent across the table towards her, scraping the air from before his eyes with one hand as though he were tearing aside a cobweb. (p. 39)

Dante virtually spits her accusations of "Blasphemer! Devil!" in Mr. Casey's face. Stephen reacts to the auditory as well as the substantive dimensions of the language: "His face was glowing with anger and Stephen felt the glow rise to his own cheek as the spoken word thrilled him" (p. 38). The association of *glowing*—implying fire and warmth—with *language* is one of the most important developments of the chapter. At Clongowes the imagined security of home was centered in images of warmth and the hearth fire as, indeed, it was at the beginning of this section. Undoubtedly that security has been shaken, but the affirmative aspect of *fire* has not been displaced entirely, even though it has been transformed considerably. The scene ends with an image that reflects much of what has taken place and foreshadows the final climactic epiphany of the chapter, the pandybat episode: "Stephen, raising his terror-stricken face, saw that his father's eyes were full of tears" (p. 39).

Section 1.4 is the longest section in Chapter I. Although the scene shifts several times, the narrative is thematically and structurally unified. The events depicted are dominated by the pandybat episode, but the unifying theme concerns guilt and punishment. The section begins with a discussion of the punishment to be given several older boys caught "smugging" in the square. Although the boys are guilty, the consensus is that the flogging they will receive if they choose to remain in school will be light. In contrast, Stephen is later falsely accused and punished most severely; the chapter ends, however, with his personal triumph over the injustice of arbitrary authority. In many respects Stephen is a different person then from what he was at the beginning of the section. To understand the important changes that take place during the pandybat episode, we must first look at several clusters of images that appear early in the section.

Like section 1.2, the scene opens on the playing field, sometime after his return to Clongowes from Christmas vacation. The changed atmosphere is characterized by the image motif *soft, grey, evening, sky,* and *air.*[3] Earlier, *grey* was used in a different context: the football flew like a heavy bird through the grey light. The sense of threat and fear so strongly associated there with birds is not immediately present here.

One reason for this shift in connotation for *grey* may be its proximiity to another image, *soft.* Another instance of the mitigating influence of this image was seen in context with Eileen's cool, white hands where connotations of the complex involving *white* and *cold,* previously seen to carry negative associations, were modified significantly. The other two occurrences of *soft* are similarly affirmative. One occurs after Stephen's fall into the ditch as he remembers his mother's soft lips; the other occurs during the early part of the Christmas dinner scene while all was still tranquillity and security. Thus, the image comes to section 1.4 with strongly positive connotations.

Before the pandying, itself, *soft* is used several times with *grey, sky,* and so on to characterize the basic pleasantness of the evening:

> And from here and from there came the sounds of the cricket-bats through the soft grey air. They said: pick, pack, pock, puck: like drops of water in a fountain slowly falling in the brimming bowl.   (p. 41)

As in the earlier scene, something is going through the air; here, it is sound, not a bird. *Soft* is next used in a repetition of its association with Eileen's hands:

> Eileen had long thin cool white hands too because she was

a girl. They were like ivory; only soft. That was the meaning of *Tower of Ivory* but protestants could not understand it and made fun of it. One day he stood beside her looking into the hotel grounds. A waiter was running up a trail of bunting on the flagstaff and a fox terrier was scampering to and fro on the sunny lawn. She had put her hand into his pocket where his hand was and he had felt how cool and thin and soft her hand was. She had said that pockets were funny things to have: and then all of a sudden she had broken away and had run laughing down the sloping curve of the path. Her fair hair had streamed out behind her like gold in the sun. *Tower of Ivory. House of Gold.* By thinking of things you could understand them. (pp. 42–43)

The strongly positive, almost idealistic, association among *cool, white,* and *hands,* constitutes a basic element of contrast and irony for the pandying to come.

Similarly, olfactory images play an important role in establishing the context for the epiphanic experience. In the previous sections Joyce often used images of smell at the very beginning of new scenes; this pattern is present here. The first concerns the older boys who were punished for stealing and drinking the altar wine: "it was found who did it by the smell." The thought of this smell makes Stephen feel weak as he remembers the "weak sour smell" of the burning incense. However, Wells states that the real reason they are to be punished is for "smugging" in the square. Again, the image invokes a chain of associations for Stephen:

But why in the square? You went there when you wanted to do something. It was all thick slabs of slate and water trickled all day out of tiny pinholes and there was a queer smell of stale water there. (p. 43)

It is olfactory imagery, then, that establishes a link in Stephen's mind between guilt, here associated with others, and his own experience of the ditch. That their guilt touches him as the foul water did is suggested by Nasty Roche's consolation, following the pandying, that Father Dolan is a "stink." This abstract transfer of guilt becomes much more direct a bit later.

The shift in emphasis from tactile imagery in 1.2 to auditory images in 1.3 is continued in 1.4, but with important differences. Auditory images are used with images of other senses in a strongly synesthetic way. For example:

> [Stephen] thought of the dark silent sacristy. There were dark wooden presses there where the crimped surplices lay quietly folded. It was not the chapel but still you had to speak under your breath. It was a holy place. He remembered the summer evening he had been there to be dressed as a boatbearer, the evening of the procession to the little altar in the wood. A strange and holy place.   (pp. 40–41)

The *quietly folded surplices* is a combination of an auditory image with what may be considered a tactile or visual image, or both. This combining of various senses with the auditory grows in significance until the actual pandybat scene.

As in the matter of the ditch, the reader learns in retrospect of Stephen's fall on the bicycle path and the breaking of his glasses. It is immediately after this that the first cluster of references to *soft, grey,* and *sky* or *air* occurs. Without his glasses, Stephen can see very little; consequently what he does see is a hazy, indistinct, more or less homogeneous mass of blending hues. A dominant characteristic of the section is that auditory images cut through this continuum and through Stephen's wandering thoughts to bring him back to the events that surround him. For example, he hears the "pick, pack, pock, puck" of the cricketbats coming through the air. These sounds are immediately linked with an unusual image: "drops of water in a fountain slowly falling into the brimming bowl." The connotations of·*water* imagery have already been discussed; however, the implications of this particular *water* image do not fit the earlier pattern. It is possible that associations with the ditch are carried, but this image is primarily auditory, not tactile. At this point, one can conclude only that the image seems to carry other, perhaps more complex, associations than previous *water* images. Later, Stephen's thoughts are interrupted by another auditory image : Athy's voice telling them that their speculations are wrong concerning the deed committed by the older boys. This is followed by Cecil *Thunder's* complaint that the entire student body may be punished by "three days silence in the refectory" and an increase in the numbers of prayers that must be said; the guilty older boys will be flogged and "sent up for twice nine." Athy jokes at their plight with the rhyme :

> It can't be helped;
> It must be done.
> So down with your breeches
> And out with your bum.
> (p. 44)

One final auditory image that must be considered before moving on to the pandybat scene is the sound of the cricket-bat :

Pock. That was a sound to hear but if you were hit then you would feel a pain. The pandybat made ,a sound too but not like that. The fellows said it was made of whalebone and leather with lead inside : and he wondered what was the pain like. There were different kinds of pains for all the different kinds of sounds. A long thin cane would have a high whistling sound and he wondered what was the pain like. It made him shivery to think of it and cold.   (p. 45)

Although the pandybat and the cricket bat are different, they are linked in Stephen's imagination by their sounds. These auditory images lead Stephen to imagine the sounds of other instruments of pain. The reference to *cane* foreshadows the cane used by Heron to force Stephen to "submit" in Chapter II. Earlier, the pandybat was associated with *turkey* and perhaps *bird* images and the sense of fear they carry for Stephen. Most important in this context, however, is the relation between the sound and the tactile senses. This link between the cane and the pandybat with *cold* ties them to all of the earlier associations with *water*, the *ditch*, and the fear, guilt, and repugnance associated with these images. Stephen is rescued from this morass by still another auditory image:

> A voice from far out on the playground cried:
> —All in!
> And other voices cried:
> —All in! All in!   (p. 45)

Although Stephen has broken his glasses and can see only indistinct masses of color, the atmosphere is relatively relaxed, as suggested by the pleasant, protective associations of the *soft, grey, air* group. The only unpleasantness resides in the associations in Stephen's mind between the sounds on the playing field and images of the pandybat and canes. This same low-keyed atmosphere is carried into the writing class, the context from which the pandying develops, and the level to which events return at the end of that scene.

The scene shifts abruptly to the writing class. The quality of Stephen's visual sense inferred earlier in conjunction with the *soft, grey, air* complex is described here:

> He had tried to spell out the headline for himself though he

knew already what it was for it was the last of the book. *Zeal
without prudence is like a ship adrift.* But the lines of the
letters were like fine invisible threads and it was only by
closing his right eye tight and staring out of the left eye that
he could make out the full curves of the capital.   (p. 46)

The silence of the room is broken only by the scratching
of the pens. Stephen thinks of the guilt of the older boys,
but his thoughts settle on the communion mass. This chain
of associations is epitomized by images of wine:

The day when he had made his first holy communion in the
chapel he had shut his eyes and opened his mouth and put
out his tongue a little: and when the rector had stooped
down to give him the holy communion he had smelt a faint
winy smell off the rector's breath after the wine of the mass.
The word was beautiful: wine.   (p. 46)

Emphasis on auditory imagery is continued after Father
Arnall comes in and the Latin lesson begins. The boys are
asked to decline the noun *mare* aloud. When Fleming gives
a wrong answer, Father Arnall's voice is quiet but "his face
was blacklooking." Like earlier images, Father Arnall's face
appears fixed, revealing his mood. After Fleming is made to
kneel in the middle of the floor, the room returns to silence
except for the scraping of the pens.

   Father Dolan's arrival is marked by a series of auditory
images:

The door opened quietly and closed. A quick whisper ran
through the class: the prefect of studies. There was an instant
of dead silence and then the loud crack of a pandybat on the
last desk. Stephen's heart leapt up in fear.   (p. 48)

When he confronts Fleming, Father Dolan metes out punishment not for lack of knowledge but for what he states is

Fleming's fundamental character: "Hoho, Fleming! An idler of course. I can see it in your eye" (p. 48). It is Fleming's face that, masklike, indicates his character. (This same remark will be repeated to Stephen.) Stephen's experience of the present situation is mostly auditory:

> He banged his pandybat down on the desk and cried:
> —Up, Fleming! Up, my boy!
> Fleming stood up slowly.
> —Hold out! cried the prefect of studies
> Fleming held out his hand. The pandybat came down on it with a loud smacking sound: one, two, three, four, five, six. (p. 49)

Although Stephen wonders whether the tactile sensation is painful, for Fleming used to rub rosin into his palms to toughen them, he concludes that the pain may have been great since the noise of the pandybat was so loud. Stephen's own fear, manifest in the image of his "fluttering heart," could raise associations with *bird* images because the pandybat was linked earlier with the word *turkey;* the association is not developed here.

As the prefect turns to go, he sees that Stephen is not writing and asks: "You, boy, who are you?" Stephen, shocked into silence, finally manages to overcome his fright and stammers out his name. After discovering from Father Arnall why Stephen is not writing, the prefect again asks Stephen his name. The close association between name and identity seen earlier is interesting in the context of Father Arnall's next remark: "Out here, Dedalus. Lazy little schemer. I see schemer in your face." Stephen wonders if "schemer" really is written on his face and if this is his true nature. The train of thought, of course, represents Stephen's basic pattern of discovery and creativity: the movement from juxtaposed images or words to an imaginative examination of their relation and meaning. This pattern, it will be recalled, was present in both songs in 1.1 and the rose cluster of 1.2. The masklike association between face and personal character is continued as Stephen looks up into the prefect's face:

> Stephen lifted his eyes in wonder and saw for a moment Father Dolan's white-grey not young face, his baldy white-grey head with fluff at the sides of it, the steel rims of his spectacles and his nocoloured eyes looking through the glasses. Why did he say he knew that trick?
> —Lazy idle little loafer! cried the prefect of studies. Broke my glasses! An old schoolboy trick! Out with your hand this moment. (p. 50)

The pandying of Stephen is accompanied by an avalanche of images with nearly a third of the words of this scene having sensual value. The imagery associated with this event, however, is important not only because of sheer numbers but also for the particular images present. Among them are:

> eyes
> air
> hand
> fingers
> pandybat
> hot
> burning
> leaf
> fire
> sound
> pain
> scalding
> teach
> prayer

When Stephen recalls the event, he adds to the list the following:

> soft
> firm
> white/grey

Contained in this list are most of the important clusters found in the preceding sections. The major themes of the chapter, developed through the gradually expanding associations among various images, all converge to this point, to this experience. The association between *eyes, fear,* and *feelings of weakness and vulnerability* has been well documented. *Air* represents the first major image of the section, and it is also one of the last. Its occurrence here in the center of the section suggests a symmetrical structure. *Hands, fingers, soft, firm,* and *white* have all been associated with Stephen's idealistic image of Eileen; and the association of her hands protecting his eyes is reinforced earlier in section 1.4. *Pandybat* was linked with *bird* images earlier, and more recently with the discussion of guilt and punishment on the playing field. It was also used in conjunction with the mysterious image of the dripping water. *Fire* and *burning* were strongly associated with the security of the hearth; while *prayer,* a rather infrequent image in this chapter, might be interpreted as a link back to the very rich scene of Stephen's first chapel experience and his ensuing dreams. That scene, it will be recalled, was permeated with bits of liturgy. *Water* imagery is present in the tears that spring to Stephen's eyes; with the strong link between *tears, eyes, white,* and the *water* of *ditch* experience, it is reasonable to assert that the image and its associations strongly underlie the scene. All of these complex associations converge in this scene.

The exact point of focus can be seen in the following passage:

> A hot burning stinging tingling blow like the loud crack of a broken stick made his trembling hand crumple together like a leaf in the fire: and at the sound and the pain scalding tears were driven into his eyes.   (p. 50)

At the exact moment the pandybat strikes, the images that characterize the experience are *leaf* and *scalding tears*. Both *leaf* and *scalding* are used here for the first time in the novel. *Scald* is certainly the more interesting of the two images, for it represents a literal fusion of two of the most important image groups of the chapter: *fire* and *water*. (The use of an image for the first and sometimes only time in the novel at the very focus of an epiphanical experience is a technique used several times by Joyce in *Portrait*.) Used to describe the tears that spring from Stephen's eyes as a result of the pandybat, *scald* further links *fire* and *water* images with two other groups of fundamental importance: the *eye/bird* complex, linked through fear in Stephen's mind as recently as that very day on the playing field. Thus, there is the convergence and fusion of virtually every major theme of the chapter in the blinding, burning pain of the pandybat.[4] Associations among these groups have fused and altered drastically; when we see them later, their relations are structurally much more complex. Consequently, Stephen is in many respects a different person after this experience from what he was earlier.

As the scene diminishes slightly in intensity, the emphasis on auditory imagery is maintained:

—Kneel down! cried the prefect of studies

and shortly later:

—Get at your work, all of you, cried the prefect of studies
from the door. Father Dolan will be in every day to see if
any boy, any lazy idle little loafer wants flogging. Every day.
Every day.

The door closed behind him.

The hushed class continued to copy out the themes. Father
Arnall rose from his seat and went among them, helping the
boys with gentle words and telling them the mistakes they had
made. His voice was very gentle and soft.   (p. 51)

Considering the entire scene, we can now see that it is
structured by the auditory imagery. The basic form is a
crescendo followed by a diminuendo. The intensity of
auditory images begins at a very low level, with the silence
of the room broken only by the scraping of the pens. The
prefect's entrance is marked by the hushed whispers of the
class and then the loud crack of the pandybat on the last
desk. The intensity of these images rises continually through
Fleming's pandying to the most intense moment of all : the
actual pandying of Stephen. After that, the level drops
slightly with the shouts of the prefect and then decreases
continually until it returns to the level from which it started:
the hushed classroom whose silence is broken only by Father
Arnall's quiet voice and the scrapings of pens.

When the prefect has gone, Father Arnall says to
Stephen and Fleming : "You may return to your places, you
two." Stephen is acutely aware of the teacher's failure to
distinguish between them :

It was cruel and unfair to make him kneel in the middle of
the class then : and Father Arnall had told them both that
they might return to their places without making any difference between them.   (p. 52)

The theme of cruelty and injustice is continued in Stephen's ensuing conversation with his classmates. Stephen has been punished severely for something of which he is not guilty. He has also been linked indiscrimately with Fleming, who was guilty, but not "justly" punished since his rosin-toughened palms were probably not hurt by the pandying. Finally, Stephen is implicitly associated with the older boys who are guilty of smugging, connoting the square and the ditch, but who will probably not be punished so severely as they deserve. As a result, Stephen's belief in his own innocence is shaken but not completely destroyed: "He began to wonder whether it might not really be that there was something in his face which made him look like a schemer and he wished he had a little mirror to see" (p. 53).

Stephen's natural reaction is similar to his earlier cringing on the sideline of the playing field: "It was best to hide out of the way because when you were small and young you could often escape that way" (pp. 54–55). However, another series of images can be seen working in this section. While in the infirmary Athy had said that Stephen's name, indeed strange as was his own, sounded like Latin while his own was distinctly Irish. In the events just after the pandying, there are five references to Rome or the Roman people:

—The senate and Roman people declared that Dedalus had been wrongly punished.

And later:

Yes, he would do what the fellows had told him. He would go up and tell the rector that he had been wrongly punished. A thing like that had been done before by somebody in history. And the rector would declare that he had been wrongly punished because the senate and the Roman people

always declared that the men who did that had been wrongly
punished. Those were the great men whose names were in
Richmal Magnall's Questions. History was all about those men
and what they did and that was what Peter Parley's Tales
about Greece and Rome were all about.   (p. 53)

Working in opposition to the theme of submission through
fear is the theme of honor associated with the Romans. In
pondering whether to report the injustice to the rector or
not, Stephen links himself with this tradition of heroism
through his name:

The great-men in the history had names like that and nobody
made fun of them. . . . It was his own name that he [Dolan]
should have made fun of if he wanted to make fun. Dolan: it
was like the name of a woman that washed clothes.   (p. 55)

As Stephen goes up the stairs to the rector's office, he thinks
of the names and portraits of the Latin Fathers of the
Church that line the corridor: Ignatius Loyola, Francis
Xavier, Lorenzo Ricci, and Stanislaus Kostka, to name a few.
On the way to the office, he must also pass the location
where the servants reported seeing the ghosts of the Marshall and his dog. Thinking of these images before, Stephen
only cringed deeper into his bed; this time he gathers the
courage to go to the prefect's door.

Inside the office, the prefect asks, "Your name is Dedalus,
isn't it?" This instance of someone's knowing and accepting
his name contrasts sharply with Father Dolan's inability to
remember it. Throughout the scene there are numerous
references to Stephen's weak eyes, filled with tears, but he
continues his account. When he is ready to leave, the rector
holds his hand momentarily, again in contrast with Father
Dolan's touch before the pandying.

Once out on the playing field, Stephen's triumph is
greeted with cheers, which soon die into the "soft, grey air."
Most of the other images present reflect similar patterns

present at the beginning of the section. Several olfactory images follow:

> There was the smell of evening in the air, the smell of the fields in the country where they digged up turnips to peel them and eat them when they went out for a walk to Major Barton's, the smell there was in the little wood beyond the pavilion where the gallnuts were. (p. 59)

Unlike the earlier images that were sickening, these are refreshing. They, along with the images of ghost, also link this experience with the evening in the chapel and the wholesome smell of the peasants. At that time the smells were diminished by the stronger associations of home; now those associations offer less security and the images appear more self-sustaining.

The final set of images repeats a reference to the soft, grey air:

> In the soft grey silence he could hear the bump of the balls: and from here and from there through the quiet air the sound of the cricket bats: pick, pack, pock, puck: like drops of water in a fountain falling softly in the brimming bowl. (p. 59)

If we look back at the entire section, we can see a structure that is beautiful in its simplicity. The pandybat scene is linked through auditory associations to the sounds of the cricket bats and to the sounds of dripping water, thus extending the structure of the central scene symmetrically on both sides to the beginning and to the final images of the section. The entire experience grows out of the continuum of experience, gains in intensity until the climactic blow of the pandybat, and then gradually diminishes until it blends back into the continuum from which it arose. Figure 3.5 represents this symmetrical structure.

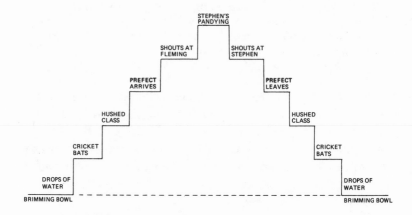

Figure 3.5

Earlier, the image of the water in the brimming bowl was unclear in its implications. Here, the image seems to characterize the continuity of human experience, the subjective state noted in Whitehead. The experience of the pandybat episode has been incorporated into this state : the effects, which are profound, are not immediately perceptible—they lie deep within the subconscious of Stephen, below the surface of his mind. The model of associations through which the individual perceives and characterizes experiences has been fundamentally altered into a structure of greater complexity. The full ramifications of these changed associations will become apparent in subsequent chapters of the novel.

Looking back at the chapter, we can see that it is organized, structurally, through the imagery. Section 1.1. functions as an overture for the chapter and for the novel. Many of the novel's basic thematic groups of images are introduced here; particularly important are the *bird/eye/fear* group and the set of auditory images emphasizing the sense of sound. In addition to introducing specific themes that are continued and developed later, the section reveals the clear relation between associations within the fictive mind of Stephen and the sequence of images in the printed text. By noting the sequence of images we can determine the associative links that exist among them in Stephen's mind. Finally, the section reveals in miniature Stephen's, and probably Joyce's, fundamental mode of creativity : the rearrangement of the components of immediate experience. In the case of "the green wothe botheth," the act is trivial; not until the associations and meanings of these restructured components are examined in retrospect does the act become meaningful.

Section 1.2 continues and develops many of the themes introduced in 1.1. The gap of some four or five years that separates them in time is bridged through recurrent image patterns: the *bird/eye/fear* motif appears at the end of 1.1 and in the first paragraph of 1.2. A new theme, concerning the relation between name and identity, is introduced here; as would be expected, it continues throughout the novel. However, the most important development concerns the dual groups centered in *fire* and *water* imagery. *Water* is closely and indelibly associated in Stephen's mind with his fall into the ditch. This image, in turn, links the experience with a variety of repugnant images including *dirt, filth, excrement, the bloated rat,* and *coldness.* When Stephen recalls this dreadful event, he invariably escapes to thoughts of home, represented literally by the hearth fire. Implied is the extension to warmth, security, and all that stands opposed to his fears associated with Clongowes.

Section 1.3, centered around the Christmas meal, contains few dramatic new developments. In tone, it opens to question the security and thrust that Stephen has associated with home. The other thematic extensions that take place are all done through language itself. In casual conversation, Stephen hears the pandybat referred to as a turkey, linking it with the *bird* motif and perhaps compromising the joy and security symbolized by the beautiful brown bird on the table. Similarly, at the height of the argument that develops, Stephen's association between *eyes* and *fear* is strengthened as he listens, mesmerized, by the heated language that encompasses the family gathering.

Section 1.4 is one of Joyce's most beautifully structured scenes. The tempo of the action and the level of Stephen's emotional involvement are perfectly balanced. The level of intensity begins low, reflected in images of coolness and softness out on the playing field. Gradually the level rises as Stephen's glasses are broken, as he listens to his classmates' conversations, and as he goes into the classroom. When the Prefect of Studies enters, the atmosphere suddenly becomes charged, then rises continually until it peaks at the very moment the pandybat strikes Stephen. From that climax, the intensity diminishes steadily in reverse order back through all previous levels until the final tranquil scene back out on the playing field. This rising and falling pattern is dramatically reflected in the auditory components of the imagery present, but it is the auditory dimension that also extends major thematic developments. Through sounds, the cricket bat is linked with the *brimming-bowl* image on the one side, and the *pandybat* on the other. As the level of intensity rises in the classroom, the auditory images get louder and louder. At the very height of the crescendo, as the bat strikes, virtually every major theme of the chapter is welded into a new and different complex. Particularly significant is the fusion of *bird, eye, water,* and *fire* themes in the phrase, "scalding tears were driven into his eyes." If we regard an epiphany as a formative experience that reshapes the personality into a significantly different structure, this moment is obviously epiphanal. After the experience, Stephen is a different, more complex, more mature individual. Images no longer carry unidimensional associations: good and bad associations have been joined. In the chapters that follow strands of the pre-pandybat links remain, but we would expect to find new and more complex associations developing. The discussions that follow trace these developments.

4
Analysis of Chapter II

Chapter II covers the period in Stephen's life from the summer following his year at Clongowes to early adolescence. The most important development during that period is the slow but inexorable dissolution of the Dedalus household, accompanied by Stephen's increasing sense of isolation from all those around him. The chapter is divided into five sections, each with from six to ten scenes. As might be expected, the subject matter represents a varied and disparate collection of actions and experiences. This diversity of material results in a narrative that states or describes Stephen's experiences much more than it "renders" them. In the preceding chapter, especially in the Christmas dinner and pandybat scenes, the reader is taken into the setting so that Stephen's experiences seem very close to the reader himself. The scenes have dramatic life of their own. Much of that quality is missing in Chapter II, with the exception of the encounter with Heron and the trip to Cork.

This difference in narrative technique is reflected in Joyce's use of imagery. Although the chapter is only some twenty percent shorter than Chapter I, it contains only about half as many images. The imagery that does appear, however, is quite important; it is primarily through recurring patterns of images that this collection of experiences is held together thematically and aesthetically. Among the most important clusters of this sort are *death, excrement,* and *laughter images.* These and other groups will be discussed in detail below.

Psychologically, the period is not very rich compared with the changes in personality that take place in the rest of the novel. The only scene that approaches epiphanic status is the encounter with the prostitute, but it is a highly qualified experience. This scarcity of insight into Stephen's personality afforded by the narrative is further indicated by the number of images relating to physical detail. This chapter contains the highest concentration of images of physical places and buildings of any chapter in the novel as well as the highest concentration of references to other human beings (see the graphic representation of these thematic groups in Appendix E). This emphasis on external detail is often used in contrast with Stephen's sense of isolation; the result is a strong tension between inner, subjective experiences and the world outside himself. This dichotomy is epitomized in the encounter with the prostitute, in which the emotional and physical intimacy that can accompany sexual experience is perverted through a strong train of negative associations in Stephen's mind; consequently, Stephen emerges, in Chapter III, with an even greater sense of isolation.

Section 2.1 is a collection of some six scenes occurring during the summer and fall after Stephen leaves Clongowes. Three of these concern Stephen's Uncle Charles. Following a portrait of the old man is a description of a typical jaunt with Stephen to the shopping district. The third and final scene involving the elderly man is a description of the "constitutional" walks by the two with Mr. Dedalus. The last three scenes of the section center much more directly on Stephen and his imaginative development. Two of these involve Stephen's reading of *The Count of Monte Cristo* while the third depicts his play with friends. All basically concern the Dedalus household or its members.

In Chapter I Joyce used images to provide structural continuity between scenes. *Bird* images linked section 1.1 to 1.2, and *fire* and *water* images established a continuity between the first section at Congowes and the Christmas dinner scene. Similarly, Joyce uses imagery to provide continuity between chapters. The *soft, cool, grey, air* sequence of images that symmetrically framed the pandybat episode at the end of ChapterI is found in a modified form in the first scene of this chapter. The following is a description of Uncle Charles's morning smoke in the garden outhouse:

> Every morning he hummed contentedly one of his favourite songs: *O, twine me a bower* or *Blue eyes and golden hair* or *The Groves of Blarney* while the grey and blue coils of smoke rose slowly from his pipe and vanished in the pure air. (p. 60)

The imagery in this passage, in addition to bridging the two chapters, also introduces a new theme. Most indicative of that theme is the image *blue*. Five of its seven occurrences in this chapter are on the first two pages. Other than the two instances in the passage concerning Uncle Charles, all of the others concern Mike Flynn. For example:

> Stephen often glanced with mistrust at his trainer's flabby stubble-covered face, as it bent over the long stained fingers through which he rolled his cigarette, and with pity at the mild lustreless blue eyes which would look up suddenly from the task and gaze vaguely into the blue distance while the

long swollen fingers ceased their rolling and grains and fibres of tobacco fell back into the pouch. (p. 61)

The four examples of the image cited thus far—the idealized *blue eyes* of the *song*, the *blue* and *grey coils of smoke* rising into the pure *air*, the *blue eyes* that stare into the distant *blue*—imply an association between *blue* and *that which is removed in time and place*, idealized, ephemeral. Later this associative link between *blue* and the *idealized remote* merges with other imagery of the section suggesting the same theme. The fifth use of *blue*, however, lacks this quality and is much more mundane:

When the morning practice was over the trainer would make his comments and sometimes illustrate them by shuffling along for a yard or so comically in an old pair of blue canvas shoes. (p. 61)

Thus, while the association discussed above is pervasive, it is not inclusive.

Chapter I closed with the image of drops of water falling softly in a brimming bowl, implying a religious connotation, perhaps suggesting a font. This *water* image is quite different from earlier *water* imagery associated with the cold, slimy ditch and with the bath; however, the image is ambiguous and interpretation can be made only from the context and tone of the passage. In the second scene of 2.1, Joyce uses a *water* image that suggests a physical realization of the preceding image, an image that existed solely in Stephen's imagination:

On the way home Uncle Charles would often pay a visit to the chapel and, as the font was above Stephen's reach, the old man would dip his hand and then sprinkle the water briskly about Stephen's clothes and on the floor of the porch. (p. 61)

The effect of this *water* image is quite different. Rendered as flat realism, the image—so far as Stephen's response is indicated—while religious in form seems wholly secular in this context. Part of the reason may be because it occurs immediately after the description of Mike Flynn's swollen and stained fingers. Thus, while *water* is denotatively associated here with the religious font, it seems much closer affectively to the earlier pattern relating *water* to *cold, filth,* and *excrement.*

The theme carried by images associated with *excrement* is expanded later in the section. Joyce describes the play of Stephen's and Aubrey Mills's group:

> The gang made forays into the gardens of old maids or went down to the castle and fought a battle on the shaggy weed-grown rocks, coming home after it weary stragglers with the stale odours of the foreshore in their nostrils and the rank oils of the seawrack upon their hands and in their hair. (p. 63)

The two leaders also regularly visited their friend, the milkman:

> When autumn came the cows were driven home from the grass: and the first sight of the filthy cowyard at Stradbrook with its foul green puddles and clots of liquid dung and steaming brantroughs sickend Stephen's heart. The cattle which had seemed so beautiful in the country on sunny days revolted him and he could not even look at the milk they yielded.   (p. 63)

This motif of excrement, filth, and dirt runs through most sections of the chapter, providing structural continuity. The graph in Appendix C.1 indicates the importance of the cluster, for the expansion here of this theme represents the largest single cluster of images-used-for-the-first-time of any scene after the first few pages of the novel. Although Stephen is overtly repulsed by these experiences, the rather dramatic relish with which they are presented foreshadows a change in connotation that takes place in Chapter III.

Perhaps the most important theme of the section concerns the conflict or dichotomy between the *inner,* imaginative world of Stephen and the *outer,* physical world. Suggested by many different images, the theme grows by accumulation until it is stated outright in the final paragraph of the section. The running style Mike Flynn imposes on Stephen is one early example of the theme:

> Mike Flynn would stand at the gate near the railway station, watch in hand, while Stephen ran round the track in the style Mike Flynn favoured, his head high lifted, his knees well lifted, and his hands held straight down by his sides.   (p. 61)

The style is contrived, artificial, and unnatural, coming not from the experience of running but from some external, abstract image of a runner that exists within Mike's mind. Eearlier, Mike Flynn was strongly associated with images of blue, implying that which is removed or distant. In this passage the "distance" or separation is between abstract form and physical reality—the model of the runner versus Stephen's act of running.

A similar dichotomy exists in Stephen's musings on the relevance of words and their position between the inner, subjective world of the individual and the outer, physical world:

> Words which he did not understand he said over and over to himself till he had learned them by heart: and through them he had glimpses of the real world about him. (p. 62)

Working in an exactly opposite way from words, however,

are the theaterlike sets Stephen builds representing scenes
from *The Count of Monte Cristo:*

> At night he built up on the parlour table an image of the
> wonderful island cave out of transfers and paper flowers and
> coloured tissue paper and strips of the silver and golden
> paper in which chocolate is wrapped. When he had broken
> up this scenery, weary of its tinsel, there would come to his
> mind the bright picture of Marseilles, of sunny trellisses and
> of Mercedes. Outside Blackrock, on the road that led to the
> mountains, stood a small whitewashed house in the garden of
> which grew many rosebushes: and in this house, he told
> himself, another Mercedes lived. Both on the outward and on
> the homeward journey he measured distance by this land-
> mark: and in his imagination he lived through a long train
> of adventures, marvellous as those in the book itself, towards
> the close of which there appeared an image of himself, grown
> older and sadder, standing in a moonlit garden with Mer-
> cedes who had so many years before slighted his love, and
> with a sadly proud gesture of refusal, saying:
> —Madam, I never eat muscatel grapes.   (pp. 62–63)

Through these physical representations Stephen's imagination gains stimulus for empathic response and exploration,
resulting in attempts to merge his own self-image with the
fictional characters from the novel by projecting himself into
the fictional world of the novel. Thus the direction of discovery is from the outside—the physical models he builds
—into his imagination, not from the inside out as with
words. Analogously, Stephen assumes a mental attitude
that leads to his stylized physical gestures and manner in his
role with the gang:

> Stephen, who had read of Napoleon's plain style of dress,
> chose to remain unadorned and thereby heightened for him-
> self the pleasure of taking counsel with his lieutenant before
> giving orders.   (p. 63)

The final and strongest statement of the theme comes in the last scene of the section. Stephen's images of himself and his life become increasingly insubstantial: the group dissolves with fall and Aubrey Mills's return to school; Mike Flynn goes into the hospital; the family's financial difficulties become increasingly obvious. Reacting to these problems, Stephen becomes more and more aware of the differences between himself and others:

> The noise of children at play annoyed him and their silly voices made him feel, even more keenly than he had felt at Clongowes, that he was different from others. He did not want to play. He wanted to meet in the real world the unsubstantial image which his soul so constantly beheld. He did not know where to seek it or how: but a premonition which led him on told him that this image would, without any overt act of his, encounter him. They would meet quietly as if they had known each other and had made their tryst, perhaps at one of the gates or in some more secret place. They would be alone, surrounded by darkness and silence: and in that moment of supreme tenderness he would be transfigured. He would fade into something impalpable under her eyes and then in a moment, he would be transfigured. Weakness and timidity and inexperience would fall from him in that magic moment. (pp. 64–65)

Dreaming of discovering his identity by merging himself with some external form or image, Stephen expects to be liberated from all previous weaknesses and inadequacies. In part this wish if fulfilled during the visit to Cork; however, the experience does not produce the liberating confirmation he imagines.

The dichotomy between inner and outer is also reflected by patterns in the narrative line itself. In five of the six sections there is a progression among the images from direct, phyical realism to abstractions or more general, imaginative images; in the sixth section, the opposite development takes place. In the first scene the images progress from *reeking, outhouse, cat, tools, songs* to *blue, eyes, coils, smoke, air.* In the next, the progression goes from the realistic images of the font to Uncle Charles's prayers and thoughts of death and the past. Similarly, in the third scene the imagery moves from details of the constitutional walks to Stephen's musings on the nature of words, while in the fourth scene we saw the movement from the images of Monte Cristo that Stephen constructed to his imaginative adventures in personal identity. The following scene, however, shows the opposite progression: from the description of Stephen's adopted Napoleonic manners, the images move toward greater concreteness in the sequence *stale, odour, foreshore, nostrils, rank, oils,* and *seawrack* to the sequence *filthy, cowyard, foul, green puddles, liquid, dung.* The cluster of excremental images serves as a nadir from which the imagery rises, progressing from acceptance of the milk and cowhairs through other realistic images such as *warm, gloves,* and *gingernuts,* through his musings on his father's misfortunes, and finally to a direct statement of the *inner/outer* theme. Graphically, the pattern can be represented as follows:

Imagination

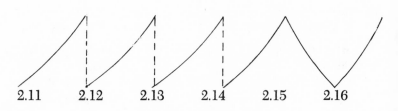

2.11   2.12   2.13   2.14   2.15   2.16

Physical Reality

The pattern is regular except for the fifth scene, which is a mirror image of that of the other scenes.

Thus the imagery in both thematic groups and patterns in the narrative line support the major substance of the section: the conflict between Stephen's inner and outer worlds. Physical reality is most immediately represented by images such as *dirt, filth,* and *excrement,* all with highly negative associations for Stephen. By contrast, the inner realm of experience is associated with a general sense of ideality. The "space" between *inner* and *outer* may be continuous with these groups representing the extremes; however, there is no indication that Stephen understands this relation. All attempts to resolve the distance between them are unsuccessful, including the imposition of form on the act of running, the role of language in experience, the escape into the fictive world of literature, the adoption of stylized behavior, and, ultimately, the search for self-identity in some "image" external to self. This motif reoccurs through the rest of the chapter, thus providing thematic continuity, but the tension that Stephen feels grows until section 2.5, where it becomes overpowering.

Section 2.2., like 2.1, consists of six distinct scenes loosely related in temporal and causative sequence but linked through associative patterns of themes and images. The first two show the family's move from their spacious quarters at Northgate to the smaller, less attractive house in Dublin. The middle two cover Stephen's growing sense of isolation, and the last pair draw heavily on remembrances from Clongowes. As in 2.1, the final scene ends with a set of images suggesting another recurrent motif that plays an important role in the remainder of the chapter and again in Chapter V.

In Chapter I, the security that Stephen associated with home was closely allied with images of the hearth fire; in the first scene of this section the hearth fire again characterizes the household:

> He understood also why the servants had often whispered together in the hall and why his father had often stood on the hearthrug, with his back to the fire, talking loudly to Uncle Charles who urged him to sit down and eat dinner.
> —There's a crack of the whip left in me yet, Stephen, old chap, said Mr. Dedalus, poking at the dull fire with fierce energy. We're not dead yet, sonny. No, by the Lord Jesus (God forgive me) nor half dead. (p. 66)

The bright, cheerful, roaring fire of the Christmas dinner scene has become a "dull fire" that won't draw (the link with the image *dead* seems more than a casual figure of speech). Later in the section a number of fire images appear:

> The firelight flickered on the wall and beyond the window a spectral dusk was gathering upon the river. Before the fire an old woman was busy making tea and, as she bustled at her task, she told in a low voice of what the priest and the doctor had said. She told too of certain changes she had seen in her of late and of her odd ways and sayings. He sat listening to the words and following the ways of adventure that lay open in the coals, arches and vaults and winding galleries and jagged caverns.
> Suddenly he became aware of something in the doorway. A skull appeared suspended in the gloom of the doorway. A feeble creature like a monkey was there, drawn thither by the sound of voices at the fire. A whining voice came from the door, asking:
> —Is that Josephine?   (pp. 67–68)

Again, the image *skull* suggests an association between the lusterless *fire* and *death*. The only aspect that is remotely pleasant is Stephen's imaginative reverie as he stares into the coals, isolated in his thoughts from the reality around him.

The house and Stephen's experiences in Dublin are also linked with the *excrement/filth/dirt* motif:

> The lamp on the table shed a weak light over the boarded floor, muddied by the feet of the vanmen. (p. 65)

And in the next scene:

> He passed unchallenged among the docks and along the quays wondering at the multitude of corks that lay bobbing on the surface of the water in a thick yellow scum, at the crowds of quay porters and the rumbling carts and the illdressed bearded policeman. (p. 66)

The motif is continued and becomes associated with several other important themes. The aunt, sitting in her cheerless kitchen, is daydreaming over what is apparently one of those romanticized portraits of young girls, encircled in unfocused darkness, found in newspapers. She muses:

> —The beautiful Mabel Hunter!
> A ringletted girl stood on tiptoe to peer at the picture and said softly:
> What is she in, mud?
> —In the pantomime, love. (p. 68)

The juxtaposition of the images *mud* and *love* is quite interesting in this context. *Mud* is a short form of mother; however, the sentence "What is she in, mud?" can be read punningly with the suggestion of mud as dirt. Another combinuation of images of dialectically opposite connotations follows immediately, further substantiating this associative pattern. When the aunt shows the picture to those present, the contrast between Mable Hunter's idealized beauty and the reality of this setting is suggested by the "reddened and blackened hands" of one of the coal boys, which "maul the edges of the paper." If we assume the double meaning of *mud,* this juxtaposition of *mud*—assciated with the theme of dirt, filth, etcetera—with love may foreshadow the experience with the prostitute in the final scene of the chapter.

Scene 2.2.b is set at a party at Harold's Cross. Stephen's thoughts blend in and out with figures present and past. He is apparently with Emma Clery, but the way his thoughts relate to her and to associations with previous experiences with Eileen makes it impossible to determine the boundary between them within his mind. The experience, which is basically pleasant, is qualified by the implications of several images. As they prepare to go:

> They seemed to listen, he on the upper step and she on the lower. She came up to his step many times and went down to hers again between their phrases and once or twice stood close beside him for some moments on the upper step, forgetting to go down, and then went down. His heart danced upon her movements like a cork upon a tide.   (p. 69)

The image *cork* here is uncomfortably similar to the cork seen earlier bobbing in the yellow scum around the Dublin quays, and its context in this passage describing Stephen's romance again prepares us for the final scenes with the prostitute.

Later in the same passage:

> He remembered the day when he and Eileen had stood looking into the hotel grounds, watching the waiters running up a trail of bunting on the flagstaff and the fox terrier scamper-

of his unjust pandying. His reaction to the tale of Stephen's
courage is one of ridicule:

> —Father Dolan and I, when I told them all at dinner
> about it, Father Dolan and I had a great laugh over it. *You*
> *better mind yourself, Father Dolan said I, or young Dedalus*
> *will send you up for twice nine.* We had a famous laugh
> together over it. Ha! Ha! Ha!
> Mr. Dedalus turned to his wife and interjected in his
> natural voice:
> —Shows you the spirit in which they take the boys there.
> O, a jesuit for your life, for diplomacy!
> He resumed the provincial's voice and repeated:
> —I told them all at dinner about it and Father Dolan and
> I and all of us we had a hearty laugh together over it. Ha!
> Ha! Ha! (p. 72)

The motif of ridicule and mockery is developed considerably
during the succeeding sections before culminating in Mr.
Dedalus's public humiliation of his son. There it merges
with the larger theme of isolation that is accumulating as
the novel progresses.

Section 2.3, the longest of the chapter, is much more
unified than the two previous sections in terms of theme as
well as temporal and causal sequence. The events portrayed
all occur on the night of the Whitsuntide play some two
years after the close of the previous scene. Although submission is the most important theme of the section, a number of other major image clusters and motifs are present
and continue to accumulate associations. Three of these
concern *water, excrement,* and *ridicule.*

Water, it will be recalled, displayed rather specific connotations throughout Chapter I; however, the final *water*

ing to and fro on the sunny lawn, and how, all of a sudden
she had broken out into a peal of laughter and had run down
the sloping curve of the path. Now, as then, he stood listlessly
in his place, seemingly a tranquil watcher of the scene before
him.   (p. 69)

Laughter, while apparently affirmative here, assumes such
specifically unpleasant connotations several scenes later that
it must be regarded as ambiguous in this context also.

The last two scenes are dominated by mental associations
with the past. When Stephen sits down to write a poem to
"E——— C———," he remembers a similar effort the day
after the Christmas dinner when he tried to write poems on
the backs of his father's second moiety notices (an interesting
juxtaposition!). Instead, he writes down a series of names
of classmates he knew at Clongowes. As before, he is unable
to write.

In the final scene, the ghosts of Clongowes are even
more pervasive and devastating. His father, at dinner, re-
counts his encounter with the former rector of Clongowes.
Stephen's reaction is immediate:

> One evening his father came home full of news which kept
> his tongue busy all through dinner. Stephen had been awaiting
> his father's return for there had been mutton hash that day
> and he knew that his father would make him dip his bread
> in the gravy. But he did not relish the hash for the mention
> of Clongowes had coated his palate with a scum of disgust.
> (p. 71)

The image of scum here suggests the earlier image of the
floating cork with its implication of the *excrement/filth*
motif. However, the most important development of the
scene and perhaps of the section concerns the image *laugh.*
Mr. Dedalus tells of the rector's account of Stephen's protest

images—the *brimming bowl* of that chapter and those of the font in the first two sections of Chapter II—are ambivalent. In section 2.3 another pattern begins to emerge. This group, largely metaphoric or imanginative, involves flowing water or great bodies of water. As Stephen walks out into the night air on the way to his encounter with Heron, the gymnasium looks to him like "a festive ark, anchored among the hulks of houses, her frail cables of lanterns looping her to her moorings" (p. 74–75). In the same paragraph: "his unrest issued from him like a wave of sound; and on the tide of flowing music the ark was journeying, trailing her cables of lanterns in her wake." Later, while talking with Heron, he recalls his feelings for Emma:

> All day he had imagined a new meeting with her for he knew that she was to come to the play. The old restless moodiness had again filled his breast as it had done on the night of the party but had not found an outlet in verse. The growth and knowledge of two years of boyhood stood between them now, forbidding such an outlet: and all day the stream of gloomy tenderness within him had started forth and returned upon itself in dark courses and eddies.   (p. 77)

It is significant that all three passages contain or suggest images of waters moving with force and that they are metaphoric or imaginative. In connotation, they are closer to the images in Chapter I of the water beneath the wall of the Dedalus home than the more prevalent association with the waters of the ditch. Later in the chapter this set of images merges with the larger theme of the dichotomy between inner and outer.

As *water* begins to change in its relations with other images in the novel, the *excrement/fiilth/dirt* motif climaxes in this section and begins to decline in importance. After the play Stephen, filled with the success of his performance but embarrassed by his family, makes brief excuses to his father and disappears down the street:

> A film still veiled his eyes but they burned no longer. A power, akin to that which had often made anger or resentment fall from him, brought his steps to rest. He stood still and gazed up at the sombre porch of the morgue and from that to the dark cobbled laneway at its side. He saw the word *Lotts* on the wall of the lane and breathed slowly the rank heavy air.
>
> —That is horse piss and rotted straw, he thought. It is a good odour to breathe. It will calm my heart. My heart is quite calm now. I will go back.   (p. 86)

He acknowledges here a predilection for the sensations he denied in the earlier cluster concerning the cow yard. Like sound images in Chapter I, the *smell of excrement* is able to cut through his reveries; in Chapter III it is this same odor that Stephen seeks out in his attempts to mortify his senses.

The theme of ridicule, established in the preceding section, is developed here around Stephen's role as the farcical pedagogue in the play. Since his interests are already strongly intellectual and literary, the part is, in a sense, a farce on his own nature. That Stephen regards the role as such is clear: "The thought of the part he had to play humiliated him" (p. 85). The same note of ridicule is present in Heron's greeting to Stephen:

> —Here comes the noble Dedalus! cried a high throaty voice. Welcome to our trusty friend!
>
> This welcome ended in a soft peal of mirthless laughter as Heron salaamed and then began to poke the ground with his cane.   (p. 75)

The whole encounter with Heron is filled with images suggesting this theme; they include *cruel* or *mirthless laughter,* *false smiles,* and *malignant joy,* to name a few.

The most important themes, however, concern *fear* and *submission.* In Chapter I, *fear* was closely associated with images of eyes and bird. Here it is most immediately related to *Heron, cane,* and *cried.* (See factor 17, Appendix D.2.) Although the source of fear is very different from Stephen's childhood fantasies of birds attacking his eyes, it is clear that elements of this association are still present. Early in the encounter, Joyce establishes a strong connection between *Heron* and images of birds. The second link—between *Heron* and *fear*—already exists and is reinforced later. In reply to his friend's taunting jest.

> Stephen shook his head and smiled in his rival's flushed and mobile face, beaked like a bird's. He had often thought it strange that Vincent Heron had a bird's face as well as a bird's name. A shock of pale hair lay on the forehead like a ruffled crest: the forehead was narrow and bony and a thin hooked nose stood out between the closeset prominent eyes which were light and inexpresisve.

As before, name and face images indicate fundamental character. Once the association is made between *Heron* and *bird* imagery, there are numerous other images and expressions that can be seen to indicate and support this relation within Stephen's mind. The following are examples:

> The excited prefect was hustling the boys through the vestry like a flock of geese, flapping the wings of his soutane nervously and crying to the laggards to make haste.   (p. 74)

> A sidedoor of the theatre opened suddenly and a shaft of light flew across the grassplots.   (p. 75)

A shaft of momentary anger flew through Stephen's mind at these indelicate allusions in the hearing of a stranger. (p. 77)

In this context the references to flock of geese, flapping wings, and the two metaphoric uses of *flew* all reinforce the metaphoric relations between *Heron, bird,* and *fear.*

The scene moves rather quickly to climax, the caning of Stephen. There are obvious similarities between this scene and the earlier, pandybat episode; yet the intensities of the two scenes are quite different. The former was truly epiphanic. while the latter breaks in intensity at the very moment of the blow. This difference is evident in the respective concentrations of images. (See figures 2.3 and 2.4.) In the earlier scene, Stephen is overwhelmed by what is happening to him; here he is in complete self-control. At the height of the experience he lapses into an abstract form of submission: he begins to recite in self-mockery the *confiteor*. Also, at the very moment of the blow, his mind is carried away by a long train of associations connected with the image *admit*. While he mechanically repeats the *confiteor*, his thoughts go back to two earlier encounters. The first concerns the charge of his writing teacher that his weekly essay contains heresy, to which Stephen had weakly submitted. The second, another encounter with Heron, concerns Stephen's defense of Byron as the greatest English poet. Although he sustains a beating from Heron and his colleagues, he refuses to betray his belief. The imagery in that scene links it with the pandybat episode:

> At last after a fury of plunges he wrenched himself free. His tormentors set off towards Jones's Road, laughing and jeering at him, while he, torn and flushed and panting, stumbled after them half blinded with tears, clenching his fists madly and sobbing. (p. 82)

The personal importance of literature in particular and aesthetics in general grows steadily until its full realization in Chapter V; in the present context, however, it is mixed with the ridicule so prevalent in this portion of the narrative.

When his thoughts return to the present, Stephen is still repeating the *confiteor,* but he is able to see himself and his relations with his tormentors with remarkable detachment:

> While he was still repeating the *Confiteor* amid the in-dulgent laughter of his hearers and while the scenes of that malignant episode were still passing sharply and swiftly before his mind he wondered why he bore no malice now to those who had tormented him. (p. 82)

The personality factor that allows him to bear no malice is, of course, his sense of isolation. He feels only remotely "in" the encounter with Heron: in effect, the *confiteor* serves as a façade of formalized actions that makes his apparent sub-mission not a submission at all: he has redirected the con-frontation. Thus, the whole notion of submission is also couched in terms of the *inner/outer* conflict, for submission inherently involves the breaking down of some inner barrier or self-image by either a different inner impulse or an outer, physical stimulus. Earlier, the relation between the *inner/ outer* dichotomy was closely related to patterns of habitual or formalized action; here that same pattern prevails and also links this complex to the theme associated with fear and birds. In the final climactic experience of the chapter, this group will again play an important part.

Like 2.3, section 2.4 concerns a unified sequence of events depicting the trip to Cork taken by Stephen and Mr. Dedalus while the family's personal property was being sold to cancel Mr. Dedalus's debts. Thematically, the section displays several variations on the isolation motif; they include *death, betrayal,* and the *past.*

Structurally the section is bounded by images of heat and cold. The section begins with the scene in the railway coach where images of cold, light, shiver, and chilly morning breeze are found. Mr. Dedalus's come-all-you contains the lines:

> My love she's handsome,
> My love she's bonny:
> She's like good whisky
>   When it is new;
> But when 'tis old
> And growing cold
> It fades and dies like
>   The morning dew.
>   (p. 88)

This association of *Cork* with *coldness,* however, is mitigated by several images of warmth: after arriving in Cork, Stephen notes the "warm sunlight" and later he refers to "the warm sunny city." The images of cold in the latter part of the section will be discussed later, since they relate to several other motifs.

The importance of the image *name* in this section is reflected in its frequency, for it occurs twice as often here as in the rest of the chapter. For Mr. Dedalus, names are an approach to the past:

> Mr. Dedalus had ordered drisheens for breakfast and during the meal he crossexamined the waiter for local news. For the most part they spoke at crosspurposes when a name was mentioned, the waiter having in mind the present holder and Mr. Dedalus his father or perhaps his grandfather. (p. 89)

As the passage indicates, he is consistently frustrated in his attempts to recapture his earlier life. For Stephen, *name* carries a different meaning. Through names he seeks to penetrate the isolation in which he is engulfed, to establish some relationship between himself and his social and physical environment:

> Nothing moved him or spoke to him from the real world unless he heard in it an echo of the infuriated cries within him. He could respond to no earthly or human appeal, dumb and insensible to the call of summer and gladness and companionship, wearied and dejected by his father's voice. He could scarcely recognise as his own thought, and repeated slowly to himself:
> —I am Stephen Dedalus, I am walking beside my father whose name is Simon Dedalus. We are in Cork, in Ireland. Cork is a city. Our room is in the Victoria Hotel. Victoria and Stephen and Simon. Simon and Stephen and Victoria. Names. (p. 92)

The theme of death is also prevalent through out the section. On the train Stephen recalls the death of Uncle Charles. His father's attempts to find old friends are almost invariably frustrated because the person has died. The image *dead* itself occurs more frequently in this section than in any other entire chapter except the last. Contrasting with these images of death is the image *foetus* that Stephen sees carved on a desk in one of his father's old lecture halls. Just as names function differently for the two, so this image evokes in Stephen a flood of images of his father's past that are not available to the elder Dedalus:

> On the desk before him he read the word *Foetus* cut several times in the dark stained wood. The sudden legend startled his blood: he seemed to feel the absent students of the college about him and to shrink from their company. A vision of their life, which his father's words had been powerless to evoke, sprang up before him out of the word cut in the desk. A broadshouldered student with a moustache was cutting in the letters with a jackknife, seriously. Other students stood or

sat near him laughing at his handiwork. One jogged his elbow. The big student turned on him, frowning. He was dressed in loose grey clothes and had tan boots.   (pp. 89–90)

The emotional impact of the experience is profound:

The word and the vision capered before his eyes as he walked back across the quadrangle and towards the college gate. It shocked him to find in the outer world a trace of what he had deemed till then a brutish and individual malady of his own mind.   (p. 90)

For Stephen to confront within the external world an aspect of himself is to breach the barrier that has isolated him. In doing so, he achieves the desire expressed at the end of section 2.1: "to meet in the real world the unsubstantial image which his soul so constantly beheld." The shocking and disconcerting aspect of the experience, however, is that the image is a manifestation of a part of Stephen's mind that he sees as evil and disgusing. Instead of associating *Foetus* with life in contrast to the images of death present, he associates it with the *excremental/filth* complex. The motif of gestation imagery, which grows in subsequent chapters, is left relatively undeveloped in the rest of Chapter II.

The crisis of the section is Simon Dedalus's public denunciation of his son. The act is accomplished in a sequence of three statements that are cumulative in their impact. The first incident, part of Simon Dedalus's "fixed" response to all he encounters, could be interpreted as only jest:

To the sellers in the market, to the barmen and barmaids, to the beggars who importuned him for a lob Mr. Dedalus told the same tale, that he was an old Corkonian, that he had been trying for thirty years to get rid of his Cork accent up in Dublin and that Peter Pickackafax beside him was his eldest son but that he was only a Dublin jackeen.   (p. 93)

The second might also be read as a figure of speech, and, hence, innocuous:

> Leave him alone. He's a levelheaded thinking boy who doesn't bother his head about that kind of nonsense.
> —Then he's not his father's son, said the little old man.
> —I don't know, I'm sure, said Mr. Dedalus, smiling complacently.　(p. 94)

But the third statement is wholly malicious:

> By God, I don't feel more than eighteen myself. There's that son of mine there not half my age and I'm a better man than he is any day of the week.
> —Draw it mild now, Dedalus. I think it's time for you to take a back seat, said the gentleman who had spoken before.
> —No, by God! asserted Mr. Dedalus. I'll sing a tenor song against him or I'll vault a fivebarred gate against him or I'll run with him after the hounds across the country as I did thirty years ago along with the Kerry Boy and the best man for it.　(p. 95)

The effect of this drunken betrayal is to seal Stephen's sense of isolation from his father and the past: "An abyss of fortune or of temperament sundered him from them" (p. 95).

The section closes as it began, with images of cold:

> His mind seemed older than theirs: it shone coldly on their strifes and happiness and regrets like a moon upon a younger earth.　(p. 95)

And shortly later:

> Nothing stirred within his soul but a cold and cruel and loveless lust. His childhood was dead or lost and with it his soul capable of simple joys, and he was drifting amid life like the barren shell of the moon.　(p. 96)

Here the major themes of the section—*death, the past,* and *cold*—coalesce in the numbing isolation Stephen experiences; even the lust within him is cold, not warm or hot.

Section 2.5 consists of two major actions: the events surrounding Stephen's winning the State Essay Prize, followed by the events leading up to the climactic scene with the prostitute. Because the narrative is more a description than a rendering of Stephen's thoughts, the final epiphany is not so dramatic as the pandybat episode. However, the concentration of imagery—as can be seen in II.4—is considerably greater than in any previous scene of the chapter. As in Chapter I, many of the major themes developed through the chapter converge in this experience.

As Mr. Dedalus sought ties with the past through names, Stephen seeks to break through his present isolation from his family and to establish some semblance of order by purchasing gifts and taking the family on an extended round of elegant meals and theater excursions. Two of the images closely associated with his "wealth" are the *squares of Vienna chocolate* he distributes and the *pot of pink paint* he buys to refurbish his room. *Chocolate* has interesting associations: Stephen earlier constructed images from *The Count of Monte Cristo* out of the papers used to wrap chocolates; these images, in turn, stimulated his fantasies and imaginative explorations. The *pink paint*, which runs out before the whole room is done, also represents an attempt to escape the deep rifts running through the household. Stephen's realization of the futility of his efforts is evident in the following passage:

How foolish his aim had been! He had tried to build a

breakwater of order and elegance against the sordid tide of life without him and to dam up, by rule of conduct and active interests and new filial relations, the powerful recurrence of the tides within him. Useless. From without as from within the water had flowed over his barriers: their tides began once more to jostle fiercely above the crumbled mole.   (p. 98)

The powerful forces within him and the oppressive squalor of the household eventually overpower all of his efforts to maintain former patterns of relationships and life style. In a sense, he has attempted to impose an order—as Mike Flynn attempted to impose a running style—that no longer has any relation with what actually exists. Even Stephen's image of ideal beauty, *Emma,* is overcome by the forces growing within him:

By day and by night he moved among distorted images of the outer world. A figure that had seemed to him by day demure and innocent came towards him by night through the winding darkness of sleep, her face transfigured by a lecherous cunning, her eyes bright with brutish joy.   (p. 99)

The result is a sense of isolation even more profound than before:

He saw clearly too his own futile isolation. He had not gone one step nearer the lives he had sought to approach nor bridged the restless shame and rancour that divided him from mother and brother and sister. He felt that he was hardly of the one blood with them but stood to them rather in the mystical kinship of fosterage, fosterchild and fosterbrother.   (p. 98)

The second part of section 2.5 concerns, presumably, Stephen's first sexual encounter with a woman. Like the inverted relation between *foetus* and *death,* the imagery underlying this scene suggests not *love* or *beauty* but *excrement* and *filth:* "He wandered up and down the dark slimy streets peering into the gloom of lanes and doorways" (p. 99). As he walks toward the brothel district he feels building within himself a tremendous cry:

> It broke from him like a wail of despair from a hell of sufferers and died in a wail of furious entreaty, a cry for an iniquitous abandonment, a cry which was but the echo of an obscene scrawl which he had read on the oozing wall of a urinal. (p. 100)

And finally: "He had wandered into a maze of narrow and dirty streets. From the foul laneways he heard bursts of hoarse riot and wrangling and the drawling of drunken singers" (p. 100).

Out of this context the prostitute approaches him wearing a "pink gown" and they go to her room:

> Her round arms held him firmly to her and he, seeing her face lifted to him in serious calm and feeling the warm calm rise and fall of her breast, all but burst into hysterical weeping. Tears of joy and relief shone in his delighted eyes and his lips parted though they would not speak.   (p. 101)

The passage contains interesting images: the image of tears bursting from eyes is reminiscent of the pandybat episode while the image of extended arms foreshadow the final scene of the novel and Stephen's departure from Ireland. Through this imagery, the experience is linked structurally to both the immediate context and the fabric of the entire novel.

As the situation progresses, Stephen is helpless to resist:

> With a sudden movement she bowed his head and joined her lips to his and he read the meaning of her movements in her frank uplifted eyes.   (p. 101)

As in the pandybat sequence, *eyes* or *face* suggests basic states of feeling. The next group of images links the experience with the theme of submission associated with the Heron encounter:

> It was too much for him. He closed his eyes, surrendering himself to her, body and mind, conscious of nothing in the world but the dark pressure of her softly parting lips. (p. 101)

There, submission was closely associated with fear of some external force; here, although the immediate cause—the prostitute's pull—is external, the submission is to the inner nature of his own personality—that nature which he saw as sordid and evil in connection with the image *foetus*.

The climax of the scene, the moment of epiphany, is similar in many ways to the pandybat experience and other epiphanies that follow. One characteristic suggested by the discussion of epiphany earlier is that these encounters are marked by the dissolution between subjective and objective levels of experience. The breaking of this barrier, no matter how slight or momentary, is particularly important here considering the pervasive sense of isolation built throughout the chapter. This sense of encounter can be seen in the following passage: "[Her lips] pressed upon his brain as upon his lips as though they were the vehicle of a vague speech; and between them he felt an unknown and timid pressure, darker than the swoon of sin, softer than sound or odour" (p. 101). Like the epiphany in Chapter I, the senses fuse synesthetically: tactile, auditory, olfactory, and visual images all coalesce in the final phrase of the passage. The intensity of the experience, however, is significantly lower than that of the earlier epiphany. Although Stephen has apparently gained some personal insight and is able to break his sense of isolation momentarily, a number of disturbing undercurrents remain. First, the image *pink* used to describe the prostitute's gown may suggest that this attempt to satisfy his physical desires and find understanding is as futile as was his attempt to change his living conditions with pink paint. More important, the situation is artificial, not personal. Their relationship is a contract based on money; consequently, it is similar to the earlier experience in the chapter where his attempts to impose external form onto reality through the prize money failed. Finally, the association between *love* and *ideality* is undercut by images from the *dirt/filth/ excrement* motif. There is every indication that this disturbing and unresolved relation permeates the experience.

Thus, the scene achieves an epiphany of sorts, as can be seen by figure II.4, but the lack of a sustained build-up for the experience itself, the many qualifying associations that run counter to any real sense of communication, and the artificiality of the experience's form suggest that any communication is momentary, if not illusory. The most lasting effects are likely to be those suggested in the structure of images present rather than any conscious realization available to Stephen.

Looking back at the chapter, we can see the domination of a single thematic pattern: Stephen's quest to integrate the ideal with the real. In the first section the theme took several forms. Images of blue consistently suggested the unattainability of the distant, the removed. Mike Flynn's coaching consisted of his attempts to impose over Stephen's natural running gait—as awkward as we might imagine it to be—an abstract, idealized form. The same distance relation is present in Stephen's attempts to escape into the fantasy world induced by his tinfoil images from *The Count of Monte Cristo.* In contrast to these unattainable images of the ideal, images strongly suggestive of the *dirt/filth/ excrement* motif dominate Stephen's immediate objective experience. These include *scum* and *slime* related to *food, foetus* related to *death,* and *slime* related to the *brothel neighborhood.* In all these cases, images that should connote the factors of life at its most fundamental level—*food, physical love,* and *procreation*—are denigrated by the overwhelming associations in Stephen's mind with his squalid physical life.

A corollary of this theme is that concerning submission. Stephen's earlier personal triumph at Clongowes when he refused to submit to his unjust punishment is transformed into ridicule by Father Dolan's and Simon Dedalus's laughter. In the frightening encounter with Heron, Stephen, ironically, withstands their demands that he submit by repeating the *Confiteor,* distancing himself psychologically from their physical blows and jeers. In the final scene with the prostitute, Stephen is unable to submit completely to his adolescent desires: in approaching the brothel he would circle until some outside force intervened; in the actual embrace, Stephen submits only when the prostitute physically pulls his lips to hers.

Over the chapter, the general intensity of imagery rises and falls in a fairly regular pattern, with each rise a little higher than the preceding one. In the prostitute scene, the richest of the chapter, Stephen's sense of physical love fuses with a complex of thematic groups, most highly negative in connotation; the ideal image of beauty that he clings to becomes even more remote, unattainable, and unrealistic. As it recedes, Stephen's sense of personal degeneracy increases. It is this context out of which the events of Chapter III grow.

5
Analysis of Chapter III

Chapter III, the middle chapter of *Portrait*, is central to the narrative both in sequence and in formal structure. Chapters I and II represent, to a large extent, a continuing development of the same thematic materials: school, friends, and home. At the end of II, however, the important new theme of submission appears in Stephen's acquiescence to his adolescent desires. Chapter III exhibits in the interrelation of this theme with that of religious ideality a major structural pattern found in the remaining chapters of the novel. As the chapter begins, the last major theme of the preceding chapter is developed and expanded; during the latter half, it recedes in importance and finally disappears. Concurrent with the starting theme's recession is the emergence of a new theme—*religious ideality*—that builds toward epiphany. This theme, similarly, follows the same pattern in IV that *submission* follows here. Chapter III is the first chapter to exhibit this full cycle of development.

The chapter has three sections. In 3.1 we see Stephen's present psychological state through direct narration of his thoughts and feelings and through depiction of habitual actions. First shown is a family meal followed by an account

of Stephen's frequent visits to the brothel district of Dublin.
The narrative then enters Stephen's imagination and shows
his attempts to deal empathically with feelings of separation
from the ideality of the Virgin Mary and from God. The
section ends with the classroom speech in which the rector
announces the retreat. Section 3.2 contains the direct narration of the retreat interspersed with short scenes depicting
Stephen's reaction to the sermons. In the first sermon Father
Arnall outlines the retreat: the announced topics for the
four sermons are Death, Judgment, Hell, and Heaven. The
sequence is followed rigorously except that the final sermon,
instead of examining heaven, further explores the horrors
of hell. The last section of the chapter extends the basic
rhythm of sermon and reaction by describing Stephen's
final, climactic reaction. This portion of the narrative begins
with his fears while alone in his room at home and the nightmare that follows. When Stephen awakens, he wanders
through the streets of Dublin, but instead of going to the
brothel, he seeks a chapel in which to make his confession.
The chapter ends with two brief scenes: the Dedalus household and Stephen's earnest prayers.

That Stephen's experiences are markedly different from
those of the first two chapters is indicated by the more
frequent images of the chapters:

Chapter I	name	smell
	cold	air
father	God	head
Dedalus	rector	bed
hand	dark	
eye	cried	
face	door	Chapter II
prefect	voice	father
day	walk	Dedalus

Heron	home	child
day	light	day
eye	garden	eye
dark	halt	fire
face		word
voice		hand
walk	Chapter III	body
hand	God	heaven
smile	sin	saint
heart	soul	confess
night	hell	death
silence	dark	face
work	pray	light
head	heart	

The central figure of authority in I and II is father, associated with Mr. Dedalus and the fathers at Clongowes; in III, the theme of authority is related to the image *God*. The prominence of images associated with the physical body in I and II has diminished considerably in III; one image, *eye*, from this group that is important here is used metaphorically. The most obvious shift in subject matter concerns religious images.[1] *God, sin,* and *soul* each occur almost twice as often as the next most frequent image, *hell*. So pervasive is this group that the first image without necessarily religious associations, *dark*, occurs only some thirty-eight times compared with 134 for *God*. The comparative positions of *hell* and *heaven* are also interesting; the former occurs twice as often as the latter. In comparing these lists, we see the strong shift in the general areas of Stephen's experience as well as the connotations of this experience, suggested by the importance of the images *sin, hell, dark, fire, confess,* and *death*.

The early scenes of Chapter III reveal Stephen's state of mind. As he sits in the darkened classroom he thinks of the evening meal:

> He felt his belly crave for its food. He hoped there would be stew for dinner, turnips and carrots and bruised potatoes and fat mutton pieces to be ladled out in thick peppered flourfattened sauce. Stuff it into you, his belly counselled him.   (p. 102)

In the preceding chapter, several meals were described, but one quoted in particular is closely related to this meal:

> There had been mutton hash that day and he knew that his father would make him dip his bread in the gravy. But he did not relish the hash for the mention of Clongowes had coated his palate with a scum of disgust.   (p. 71)

The earlier association between scum and the ditch heightens our sense of Stephen's repulsion. The kind of food that had been impalatable to him earlier is not only acceptable now but desired. The attraction suggests a beast, craving for fats and starches. In later meals (3.2), this suggestion is more direct.

The sensual response Stephen experienced with the prostitute in Chapter II indicate at least a partial break in his sense of isolation; here the encounter is reduced to habit. It has become his custom to wander after dark into the brothel district: "He would pass by them calmly waiting for a sudden movement of his own will or a sudden call to his sinloving soul from their soft perfumed flesh" (p. 102). The necessity to await an impulse from his "lower" nature before acting reenforces his sense of himself as bestial. The earlier impression of breaking through the barrier between outer and inner has been dissipated: there is no communication—only submission to physical desires.

In the scene that follows, Stephen uses formalized structures to examine the distance between inner, personal reality and the outer, physical world. The immediate images that evoke this empathic projection are two equations in his textbook. In his imagination, the first equation begins "to spread out a widening tail, eyed and starred like a peacock's" (pp. 102–3). The eyes in this passage are more closely associated with stars than with Stephen's own eyes or with his earlier sense of vulnerability and fear: "The indices appearing and disappearing were eyes opening and closing; the eyes opening and closing were stars being born and being quenched" (p. 103). The significance of this train of associations is increased by Stephen's strong involvement:

> The vast cycle of starry life bore his weary mind outward to its verge and inward to its centre, a distant music accompanying him outward and inward. What music? The music came nearer and he recalled the words, the word of Shelley's fragment upon the moon wandering companionless, pale for weariness. The stars began to crumble and a cloud of fine stardust fell through space.   (p. 103)

Fear of physical harm, earlier associated with *eyes* and *bird* images, has been replaced by his overwhelming sense of isolation. Shelley's fragment about the moon wandering companionless links this passage with the scene in the Cork bar where Stephen experienced childhood's end, realizing the emotional distance separating him from his father. There the metaphoric representation of phenomenological isolation as spatial distance was inchoate; here the imagery makes that metaphor much more substantial.

Stephen's musings on the second equation clarify the reasons he feels are responsible for his condition:

It was his own soul going forth to experience, unfolding itself
sin by sin, spreading abroad the balefire of its burning stars
and folding back upon itself, fading slowly, quenching its own
lights and fires. They were quenched: and the cold darkness
filled chaos. . . . The chaos in which his ardour extinguished
itself as a cold indifferent knowledge of himself. He had
sinned mortally not once but many times and he knew that,
while he stood in danger of eternal damnation for the first
sin alone, by every succeeding sin he multiplied his guilt
and his punishment. His days and works and thoughts could
make no atonement for him, the fountains of santifying grace
having ceased to refresh his soul.　(p. 103)

These scenes portray Stephen's general psychological state
at this time. The events and attitudes that were tumultuous
or climactic in the preceding chapter have become habit;
although capable of empathic projection outward toward
physical reality and life, he is preoccupied with his own
inner sense of guilt and sin, manifested in a cold indifference
that verges on nonentity. Stephen's sense that his is a dark,
bestial, and loathsome personality and the emotional isolation he feels because of this is closely associated with the
large number of images connoting physical distance.

Two other groups of images central to the major development of the chapter are *light* and *dark* images. Like *fire* and
water in Chapter I, these images carry opposite connotations. Their importance for the chapter is apparent in the
graph in Appendix E, which indicates that the greatest
concentration of this group by far is in Chapter III; however,
the importance of an image group is often a matter of place-
ment as well as frequency. In Chapter I, Joyce uses *fire* and
water images almost emblematically, ending the traumatic
Clongowes scene with a *water* image and beginning the
succeeding Christmas dinner scene with a *fire* image. In
section 3.1, Joyce similarly begins most scenes with an
image denoting light or its absence. The chapter begins:

The swift December dusk had come tumbling clownishly after its dull day and, as he stared through the dull square of the window of the schoolroom, he felt his belly crave for its food. (p. 102)

The images of dusk and the two references to *dull* describe the amount and kind of light present. Later, his visits to the brothels are on "gloomy secret" nights. Referring to one of the equations, "the dull light fell more faintly upon the page whereon another equation began to unfold itself slowly and to spread abroad its widening tail" (p. 103). The central image in the following summary statement is one of darkness:

At his first violent sin he had felt a wave of vitality pass out of him and had feared to find his body or his soul maimed by the excess. Instead the vital wave had carried him on its bosom out of himself and back again when it receded: and no part of body or soul had been maimed but a dark peace had been established between them. (p. 103)

In all of these scenes, images of darkness or of dim, unattractive light reinforce Stephen's sense of the darkness of his own inner nature.

In contrast to the *dark* images associated with Stephen's sense of self is the *light* motif. This theme is punningly suggested in the first sentence describing Stephen's room: "On the wall of his bedroom hung an illuminated scroll, the certificate of his prefecture in the college of the sodality of the Blessed Virgin Mary" (p. 104). The important relation between *light* and *religious ideality* becomes apparent immediately:

His sin, which had covered him from the sight of God, had led him nearer to the refuge of sinners. Her eyes seemed to regard him with mild pity; her holiness, a strange light glowing faintly upon her frail flesh, did not humiliate the sinner who approached her. (p. 105)

Later reference is made to Mary, "whose emblem is the morning star, *bright and musical, telling of heaven and infusing peace*" (p. 105). The association between the *religious ideality* of God and Mary and images of *light* with the further development that religious acceptance of the individual is indicated by his existing within the "sight" of God makes Stephen's negative sense of self even more dramatic. The passage also suggests a different connotation for *eyes* from the earlier association with *fear*.

There are some seven *eye* images in section 3.1, occurring in a variety of contexts. The first occurs in the brothel, where Stephen notes details such as a "ring of porter" with his eyes (p. 102). In the passages concerning the equations, *eyes* are associated with stars and Stephen's attempt to resolve his isolation. The image's final occurrence in the section is the rector's "dark stern eyes" whose "dark fire kindled the dusk into a tawny glow" (p. 108). The implications of fire associated with the eyes of a religious personage become clear in 3.2; here we can simply note the general environment of these images: *stars, religious personages, fire,* and Stephen's *sense of isolation*.

Water imagery also changes in its connotations during the chapter before figuring dramatically in the epiphanic scene of Chapter IV. In Chapter I *water* imagery was strongly associated with Stephen's fall into the ditch before being explicitly identified with *filth* and *excrement* in Chapter II. In contrast, the image of the brimming bowl following Stephen's pandying carried quite different, even mysterious, connotations. Elements of both associative patterns are present in 3.1. In questioning "the darkness of his own state," Stephen felt himself sinking into a "swamp of spiritual and bodily sloth" (p. 106); however, a different *water* image occurs in the passage assessing Stephen's psychological state. The isolation he feels because of his sinful nature is characterized as follows: "His days and works and thoughts could make no atonement for him, the fountains of sanctifying grace having ceased to refresh his soul" (p. 103). In a passage from the same scene quoted above in the discussion of *light/dark* imagery, the entire experience is characterized as a "wave" of vitality that passes out of him. In these instances, the wave and the fountain suggest positive, life-giving forces that contrast with Stephen's dark inner state. This connotation is strengthened in the section's final scene: "A little wave of quiet mirth broke forth over the class of boys from the rector's grim smile. Stephen's heart began slowly to fold and fade with fear like a withering flower" (p. 107). The flower is withered—dying—from the lack of water; *aridness,* as we would suspect, carries opposite connotations from the life-giving effects of water. This same image is repeated as the final image of the section, emphasizing its importance and giving symmetry to the scene: "Stephen's heart had withered up like a flower of the desert that feels the simoon coming from afar" (p. 108).

One final image group that warrants special attention is that concerned with cyclical or rhythmic motion. As Stephen would approach the brothel district, "He would follow a devious course up and down the streets, circling always nearer and nearer in a tremor of fear and joy, until his feet led him suddenly round a dark corner" (p. 102). While he was there, Stephen's gaze fixed itself on the "ring of porter," an image characterizing the experience. Images of cycles are also important in the sections dealing with the equations. For example: "The vast cycle of starry life bore his weary mind outward to its verge and inward to its centre, a distant music accompanying him outward and inward" p. 103). And later, "the vital wave had carried him on its bosom out of himself and back again when it receded" (p. 103). The association between *cyclical movement* and *music* is interesting, for it is the "music" of the Latin prayers that attracts Stephen most to the Roman Catholic Mass. Later, Stephen associates the auditory sense with temporality in his aesthetic theory, suggesting, perhaps, a relation between cyclical, rhythmic motion and aesthetic structure. Section 3.2, we shall see, is developed in rhythmic patterns; Joyce thus foreshadows aesthetic structure by the thematic use of imagery.

Looking back, we can now see that the major image groups coalesce to support the one dominant theme of the section: Stephen's sense of isolation and degradation. Early in the chapter he is helpless in the grip of his physical appetites, which he feels are bestial. The resulting sense of isolation is developed in several contexts. The empathic projections stimulated by the two equations evoke a metaphoric relation between emotional distance from those around him and physical distance. Similarly, he feels that his base nature is far removed from the purity and ideality he associates with God and Mary, making their grace unattainable. This aspect of the theme is heavily supported by light and eye imagery. This section represents a nadir for Stephen, out of which grows the sequence of events that culminate in the religious epiphany that ends the chapter. Thus Stephen's self-image swings 180 degrees in the course of the chapter: from a sense of bestiality and spiritual isolation to an experience of religious ideality and union.

The most striking characteristic of section 3.2 is its complex blend of rhythms. The narrative regularly alternates from sermon to effect. It begins with Father Arnall's outline of the retreat, followed by a description of Stephen's walk home. The next day, after sermons on death and judgment, comes the section's longest introspective view of Stephen. The third sermon describes the sensual qualities of hell; the fourth, its psychological horrors. The two are separated by a brief account of classroom activities and Stephen's reactions. Section 3.3 is the final oscillation: the portrayal of the retreat's cumulative effects on Stephen, climaxing in his epiphanic confession. Thus there is a regular alternation from the sermons, narrated without authorial comment just as though the reader were hearing them, to close scrutiny of Stephen's activities and mental state. A similar oscillating pattern was seen in Stephen's empathic projections induced by the equations; here the same pattern is reflected in narrative point of view.

Another pattern of rhythmic alternation is present in the modulated use of imagery, as indicated in II.g. In terms of density of imagery, the lowest point of the chapter occurs during Father Arnall's outline of the retreat. The imagery then follows a remarkably regular pattern of alternating richness and sparsity. Rising to a high point during the sensual description of death, the level of richness falls during the more abstract sermon on judgment. The second cycle begins with Stephen's musings on Emma and the Virgin Mary and then dips with the introduction of the first sermon on hell. The level of intensity increases dramatically during the sensual description of hell before dipping once again during the preacher's metaphoric comparison with language. The final rise and fall in intensity corresponds with the description of Stephen's classroom thoughts and the description of the psychological horrors of hell. Thus, the pattern of intensity of imagery alternates regularly, rising during some experiences rendered in a highly objective manner, falling during others; invariably it rises during the glimpses we get of Stephen's thoughts. The pattern continues through section 3.3, culminating in the religious epiphany.

The highest concentrations of religious imagery, the thematic group with the highest frequency in Chapter III, occur in sections 3.2, 3.3, and the first half of Chapter IV. This concentration is apparent in the graph of its distribution (Appendix E). Most of these occurrences reflect the subject matter of the narrative; some assume interesting connotations in their associations with other, secular images. These latter religious images will be discussed in connection with the specific secular images that lend them these connotations.

Another important group includes *fire* and *heat* images. The distribution of this group over the novel shows that in one scene there are over twenty occurrences—more than twice as many as in any other scene in the novel (see Appendix E). That scene, the description of hell, will be given special attention; there are several other instances before and after that point that warrant attention. During the first sermon, Stephen is reminded of his days at Clongowes:

The figure of his old master [Father Arnall], so strangely rearisen, brought back to Stephen's mind his life at Clongowes: the wide playgrounds, swarming with boys, the square ditch, the little cemetery off the main avenue of limes where he had dreamed of being buried, the firelight on the wall of the infirmary where he lay sick, the sorrowful face of Brother Michael. (pp. 108–9)

Occurring in this context, the image of firelight on the infirmary wall is interesting. In Chapter I, *fire* was associated most strongly with the hearth, suggesting the security of home, while *water* connoted all that was most threatening and unpleasant about Clongowes. In the pandybat episode they were fused associatively in the image of scalding tears. Here, the earlier strains of pleasant associations with fire have been overpowered by negative ones. This change becomes even more dramatic in the sermons to follow.

In his first statement about the nature of hell, the preacher states: "Hell is a strait and dark and foulsmelling prison, an abode of demons and lost soul, filled with fire and smoke" (p. 119). The cultural association between *hell* and *fire* becomes a heavily emphasized link in Stephen's own experience during the sermons. Another association, that between *fire* and *darkness,* is also reinforced in the passages that follow. For example,

> The fire of hell gives forth no light. As, at the command of God, the fire of the Babylonian furnace lost its heat but not its light so, at the command of God, the fire of hell, while retaining the intensity of its heat, burns eternally in darkness. It is a neverending storm of darkness, dark flames and dark smoke of burning brimstone, amid which the bodies are heaped one upon another without even a glimpse of air. (p. 120)

When the tactile qualities of hell are characterized, *fire,* as one would suspect, is again the dominant image:

> The torment of fire is the greatest torment to which the tyrant has ever subjected his fellow creatures. Place your finger for a moment in the flame of a candle and you will feel the pain of fire. But our earthly fire was created by God for the benefit of man, to maintain in him the spark of life and to help him in the useful arts whereas the fire of hell is of another quality and was created by God to torture and punish the unrepentent sinner. Our earthly fire also consumes more or less rapidly according as the object which it attacks

is more or less combustible so that human ingenuity has even succeeded in inventing chemical preparations to check or frustrate its action. But the sulphurous brimstone which burns in hell is a substance which is specially designed to burn forever and forever with unspeakable fury. Moreover our earthly fire destroys at the same time as it burns so that the more intense it is the shorter is its duration: but the fire of hell has this property that it preserves that which it burns and though it rages with incredible intensity it rages forever. (p. 121)

Later, in the final roll call of hell's sensory tortures, the sense of touch is tormented by "redhot goads" and "cruel tongues of flame" (p. 122). This overwhelming association between *fire* and *hell* implies a further link with *sin* and *guilt*; consequently the preacher's appeal to Stephen and the others to confess to a God "burning with love for mankind, ready to comfort the afflicted" (p. 134) is highly ambivalent in associations.

The thematic use of *light*-and-*dark* imagery in 3.1 is continued and expanded here, linking it with other important groups in the chapter. One early occurrence of a light image is the following: "So he had sunk to the state of a beast that licks his chops after meat. This was the end; and a faint glimmer of fear began to pierce the fog of his mind" (p. 111). The image *glimmer* suggests faintness or darkness, perhaps light from a fire; if so, this sequence would establish associations among *fire, darkness,* and *fear,* a pattern that becomes a dominant motif later in the section. The negative connotations that images of darkness have for Stephen are reinforced considerably before the hell sermons. First, *darkness* is identified with death:

Death and judgment, brought into the world by the sin of our first parents, are the dark portals that close our earthly existence, the portals that open into the unknown and the unseen, portals through which every soul must pass. (p. 114)

Next, it is used to epitomize Stephen's sense of his own sinful, bestial nature: "Like a beast in its lair his soul had laid down in its own filth but the blasts of the angel's trumpet had driven him forth from the darkness of sin into the light" (p. 115).

The most consistent and dramatic use of *dark* occurs in the sermons on hell. The preacher gives a one-sentence description characterizing the sensual horrors of hell: "Hell is a strait and dark and foulsmelling prison. . ." (p. 119). *Dark,* along with *fire,* plays a major role in describing hell. It occurs some ten times in a span of text approximately five hundred words long, always in the context of *fire* images. *Darkness* is also used to epitomize the mental horrors of hell:

> Just as every sense is afflicted with a fitting torment so is every spiritual faculty; the fancy with horrible images, the sensitive faculty with alternate longing and rage, the mind and understanding with an interior darkness more terrible even than the exterior darkness which reigns in that dreadful prison. (p. 130)

The chain of associations is drawn full circle and completed. *Darkness,* which began as an image connoting Stephen's sense of his own sinful and bestial nature, is strongly associated with both the sensual, emblematic images of hell and the general psychological state of all sinners. Stephen's intense inner feelings are linked with what is presented to him as factual, an image within the objective world with which he can identify; as before, that image has highly negative connotations.

The association between *food* and Stephen's sense of

bestiality suggested in 3.1 is developed more directly here. In a passage already quoted, Stephen acknowledges that he has sunk "to the state of a beast that licks his chaps after meat" (p. 111). Later, in the same scene:

> His soul was fattening and congealing into a gross grease, plunging ever deeper in its dull fear into a sombre threatening dusk, while the body that was his stood, listless and dishonoured, gazing out of darkened eyes, helpless, perturbed and human for a bovine god to stare upon. (p. 111)

In both passages his inner, psychological state is closely associated with images of food that is thick, greasy, verging on congealing. The association between *thick, scummy food* and the earlier theme of *filth* and *excrement* is here linked directly with bestial imagery and Stephen's own self-image. This train explains the underlying pattern of associations found in the dream of section 3.3. A foreshadowing of that experience appears just before the first sermon on hell:

> His monstrous dreams, peopled by apelike creatures and by harlots with gleaming jewel eyes; the foul letters he had written in the joy of guilty confession and carried secretly for days and days only to throw them under cover of night among the grass in the corner of a field or beneath some hingeless door or in some niche in the hedges where a girl might come upon them as she walked by and read them secretly. Mad! Mad! (pp. 115–16)

In the second sermon on hell, this pattern of associations is extended to include the psychological dimension of sin:

> —Sin, remember, is a twofold enormity. It is a base consent to the promptings of our corrupt nature to the lower instincts, to that which is gross and beastlike; and it is also a turning away from the counsel of our higher nature. (p. 127)

Stephen's sense of self is thus linked with major image groups connoting all that he finds personally abhorrent as well as more general negative concepts such as sin.

It is not surprising that *light,* the opposite of *darkness,* should carry opposite connotations. *Light* is used in a highly emblematic way throughout the section. For example:

> Saint Thomas, the greatest doctor of the church, the engelic doctor, as he is called, says that the worst damnation consists in this that the understanding of man is totally deprived of divine light and his affection obstinately turned away from the goodness of God. (p. 127)

The loss of grace is indicated by one's losing sight of "the shining raiment of the blessed spirits" (p. 123). Similarly, the prelapsarian state is characterized by light imagery: "Adam and Eve were then created by God and placed in Eden, in the plain of Damascus, that lovely garden resplendent with sunlight and colour, teeming with luxuriant vegetation" (p. 117).

While pure light characterizes religious ideality, the reality of the church proper appears in a different light. Sitting in the chapel before the sermon begins, Stephen observes:

> The chapel was flooded by the dull scarlet light that filtered through the lowered blinds; and through the fissure between the last blind and the sash a shaft of wan light entered like a spear and touched the embossed brasses of the candle-sticks upon the altar that gleamed like the battleworn mail armour of angels.   (p. 116)

Again, before the final sermon:

> The daylight without was already failing and, as it fell slowly through the dull red blinds, it seemed that the sun of the last

day was going down and that all souls were being gathered
for the judgment.   (pp. 126–27)

The light here is red or scarlet; earlier, *red* was used in conjunction with images of green to suggest the dichotomy
between church and country. That association between
Catholicism and *red* is maintained here. Later, thinking of
Emma, Stephen's imagination wanders: "In the wide land
under a tender lucid evening sky, a cloud drifting westward
amid a pale green sea of heaven, they stood together,
children that had erred" (p. 116). Because of their associative
links with church and heaven, the functioning of *red* and
green as opposite images suggests that the same distance
relation holds for *church* and *heaven* as well. This metaphoric broadside at institutional Catholicism is expanded by
the link between *scarlet light* and *fire* that follow.

In the passage above, *green* is linked with *sea* as well as
heaven. That association is expanded in the following passage:

> Rain was falling on the chapel, on the garden, on the col-
> lege. It would rain for ever, noiselessly. The water would
> rise inch by inch, covering the grass and shrubs, covering
> the trees and houses, covering the monuments and the moun-
> tain tops. All life would be choked off, noiselessly: birds,
> men, elephants, pigs, children: noiselessly floating corpses
> amid the litter of the wreckage of the world. Forty days and
> forty nights the rain would fall till the waters covered the face
> of the earth. (p. 117)

The paradoxical redemptiveness of rain falling and consum-
ing all foreshadows in opposite terms the imagery of falling
ashes that Stephen notes as he enters the church to make his
confession in 3.3. Here, as in Chapter I, *fire* and *water* carry
opposite connotations. The strong associations among *red*,

fire, hell, and *Catholicism* is parallel and opposite that among *green, water,* and *heaven.* This latter group becomes a major pattern in Chapter IV that follows; here it mainly establishes a basis of opposition for the other complex.

Closely associated with *light* imagery are *eye* images. In the present context, *eyes* most often indicate awareness of Stephen by some other person or by God. The preacher characterizes the retreat as "a most salutary practice for all who desire to lead before God and in the eyes of men a truly christian life" (p. 109). A little later:

> Time was to sin and to enjoy, time was to scoff at God and at the warnings of His holy church, time was to defy His majesty, to disobey His commands, to hoodwink one's fellow man, to commit sin after sin and sin after sin and to hide one's corruption from the sight of men. (p. 112)

Earlier, *eyes* were associated with fear of physical vulnerability; in this context, the basis for fear has become moral and pschological. This transformation from concern for the physical to concern for abstract fears reflects the general shift toward the novel's preoccupation with Stephen's phenomenal world. The most important use of *eyes* is to indicate God's awareness of man and man's vulnerability to Him. The first sermon ends with the admonition: "He who remembers the last things will act and think with them always before his eyes" (p. 111). In the conclusion of the first hell sermon, the preacher characterizes hell as the state where one is being forced to depart from God's sight. Thus, *heaven* is characterized by *light, eyes,* and *the presence of God;* hell is characterized by the deprivations of these images: *darkness* and *dismissal from sight and awareness.*

In Chapters I and II the imagery was largely direct and immediate, part of Stephen's perception of the physical world; in Chapter III, particularly with *light* and *eye* imagery, it is increasingly metaphoric or abstract. More and more Stephen dwells in his own thoughts. He explores these mental images, related and embedded in languagelike patterns of associations, by examining the semantic and auditory similarities of the words associated with them. The affective dimension of Stephen's experience is thus moving away from experiences of physical reality—objective experience—toward greater preoccupation with his own thoughts and with language itself. Because *language* grows steadily in importance through the rest of the novel, Stephen's early awareness of its function and power demands attention.

As the series of sermons opens, the preacher defines the word *retreat:*

> —Now what is the meaning of this word *retreat* and why is it allowed on all hands to be a most salutary practice for all who desire to lead before God and in the eyes of men a truly christian life? A retreat, my dear boys, signifies a withdrawal for a while from the cares of our life, the cares of this workaday world, in order to examine the state of our conscience, to reflect on the mysteries of holy religion and to understand better why we are here in this world.   (p. 109)

The withdrawal process described is similar to the cycle of empathic projection that Stephen followed with the equations. Each sermon begins the same way—with a quotation from the Bible. Typical is the following:

> —*Remember only thy last things and thou shalt not sin for ever*—words taken, my dear little brothers in Christ, from the book of Ecclesiastes, seventh chapter, fortieth verse. In the name of the Father and of the Son and of the Holy Ghost. Amen.   (p. 108)

The preacher continually emphasizes the words of the passage; for example, the reality of the trinity is closely related to its constituent names.

As Stephen stares out the window, the letters of a word epitomize his morbid image: "The letters of the name of Dublin lay heavily upon his mind, pushing one another surlily hither and thither with slow boorish insistence" (p. 111). The letters' hither-and-thither movement foreshadows the dream of section 3.3, where Stephen's self-concept is linked associatively with the excremental fiends of hell.

The capacity of language to characterize reality is evident in the first sermon on hell. Near the end, after vividly outlining hell's sensual horrors, the preacher attempts to consolidate the cumulative effect:

> —Last of all consider the frightful torment of those damned souls, tempters and tempted alike, of the company of the devils. These devils will afflict the damned in two ways, by their presence and by their reproaches. . . . They mock and jeer at the lost souls whom they dragged down to ruin. It is they, the foul demons, who are made in hell the voices of conscience. Why did you sin? Why did you lend an ear to the temptings of fiends? Why did you turn aside from your pious practices and good works? (p. 123)

He continues:

> Such is the language of those fiendish tormentors, words of taunting and of reproach, of hatred and of disgust. . . .
> —O, my dear little brothers in Christ, may it never be our lot to hear that language! (p. 124)

For Stephen, languages focuses and characterizes experience with great personal impact and significance. At the climax of the sermon, the experience is concentrated in the shriek Stephen hears in his own mind: "Hell! Hell! Hell! Hell!"

(p. 125). One of the major functions of language in general is to characterize and represent experience, but seldom is the reader given a more direct and sustained example of a single word characterizing and representing such a large complex of experience. The ramifications of this experience extend through the rest of the novel; the immediate effect on Stephen is a clearer sense of language:

> The voices that he knew so well, the common words, the quiet of the classroom when the voices paused and the silence was filled by the sound of softly browsing cattle as the other boys munched their lunches tranquilly, lulled his aching soul. . . .
>
> The English lesson began with the hearing of the history. Royal persons, favourites, intriguers, bishops, passed like mute phantoms behind their veil of names.   (p. 125)

The power of language to embody, define, and reflect the unconscious associations of experience is now raised to the level of consciousness. Stephen's awareness of the role of language in shaping experience prepares us for the aesthetic theory and his choice of vocation.

Before turning to section 3.3, we should note briefly one last image cluster. To give a sense of the concept of eternity, the preacher uses a *bird* image:

> Now imagine a mountain of that sand, a million miles high, reaching from the earth to the farthest heavens, and a million miles broad, extending to remotest space, and a million miles in thickness: and imagine such an enormous mass of countless particles of sand multiplied as often as there are leaves in the forest, drops of water in the ocean, feathers on birds, scales on fish, hairs on animals, atoms in the vast expanse of air: and imagine that at the end of every million years a little bird came to that mountain and carried away in its beak a tiny grain of that sand. How many millions and millions of

> centuries would pass before that bird had carried away even
> a square foot of that mountain, how many eons upon eons
> of ages before it had carried away all. (p. 132)

The image is realistic, but birds have carried special significance for Stephen. Earlier, they were associated with fear
and Stephen's feelings of physical inadequacy; here, that
motif is sustained but in an abstract form.

Section 3.3 consists of two major parts—the scene in
Stephen's room the night following the retreat, and his
confession the next day. The density of imagery reflects the
high level of emotional intensity. The rhythmic patterns of
rise and *fall* present in 3.2 are continued in this section with
two complete cycles: the first build-up leads to the dream;
the second corresponds with Stephen's search for a chapel.
The chapter ends with the epiphanic confessional followed
by a denouement of two less intense scenes at home. These
scenes complete the undulating pattern of increasing
emotional intensity that began with the first sermon. At the
moment of epiphany, Stephen's image of himself and his
relation with religious ideality are redefined; he is a different
person. The changes that have occurred are marked
—almost emblematically—by the imagery in the last two
brief scenes.

As the section begins Stephen is going to his room for
the evening:

> He waited in fear, his soul pining within him, praying silently
> that death might not touch his brow as he passed over the
> threshold, that the fiends that inhabit darkness might not be
> given power over him. He waited still at the threshold as at
> the entrance to some dark cave. Faces were there; eyes:
> they waited and watched. (p. 136)

The repeated references to the "dark room," the "visual gloom," and the cavelike atmosphere of the room set the tone for the scenes there. The rather ambivalent associations of *darkness* before the sermons have been replaced by the strong association with *hell*. The sense of fear evoked by *darkness* earlier in the chapter is present in this passage. That fear is centered, however, in *face* and *eye* images. In Chapter I, particularly the pandybat section, Stephen felt that his face indicated, almost masklike, his true character; the image *eyes*, the central organ of perception, has been metaphorically linked with religious acceptance. Here, the older connotations of fear and vulnerability associated with *eyes* and *face* in Chapters I and II are present, but complicated by more recent associations. The specific fears are revealed in the dream that follows.

The dream sequence begins with a description of setting:

A field of stiff weeds and thistles and tufted nettlebunches. Thick among the tufts of rank stiff growth lay battered canisters and clots and coils of solid excrement. A faint marshlight struggled upwards from all the ordure through the bristling greygreen weeds. An evil smell, faint and foul as the light, curled upwards sluggishly out of the canisters and from the stale crusted dung.   (p. 137)

The "solid excrement" image links the passage with the *filth/excrement* motif developed concurrently and associatively with Stephen's visit to the brothel in Chapter II. Inhabiting this scene are:

Goatish creatures with human faces, hornybrowed, lightly bearded and grey as indiarubber. The malice of evil glittered in their hard eyes, as they moved hither and thither, trailing their long tails behind them. A rictus of cruel malignity lit up greyly their old bony faces. (p. 137)

Their circling movement is similar to Stephen's earlier habit of slowly circling the brothel district, awaiting an impulse to resolve his indecision. Here the image of circling creatures carries similar connotations of personal shame—with an added association with the fiends of hell. This close relation of *hell, fiends, excrement,* and *self* is articulated in the next paragraph.

> He flung the blankets from him madly to free his face and neck. That was his hell. God had allowed him to see the hell reserved for his sins: stinking, bestial, malignant, a hell of lecherous goatish fiends. For him! For him!   (p. 138)

The abstractions of hell have been transformed by Stephen's imagination into images with strong, personal associations that go to the core of his sense of identity.

Earlier in the chapter, *heavy foods* were linked with *bestiality.* The convulsive vomiting that follows functions as an exorcism, cleaning the corruption that Stephen believes has filled his bowels. Having rid himself of this, he rushes to the window:

> The rain had drawn off; and amid the moving vapours from point to point of light the city was spinning about herself a soft cocoon of yellowish haze. Heaven was still and faintly luminous and the air sweet to breathe, as in a thicket drenched with showers; and amid peace and shimmering lights and quiet fragrance he made a covenant with his heart.   (p. 138)

Unlike earlier associations of stagnant water, the rain connotes redemption in its association with light. For the first time in the novel Stephen feels that he can pray sincerely, and he does.

Stephen searches for a church in which to make his confession:

He walked on and on through the illit streets, fearing to stand still for a moment lest it might seem that he held back from what awaited him, fearing to arrive at that towards which he still turned with longing.   (p. 140)

Earlier he circled through dark streets to the brothel; here his course is straight, suggesting purpose and direction.

The chapel experience is similar in form to the earlier epiphanic experiences. The intensity of imagery builds steadily (see II.5); many of the images present carry strong associations with earlier experiences. The exact moment of epiphany, however, is indicated by striking images used only casually before.

The narrative focuses on Stephen's sensations and self awareness :

> His blood began to murmur in his veins, murmuring like a sinful city summoned from its sleep to hear its doom. Little flakes of fire fell and powdery ashes fell softly, alighting on the houses of men. They stirred, waking from sleep, troubled by the heated air. . . . Little fiery flakes fell and touched him at all points, shameful thoughts, shameful words, shameful acts. Shame covered him wholly like fine glowing ashes falling continually. To say it in words ! His soul, stifling and helpless, would cease to be.   (p. 142)

The tone of the passage suggests a gentleness similar to the redemptive rain; also present, however, are *fire* and *ash* images with their strong negative associations from the sermons. The image *murmuring* connotes fear, from its earlier association with the faces Stephen saw in his darkened room. Thus, the tone of redemption and gentleness is mixed with images suggesting fear and hell.

As Stephen begins his confession, he "repeats the *confiteor* in fright" (p. 143). The *confiteor* was the prayer

Stephen mockingly repeated when commanded to confess by Heron. There the *confiteor* was a shield used to protect the integrity of his aesthetic beliefs from submission to his tormentors; here he repeats it in submission to the orthodoxy of Roman Catholicism.

As he makes his confession,

> His sins trickled from his lips, one by one, trickled into shameful drops from his soul festering and oozing like a sore, a squalid stream of vice. The last sins oozed forth, sluggish, filthy. There was no more to tell. He bowed his head, overcome.   (p. 144)

Sin and personal shame were associated with *excrement* and *filth* in the dream sequence. Just as the foul matter was purged from his stomach there, these elements are purged from his personality here. Religious epiphany follows: "The old and weary voice fell like sweet rain upon his quaking parching heart. How sweet and sad!" (p. 145).

His confession concludes:

> He knelt to say his penance, praying in a corner of the dark nave: and his prayers ascended to heaven from his purified heart like perfume streaming upwards from a heart of white rose.   (p. 145)

The suggested purity of the rose contrasts sharply with the *excrement* motif so strongly associated with Stephen in this chapter. The only undercurrent to the ideality of this epiphany is the dark knave, perhaps a realistic, descriptive image, perhaps carrying an ominous note. Nevertheless, Stephen's experience is one of ideality and purity symbolized by the rose.

The repetition of *white* sustains this tone through the next two scenes. In the first, the squalor of his life disappears before Stephen's eyes as he thinks of his confession. The next scene, a prayer that Stephen dreams, is characterized by *light* images and the white flowers on the altar.

The epiphany grows out of a dream and ends with a dream, but the dreams are as opposite from one another in connotation and form as possible. This symmetry of organization is remarkably like that of the pandybat episode. Stephen is a different person after his epiphanic experience here also. Associations among images have reformed, coalesced, and become more complex. Stephen's sense of religious redemption marks a psychological state the opposite of that at the beginning of the chapter.

Stephen's present self-image is closely associated with images of religious ideality: *light, heaven,* and *water.* This last image is particularly interesting; although its proximity to images of heaven marks a shift in connotations, the exact nature of that shift remains ambivalent until Chapter IV. Earlier, Stephen's negative self-image was marked by a complex of images that eventually included *beasts, darkness, hell,* and *fire.* This state was marked by Stephen's overwhelming sense of isolation; the distance between his own inner nature and the rest of the physical and spiritual universe was too great to traverse.

His attempts to break through this barrier take several different forms. One in particular, his rhythmic attempts to emphatically project his consciousness out through physical distances, is important; this thematic pattern is similar to structural rhythms that give aesthetic coherence to the novel. After section 3.1, the remainder of the chapter consists of regularly alternating narrations of sermon followed by reaction. The last section of the chapter marks a single sustained reaction that culminates in the religious epiphany.

Reflecting and supporting this pattern is an undulating modulation of image intensity. The final height of intensity and the length of the build-up suggest that this epiphanic experience is stronger than the preceding one involving the prostitute.

Taken as a whole, the chapter is the first to exhibit the basic thematic structure found in succeeding chapters. The matter of the preceding epiphanic experience—submission to physical sensuality—is rigified into habit early in Chapter III. After that, it continually diminishes until it disappears before the chapter's end. Concurrent with the decreasing importance of this theme is the rise of a new theme— identification with religious ideality—that culminates in epiphany. Similarly this experience—fresh and personally meaningful here—is reduced to habit before being replaced by a major new development in Chapter IV.

6
Analysis of Chapter IV

Chapter IV is almost identical in structure to ChapterIII. It consists of three sections: the first continues the subject matter of the previous epiphanic experience; the middle section is a transition toward what is to follow; and the final section is the build-up and epiphanic experience that marks another developmental level for Stephen. The epiphanic experiences of II and III—the encounter with the prostitute and Stephen's confession—mark opposite psychological states. In Chapter IV Stephen once again finds himself at a stage of development opposite that of the preceding chapter; however, he is not back where he started from in II. The substance of the experience, the sensual data for his mind, is somewhat similar to that of the earlier epiphany—both involve a girl and Stephen's immediate reactions to her— but his point of view and self-image have expanded. He has progressed one-half of a cycle, one turn of the screw, in a pattern that is helical, not circular.

Although the first section of Chapter IV is dominated by religious imagery, a comparison of the most frequent images of Chapters III and IV reveals an important shift in the nature of that religious concern:

Chapter III	Chapter IV
God	soul
sin	priest
soul	sin
hell	eye
dark	face
pray	voice
heart	God
child	pray
day	air
eye	silence
fire	spirit
word	name
hand	day
body	faint
heaven	order
saint	sea
confess	slow
death	water
face	light

In terms of prominence, *God* has dropped from position one to position seven; *soul* has risen from three to one; *priest*, the second most frequent image in IV, is not among the twenty most frequent images of III at all; *hell* has similarly disappeared from the list of IV. These repositionings suggest that the shift in religious concern from the abstract and distant of 3.2 to the more personal and immediate of 3.3 has continued with increasing emphasis on the personal and institutional aspects of religious experience as opposed to the mythic and abstract. At the same time the growing importance of *eye, face, voice, air,* and *name*—all images associated earlier with identity—suggests an increasing, secular self-awareness. The relative low position in the list for Chapter IV of *sea* and *water* is deceptive; collectively, with other images denoting water, they comprise a major thematic group (see Appendix E).

The transformation in 4.1 of Stephen's religious epiphany is similar to the change that took place in 3.1 with regard to his previous epiphanic experience: the matter of personal, meaningful experience is transformed into action. The religious fervor Stephen felt after his confession is formalized here through various frameworks of time used to partition the day into devotional areas.[1] For example:

> Sunday was dedicated to the mystery of the Holy Trinity, Monday to the Holy Ghost, Tuesday to the Guardian Angels, Wednesday to Saint Joseph, Thursday to the Most Blessed Sacrament of the Altar, Friday to the Suffering Jesus, Saturday to the Blessed Virgin Mary. (p. 147)

Overlaying the partitioning of the week is another division based on the hours of the day:

> His daily life was laid out in devotional areas. . . . Every morning he hallowed himself anew in the presence of some holy image or mystery. (p. 147)

And later:

> Every part of his day, divided by what he regarded now as the duties of his station in life, circled about its own center of spiritual energy. His life seemed to have drawn near to eternity; every thought, word and deed, every instance of consciousness could be made to reverberate radiantly in heaven; and at times his sense of such immediate repercussion was so lively that he seemed to feel his soul in devotion pressing like fingers the keyboard of a great cash register and to see the amount of his purchase start forth immediately in

heaven, not as a number but as a frail column of incense or
as a slender flower.   (p. 148)

The emphasis on the temporal dimension of experience
is interesting in several respects. In the context of religious
experience, *time* was associated with the image of a bird
moving mountains of sand. Earlier, *birds* connoted fear and
feelings of physical inadequacy; these associations, while not
apparent here, may lie beneath the surface of Stephen's
mind. In evaluating his present state of religious grace,
Stephen is haunted by the doubt that his confession may
have been motivated primarily by fear rather than true
repentance. Thus, the abstractions of time and space are
linked, somewhat precariously here, through *bird* images and
fear. The temporal side of this complex is developed in 4.1;
the spatial, in 4.3. Their final coalescence within Stephen's
experience plays a major role in the epiphany on the beach.

In Chapter III, images of flower and the frail column of
incense were closely related to Stephen's religious epiphany;
in the context of the *giant cash register in the sky*—a highly
grotesque image—they appear wooden and awkward. Other
images of flowers and roses are literally transformed into
wooden forms through a cultural pun:

> The rosaries too which he said constantly—for he carried
> his beads loose in his trouser's pockets that he might tell
> them as he walked the streets—transformed themselves into
> coronals of flowers of such vague and unearthly texture that
> they seemed to him as hueless and odourless as they were
> nameless. (p. 148)

That Joyce appreciated the pun is strongly suggested by the
association between rosaries and flowers in this passage. The
transformation of a vivid image with strong, personal connotations into one with awkward and grotesque associations is

parallel to the larger process of transforming a personally meaningful religious experience into a collection of habitual actions.

Like the catalogue of senses in the hell sermon, Stephen lists the mortifications affecting each of his five senses:

> Each of his senses was brought under a rigorous discipline. In order to mortify the sense of sight he made it his rule to walk in the street with downcast eyes, glancing neither to right nor left and never behind him. . . . To mortify his hearing he exerted no control over his voice which was then breaking, neither sang nor whistled and made no attempt to flee from noises which caused him painful nervous irritation such as the sharpening of knives on the knifeboard, the gathering of cinders on the fireshovel and the twigging of the carpet. To mortify his smell was more difficult as he found in himself no instinctive repugnance to bad odours. . . . He found in the end that the only odour against which his sense of smell revolted was a certain stale fishy stink like that of longstanding urine: and whenever it was possible he subjected himself to this unpleasant odour. To mortify the taste he practised strict habits at table, observed to the letter all the fasts of the church and sought by distraction to divert his mind from the savours of different foods. But it was to the mortification of touch that he brought the most assiduous ingenuity of inventiveness. He never consciously changed his position in bed, sat in the most uncomfortable positions, suffered patiently every itch and pain, kept away from the fire, remained on his knees all through the mass except at the gospels, left parts of his neck and face undried so that the air might sting them and whenever he was not saying his beads, carried his arms stiffly at his sides like a runner and never in his pockets or clasped behind him.   (pp. 150–51)

Again, the intensity of the images and the experience is reduced: the fires of hell have been transformed into the itch of wool. The last image of the passage—the runner with stiffened arms—suggests the rigid, overly formalized stance that Mike Flynn insisted upon in Chapter II.

Another group of images important in both Chapters III and IV is that concerning mathematical equations. In 3.1 equations were directly related to Stephen's sense of contact with the physical world through his empathic projections outward to the limits of the universe and then inwards to the center of his being. This set of images associated with the relation between inner and outer realities is present here and grows in importance through the rest of the novel. In 4.1, however, the group appears in a distinctly religious context:

> He saw the whole world forming one vast symmetrical expression of God's power and love. Life became a divine gift for every moment and sensation of which, were it even the sight of a single leaf hanging on the twig of a tree, his soul should praise and thank the Giver. The world for all its solid substance and complexity no longer existed for his soul save as a theorem of divine power and love and universality. (pp. 149–50)

Stephen's idealism borders on solipsism: the physical world exists for him only as part of some abstraction or model within his own mind. Opposing this isolation are his attempts at mortification, making him more aware of sensual stimuli from the external world. The resolution of these inner and outer forces in religious terms seems doomed to failure through a ceaseless cycle of confession, repentance, absolution, sin, confession. . . Stephen is acutely aware of his ambivalent motives:

> A restless feeling of guilt would always be present with him: he would confess and repent and be absolved, confess and repent again and be absolved again, fruitlessly. Perhaps that

first hasty confession wrung from him by the fear of hell had not been good? Perhaps, concerned only for his imminent doom, he had not had sincere sorrow for his sin? But the surest sign that his confession had been good and that he had had sincere sorrow for his sin was, he knew, the amendment
    —I have amended my life, have I not? he asked himself. (p. 153)

This ambivalence—which he sees as weakness in this context —reflects the complexities of association and connotation that underlie all images and experiences. Stephen's realization of this fact, formalized in the aesthetics, grows experientially through the remainder of the chapter.

Section 4.1 thus introduces few new images or themes; primarily, it reveals the reduction of an experientially meaningful experience into a formalized set of rituals devoid of personal relevance. This process prepares us for Stephen's rejection in 4.2 of a clerical life.

Section 4.2 is an important transition: religious imagery declines in importance while images associated with language, perception, and aesthetics emerge as major motifs. Stephen listens to the priest's bid to join the order and then, almost on a whim, turns down the offer. During the section, the dichotomy between *inner* and *outer reality* assumes added personal importance for Stephen as the narrative focuses at the interface between them: Stephen's perceptual awareness. The resolution of the distance between *inner* and *outer,* here a matter of personal experience, becomes in Chapter V the basis of Stephen's theory of aesthetics, repeating once again the pattern of formalizing the material of one chapter into habit or abstraction in the succeeding chapter.

On an experiential level, the interface between subjective and objective is a matter of conscious concern for Stephen:

> The director stood in the embrasure of the window, his back to the light, leaning an elbow on the brown crossblind and, as he spoke and smiled, slowly dangling and looping the cord of the other blind. Stephen stood before him, following for a moment with his eyes, the waning of the long summer daylight above the roofs or the slow deft movements of the priestly fingers. The priest's face was in total shadow but the waning daylight from behind him touched the deeply grooved temples and the curves of the skull. (pp. 153–54)

And a bit later:

> Stephen smiled again in answer to the smile which he could not see on the priest's shadowed face, its image or spectre only passing rapidly across his mind as the low discreet accent fell upon his ear. (p. 155)

Where senses fail, the context of experience, the subjective continuum, completes the picture. Ordinary experiences blend into and alter slightly the fabric of mind, but only at moments of epiphanic intensity is the continuity broken and major realignments of associations established.

That the rector stands with "his back to the light" and that his eyes are hidden from Stephen's view is particularly suggestive since *eyes* and *light* were emblems for the ideality of God in the preceding chapter. It is impossible to tell whether Joyce intended to place the priest and, by implication, the order in an associative position opposite God and His ideality or whether this portrayal is merely realistic; the imagery strongly suggests the former. The negative tone of the passage is extended by the deathlike image *skull*.

Concern for the perceptual process is continued through

the section, particularly in relation to language. The role of
language in formalizing and retaining the data of experience
is evident in the following passage:

> The names of articles of dress worn by women or of
> certain soft and delicate stuffs used in their making brought
> always to his mind a delicate and sinful perfume. As a boy
> he had imagined the reins by which horses are driven as
> slender silken bands and it shocked him to feel at Stradbrook
> the greasy leather of harness. It had shocked him too when
> he had felt for the first time beneath his tremulous fingers the
> brittle texture of a woman's stocking for, retaining nothing
> of all he read save that which seemed to him an echo or a
> prophecy of his own state, it was only amid softworded
> phrases or within rosesoft stuffs that he dared to conceive
> of the soul or body of a woman moving with tender life.
> (p. 155)

Words or auditory images focus the various experiences and
images embedded within the mind; the auditory dimension
of language here forms the associative link between the
image of woman and the soft clothes Stephen imagines.
Soft words reconcile the ideality within his mind and the
reality of his sense impressions.

The proposition to join the order evokes for Stephen
images of the various clerics he has known.

> He had assumed the voices and gestures which he had noted
> with various priests. He had bent his knee sideways like such
> a one, he had shaken the thurible only slightly like such a one,
> his chasuble had swung open like that of such another as he
> had turned to the altar again after having blessed the people.
> (p. 158)

In many respects, this reverie represents Joyce's primary
mode of creation—the rearrangement of the components of
experience followed by retrospective examination of that

arrangement.[2] These images, originally coming from objective experience, are drawn here from his subjective. A link between psychological isolation and social isolation comes in the same paragraph: "In vague sacrificial or sacramental acts alone his will seemed drawn to go forth to encounter reality" (p. 159). This theme is continued as he leaves the school:

> Stephen passed out on the wide platform above the steps and was conscious of the caress of mild evening air. Towards Findlate's church a quartet of young men were striding along with linked arms, swaying their heads and stepping to the agile melody of their leader's concertina. The music passed in an instant, as the first bars of sudden music always did, over the fantastic fabrics of his mind, dissolving them painlessly and noiselessly as a sudden wave dissolves the sandbuilt turrets of children. (p. 160)

It is through his auditory sense that his thoughts are interrupted and his attention directed toward the physical world; the fabric of mind dissolves to allow perception of the objective to replace reverie. The image of mind developed in the aesthetic theory is similar to this but with the difference that epiphanic experiences rend and re-form this fabric instead of simply blending into it.

The dilemma Stephen faces in choosing between life in the "real" world and a life as a cloistered Jesuit is focused by his name: The Reverend Stephen Dedalus, S.J. Stephen's mind encompasses a wide variety of associations, but it is inevitably drawn toward images of reality, not the abstractions of Roman Catholicism:

> His name in that new life leaped into characters before his eyes and to it there followed a mental sensation of an undefined face or colour of a face. The colour faded and became strong like a changing glow of pallid brick red. Was it the

> raw reddish glow he had so often seen on wintry mornings
> on the shaven gills of the priests? The face was eyeless and
> sourfavoured and devout, shot with pink tinges of suffocated
> anger. Was it not a mental spectre of the face of one of the
> jesuits whom some of the boys called Lantern Jaws and others
> Foxy Campbell?   (p. 161)

The image of himself as a priest, a composite of gestures,
grows more detailed and Stephen sees the origin of the
image's components. The choice he will make is determined;
the interesting aspect of the passage is the role his name
plays. In section 4.3 the prophetic nature of his name is
extended further, emphasizing the power of language to
resolve the dichotomy between inner and outer experiences
within perception itself. On an experiential level, this resolution occurs in the epiphany itself; the formal or philosophic
resolution comes in the following chapter.

Section 4.2 is thus a thematic crossroads for the chapter.
Images associated with institutional and conventional religion virtually disappear after this point in the narrative
while images associated with the perceptual process, particularly language, steadily grow in importance through the
scene that follows. This same pattern was present in Chapter
III with regard to images of the brothel and religious
images, and a similar pattern will be seen again in
Chapter V.

Section 4.3 consists of a single continuous action that
culminates in one of Joyce's most beautiful epiphanies. It
begins :

> From the door of Byron's publichouse to the gate of Clon-
> tarf Chapel, from the gate of Clontarf Chapel to the door of
> Byron's publichouse and then back again to the chapel and

then back again to the publichouse he had paced slowly at
first, planting his steps scrupulously in the spaces of the patch-
work of the footpath, then timing their fall to the fall of
verses.   (p. 164)

The repetitive walk between Byron's pub and Clontarf
Chapel marks Stephen's inability to choose between a life
as a cleric and a life as an artist. The indecisive oscillation
between polar opposites, implying no sense of resolution, is
one form of the *hither/thither* motif present throughout the
section. The linearity of the motion offers an interesting
contrast to the cycle images of Chapters II and III. During
the period when Stephen visited the brothels regularly, cycle
images reflected his indecision; here, indecision is marked by
the linear pattern. In the epiphany to come, when Stephen
is able to see clearly the choice he must make, the linear,
hither/thither motif disappears and cycle images are associ-
ateded with the vitality of the great life cycle.

As Stephen walks through town the narrative enters his
thoughts, revealing an interesting and important cluster of
images associated with music:

It seemed to him that he heard notes of fitful music leaping
upwards a tone and downwards a diminished fourth, upwards
a tone and downwards a major third, like triple-branching
flames leaping fitfully, flame after flame, out of a midnight
wood. It was an elfin prelude, endless and formless; and, as
it grew wilder and faster, the flames leaping out of time, he
seemed to hear from under the boughs and grasses wild
creatures racing, their feet passed in pattering like rain upon
the leaves.Their feet passed in pattering tumult over his mind,
the feet of hares and rabbits, the feet of harts and hinds and
antelopes, until he heard them no more and remembered only
a proud cadence from Newman: *Whose feet are as the feet
of harts and underneath the everlasting arms.*   (p. 165)

Experientially, *music* exists in time, its essence defined in terms of ratios of vibrations on the microscopic level and in terms of intervals and pauses on a larger scale. This image group is linked in Stephen's imagination first with flames and then with dreamlike animals. Both associations link this passage with the preceding chapter. The *flame* image suggests a tie with the theme of religion; *the dreamlike animals* suggest the figures Stephen dreamed about in section 3.3, but purified, perhaps by the *rain* images. In the preceding chapter, the dream was the immediate cause propelling Stephen toward his religious epiphany. Here, the music of language, associated with dreamlike animals of opposite connotations, is one of several factors that lead to the aesthetic epiphany. Both experiences come from internal forces: the first is motivated largely by fear, the second by insight and choice. The links between these passages suggest that the secular epiphany to come should carry levels of emotional intensity at least equivalent to those of the religious experience. This expectation is confirmed by the graph in II.6.

In the passage that follows, Stephen examines for the last time the choice of assuming a religious life:

> All through his boyhood he had mused upon that which he had so often thought to be his destiny and when the moment had come for him to obey the call he had turned aside, obeying a wayward instinct. Now time lay between: the oils of ordination would never anoint his body. He had refused. (p. 165)

Time, a major characteristic of music, is given a degree of spatiality in the words *lay between*. This union of time and space foreshadows the epiphanic fusion that takes place later on the beach.

The changes occurring in Stephen are reflected in the

image that follows: "He turned seaward." Earlier, *fire* and *religion* were closely associated; in Chapter I *fire* carried connotations opposite those of *water*. In turning *seaward* Stephen is turning away from religious institutions and toward something else. *Sea* images have often been interpreted as archetypal symbols for the deepest aspects of man's subconscious. In turning seaward, Stephen may well be seeking those aspects of himself that are most personal, most universal; such is the role of the artist. As yet, Stephen has not seen clearly his vocation.

The interplay between *fire* and *water* imagery begun in Chapter I is completed here. There *fire* and *water* carried highly positive and negative connotations, respectively. In the pandybat episode they were fused in the image of scalding tears. In Chapter III, *fire* was linked with images of hell, implying connotations opposite the earlier security of the hearth. This pattern of reversal is completed here with *sea*, carrying highly positive connotations. The respective dominance in Chapters III and IV of these two themes is evident in the graphs of Appendix E. While they have changed drastically in connotations, the earlier associations that they still carry makes them much more complex. This changing blend of associations is more complete than earlier polar qualities and is indicative of the maturation process itself.

The accumulation of images with distinct temporal or spatial qualities is continued. Two groups with strong spatial dimensions are *sea* and *cloud* images. In this short section occur twelve of the twenty-five references to sea found in the entire novel; nine other images (such as *seaborne* and *seabird*) contain *sea* as a prefix. Eight of the twenty-four occurrences of *cloud* also occur here. Together, *cloud* and *sea* encapsulate the space between them and suggest opposite aspects of reality and experience. The clouds floating overhead carry for Stephen a number of associations, including suggestions of removal and ideality. The sea, closer to Stephen, seems more immediate and personal, as its archetypal associations would suggest. Together they focus the inner and outer facets of experience. Stephen's attempts to reconcile the distance between them may be interpreted as another attempt to reconcile the subjective and objective components of perception, a theme most recently manifest in his sense of isolation. This union takes place experientially in the epiphany to come.

A number of images and events prepare Stephen for this experience. One important group of images concerns language itself: "A day of dappled seaborne clouds" (p. 166). The proximity of *seaborne* and *clouds,* we have seen, foreshadows the epiphany; here, they remain separate, although close. The medium in which they can approach one another is not space or air, but language :

> The phrase and the day and the scene harmonised in a chord. Words. Was it their colours? He allowed them to glow and fade, hue after hue: sunrise gold, the russet and green of apple orchards, azures of waves, the grey-fringed fleece of clouds. No, it was not their colours: it was the poise and balance of the period itself. Did he then love the rhythmic rise and fall of words better than their associations of legend and colour? Or was it that, being as weak of sight as he was shy of mind, he drew less pleasure from the reflrection of the glowing sensible world through the prism of a language many-coloured and richly storied than from the contemplation of an inner world of individual emotions mirrored perfectly in a lucid supple periodic prose?   (pp. 166–7)

Language serves a triple role. It enables Stephen to organize his immediate experience: it provides a context of both space and time—suggested by day—for the two dominant components of his experience, the images *clouds* and *sea*. Second, the phrase evokes a number of associations within his mind, linking the experience with other images and experiences. Finally, the phrase has an auditory dimension independent of semantic meaning or association. The cadence of the various sounds augments Stephen's immediate experience; his perceptual experience, here and now, would be different if he did not think these words. Thus the conceptual component of this phrase draws these two spatial images closer together while the auditory component draws together the temporal and spatial modes of perception. This unifying role of language grows in importance throughout the remainder of the novel.[3]

Two other *cloud* images follow. The first, a "flying squall" that appears on the horizon, suggests an earlier, metaphoric use of *cloud*. Feeling betrayed by his mother's opposition to his attending the university, Stephen remembers that

> a dim antagonism gathered force within him and darkened his mind as a cloud against her disloyalty: and when it passed, cloudlike, leaving his mind serene and dutiful towards her again, he was made aware dimly and without regret of a first noiseless sundering of their lives. (pp. 164–65)

The second contains a number of other images important in this scene:

> Disheartened, he raised his eyes towards the slowdrifting clouds, dappled and seaborne. They were voyaging across the deserts of the sky, a host of nomads on the march, voyaging high over Ireland, westward bound. The Europe they had come from lay out there beyond the Irish Sea, Europe of strange tongues and valleys and woodbegirt and citadelled and of entrenched and marshalled races. He heard a confused music within him as of memories and names which he was almost conscious of but could not capture even for an in-

stant; then the music seemed to recede, to recede, to recede: and from each receding trail of nebulous music there fell always one long-drawn calling note, piercing like a star the dusk of silence. Again! Again! Again! A voice from beyond the world was calling.

—Hello, Stephanos!

—Here come The Dedalus! (p. 167)

The phrase *a day of dappled, seaborne clouds* links the predominantly spatial image, *cloud*, with *day*, a temporal image in this context. Another temporal image, *music*, organizes names and images within his memory, implying that the structure of Stephen's mind is a harmonious and organic composition where inner and outer realities, time and space, subjective and objective can merge in the perceptual process.

The scene dissolves in a set of images linking the inner and outer components of this experience. The shouts Stephen hears come from without, but they blend into his train of thought before submerging into his subconscious memory. The specific images he hears are his name fractured into its components: Stephen and Dedalus. These names come from different cultures and signify different aspects of his personality. In 3.2, the rector addressed his attention and prayers to one facet of Stephen's self. He instructs him: "And let you, Stephen, make a novena to your holy patron saint, the first martyr, who is very powerful with God, that God may enlighten your mind" (pp. 159-60). Stephen is exhorted to adhere to religious dogma as the earlier Stephen adhered to religious ideality to the point of martyrdom. That aspect of Stephen's identity has passed; it is the other aspect, suggested by his inherited name, that is dominant here:

> Now, as never before, his strange name seemed to him a prophecy. So timeless seemed the grey warm air, so fluid and impersonal his own mood, that all ages were as one to him. A moment before the ghost of the ancient kingdom of the Danes had looked forth through the vesture of the haze-wrapped city. Now, at the name of the fabulous artificer, he seemed to hear the noise of dim waves and to see a winged form flying above the waves and slowly climbing the air. What did it mean? Was it a quaint device opening a page of some medieval book of prophecy of the end he had been born to serve and had been following through the mists of childhood and boyhood, a symbol of the artist forging anew in his workshop out of the sluggish matter of the earth a new soaring impalpable imperishable being?   (pp. 168–69)

The name *Dedalus* links Stephen with the ancient myth of Icarus and Daedalus, who fled the labyrinth on waxen wings. Earlier, the physical distance between *sea* and *clouds* characterized the psychological distance between inner and outer. The image of the "hawk-like man flying sunward" who is able to fly literally from the sea to the clouds helps to resolve this dichotomy. The connotations of courage and artistic potency present in these *bird* images is opposite the earlier associations of fear and physical inadequacy. The image of *hawklike man* also links Stephen's self-image with the artificer, creating in his own soul works of art from the materials of experience. His awareness of the vocation he will follow is clear:

> Yes! Yes! Yes! He would create proudly out of the freedom and power of his soul, as the great artificer whose name he bore, a living thing, new and soaring and beautiful, impalpable, imperishable.   (p. 170)

That "thing" he will create is art. The process being described, the movement from experience to formalization, reflects the same process operating in the narrative: the process in which experiential matter of epiphany is formalized into habit and ritual.

Empathetically, Stephen's imagination takes him one step further:

> His soul was soaring in an air beyond the world and the body he knew was purified in a breath and delivered of incertitude and made radiant and commingled with the element of the spirit. (p. 169)

Stephen identifies with Icarus, son of Daedalus; earlier he had identified with Daedalus. The fusion of father and son (in Stephen's imagination) foreshadows Stephen's quest for father in *Ulysses*. In the present context, this empathic association represents another instance of the *space/time* motif: by identifying with both father and son, Stephen has fused cause and effect, preceder and follower; the role of Icarus/Daedalus in resolving the spatial dichotomy has already been discussed. These thematic strands involving *sea, clouds, birds, Icarus/Daedalus, space/time, inner/outer* all

fuse in the epiphanic experience on the beach.

From this point in the narrative the level of emotional intensity builds steadily toward climax. The transition from preparation to resolution is marked by an important image; as Stephen starts towards the sea, "he clambered down the slope of the breakwater" (p. 170). The image *breakwater*, a realistic detail, represents on another level the boundary or choice in Stephen's mind between the religious life and life as an artist. It also links this passage with an earlier epiphany. Prior to this section the image occurred only in Chapter II, where Stephen sought to erect a barrier between himself and the sordid life that surrounded him. Here Stephen willingly crosses the breakwater, indicating his readiness for fundamental change.

As he walks along the inlet he looks down into the sea around his feet and sees

> the endless drift of seaweed. Emerald and black and russet and olive, it moved beneath the current, swaying and turning. The water of the rivulet was dark and endless drift and mirrored the highdrifting clouds. The clouds were drifting above him silently and silently the seatangle was drifting below him; and the grey warm air was still: and a new wild life was singing in his veins.   (p. 170)

The surface of the water reflects the clouds, but Stephen can also look through the reflection on the surface and see an endless motion of vague but distinguishable forms below. If we explore the archetypal associations of this set of images as well as those actually present in *Portrait*, this complex suggests the model of mind developed in the aesthetic theory. Taking the sea as a metaphor for *mind*, the surface—the interface between *water* and *air* or *water* and *reflected sky*—corresponds to the perceptual interface between the subjective and objective levels of experience. These physical stimulae interact with images and associations already present in the mind. Some external images are reflected while others make more impact and are absorbed into the subjective continuum of the personality. The long strands of seaweed floating in the current suggest the trains of associations that float within the flux of experience. Firmly rooted, these strands shift constantly but slightly. Only during stormlike agitation are they uprooted and their fundamental structural relations changed.

The level of emotional intensity builds toward epiphany as Stephen walks on the beach, becoming more and more aware of his surroundings. The very height of the experience is marked by the image of a girl standing in the water. At that moment a number of associative relations fuse; emblematic of this process is the image *seabird*, in which two important thematic groups, *sea* and *bird*, are welded together in language just as *scald* fused *fire* and *water* in Chapter I. *Seabird*, however, plays an even larger role in integrating the major themes of the chapter and the novel. Clouds, with this connotation of the ideal, the distant, are reflected in the sea, suggestive of the mind itself. Earlier, the ideal was linked with images of blue and religious images, both sets too distant psychologically to be attained. Here, Stephen's projection to his birdlike namesakes flying between these two limits of reality suggests at least the possibility of their fusion within Stephen's perception of reality; however, their actual fusion comes not through the image of Daedalus/Icarus but through the medium of language— the fusion of *sea* and *bird* into *seabird*. When this juxtaposition of the components of experience fuse experientially, when Stephen *sees* their union, this entire complex of association fuses into a unified structure embodying a number of themes.

In addition to *seabird*, other images with dialectical connotations are also present here. One in particular is noteworthy: near the height of the epiphany a cry comes to Stephen's lips: "—Heavenly God! cried Stephen's soul, in an outburst of profane joy" (p. 171). This invocation of religious imagery in a secular utterance recalls the two previous epiphanic experiences. The "outburst of profane joy" links this passage with that concerning the prostitute— sound imagery was used metaphorically there also; "Heavenly God," similarly, links it with the religious epiphany. Their juxtaposition at the very moment of epiphany suggests a fusion of opposite epiphanic experiences. On one level, Stephen is closer to his earlier, "profane'" state than to his "religious" state; from a more comprehensive perspective, however, we see that he has progressed to an entirely new level, embodying most of his past, but transcending it also. The pattern of development is thus helical, not circular. Experientially, he has now realized his vocation as artist, creator, aesthetician.

The result of this experience on the structure of Stephen's mind is apparent in the following passage :

> He closed his eyes in the languor of sleep. His eyelids trembled as if they felt the vast cycle movement of the earth and her watchers, trembled as if they felt the strange light of some new world. His soul was swooning into some new world, fantastic, dim, uncertain as under sea, traversed by cloudy shapes and beings. A world, a glimmer, or a flower? Glimmering and trembling, trembling and unfolding, a breaking light, an opening flower, it spread in endless succession to itself, breaking in full crimson and unfolding and fading to palest rose, leaf by leaf and wave of light by wave of light, flooding all the heavens with its soft flushes, every flush deeper than the other.   (p. 172)

The indecisive *hither-and-thither* movement has been replaced by the cyclical process inherent in life and art. Stephen's awareness of this motion pattern leads him to a new level of awareness—"uncertain as under sea, traversed by cloudy shapes and beings." The *cloud/sea* images echo the *cloud/sea* group as Stephen, earlier, walked on the beach. There the metaphoric relation with mind was implicit; here it is explicit. Structurally, the group provides continuity for the entire experience—buildup, epiphany, denouement—by framing it symmetrically. A similar structural pattern was present in the pandybat episode in the *pick, pack, pock, puck* sound images which, in turn, were linked with the *brimming bowl.* The *flower* images link the experience with the earlier religious epiphany; their association with images of cyclical development, however, reflects Stephen's new level of awareness. *Light,* similarly, links the experience with Chapter III, where it symbolized the ideality of God; here, it has been transformed to suggest aesthetic inspiration. The imagery of the passage thus binds this particular epiphany to the other major epiphanies of earlier chapters; because so many rich and varied trains of association converge here, this particular epiphany may be the most important of the novel.

Stephen's sense of vocation is the matter for Chapter V and the ultimate cause for all subsequent actions portrayed. It is not surprising that the particular artistic medium he chooses for expression is language. Throughout section 4.3 there is a dependent relation between language and experience. The rise in emotional intensity was produced by the organic fusion of external stimuli with internal associations and stimuli evoked through language. As Stephen became more and more aware of objective reality, he became more and more emotionally aroused and hence able to focus more attention on his experiences, thus producing even greater excitement, and so on. At the height of the experience, the phenomenological fusion of subjective and objective is emblematically concentrated in the words that burst from his lips. *Language* both evokes and encompasses the experience; but *language* alone is not sufficient. There is the clear need of objective experience and the real world. It is the balance between *inner* and *outer* present in this particular epiphany that distinguishes it from the more physical epiphany with the prostitute and the more idealistic epiphany in the chapel. The momentum of this experience carries over into Chapter V and culminates in Stephen's statement of aesthetic theory. There has been much critical discussion concerning the valdity of that theory. The pattern we have seen, where meaningful personal experience is reduced if not destroyed by abstraction, suggests that Stephen's greatest aesthetic insights occurs here, not in Chapter V. It is ironic, perhaps paradoxical, that the later statement describes the perceptual process embodied in Stephen's experience and hence is important from a critical point of view while, within the fictive world of the novel, a walk on a beach carries greater personal meaning for Stephen.

7
Analysis of Chapter V

Chapter V, by far the longest chapter of the novel, is divided into four sections spanning Stephen's university days and culminating in his preparations to leave Ireland. It begins with a section that formalizes the subject matter of Stephen's last epiphanic experience into a general theory of aesthetics based on the perceptual process. As one would expect, language figures heavily in the theory's inherent model of mind. By focusing on Stephen's train of thought, the narrative in section 5.2 reveals a mind conforming to that model in the act of creation: after a dream, Stephen awakens and composes a villanelle. In the section that follows, Stephen walks with Cranly, discussing whether he should make a confession to please his mother. Stephen finally rejects all submissions to social or religious forms that he finds meaningless or that infringe upon his integrity. The scene ends when both Stephen and Cranly realise that their friendship is an empty bond and that their former relationship is at an end. The final section is composed of entries from Stephen's journal, the last of which records his determination to

167

achieve through his vocation as artist the spiritual and aesthetic potential of Ireland. To do so, he realizes that he must leave Ireland.

During the first four chapters of the novel, a number of experiences and images develop associative links that grow in complexity and richness. In the final chapter the process culminates both abstractly and experientially. The abstract culmination of this process is the aesthetic theory; however, in and around that theory associations among images expand and coalesce into organic patterns that reflect Stephen's mind. Instrumental in this process—both theoretically and experientially—is language itself; the list of most frequent images in the chapter underscores its relevance and import-ance. *Word* and *voice* rank second and fourth on the list while language, which was not included as an image, occurs some eleven times in Chapter V out of a total of twenty-six for the novel. In all, there are some 187 images in Chap-ter V that relate to language. The prominence of *art* images indicates the particular orientation of language as medium for art. Since the theoretical aspects of the aesthetics have been discussed, emphasis in the discussions that follow will be on images and their associative relations.

Most Frequent Images of Chapter V

eye
word
face
voice
hand
art
dark
soul
light
image

walk
day
night
silence
smile
heart
head
laugh
round
god
soft
woman

Section 5.1 begins with a breakfast scene in the Dedalus household:

> He drained his third cup of watery tea to the dregs and set to chewing the crusts of fried bread that were scattered near him, staring into the dark pool of the jar. The yellow dripping had been scooped out like a boghole and the pool under it brought back to his memory the dark turf-coloured water of the bath in Clongowes.   (p. 174)

The train of associations is clear:

watery tea
↓
bread
↓
dark pool
↓
yellow
↓
boghole
↓
water
↓
Clongowes

Bread, tea, and *yellow* are all part of the associative link
with Clongowes, but images connoting stagnant water—
dark pool, boghole, and *turfcoloured water*—are the major
factor responsible for stimulating this train of thought (there
are six images suggesting water in these two sentences). The
chain of associations among *water/boghole/yellow/excre-
ment/food* is very different in connotations from those of
the *sea* images in the last chapter. There, *moving water* was
closely linked emblematically with Stephen's mind as well
as the life cycle in general; here, the *stagnant water* group
suggests excrement and death (the latter coming from
Stephen's memory of the dead rat floating in the ditch). At
this stage of development *water* is tied in Stephen's mind to
both groups : sometimes he may be conscious of only one,
but the other chain of associations is present and active
below the surface of his consciousness. This paradoxical
linking of *water/yellow/life/death/excrement/creative force*
winds its way through the section before playing a major
role during Stephen's statement of his aesthetic theory.

As Stephen walks toward town, he is aware of specific
relations among images and experiences as well as the mental processes that embody and produce them. Behind the
house he hears the screams of a mad nun :

—Jesus! O Jesus! Jesus!
He shook the sound out of his ears by an angry toss of his
head and hurried on, stumbling through the moldering offal,
his heart already bitten by an ache of loathing and bitterness.
His father's whistle, his mother's mutterings, the screech of
an unseen maniac were to him now so many voices offending
and threatening to humble the pride of his youth. He
drove their echoes even out of his heart with an execration.
(pp. 175–76)

Earlier, the auditory sense—the sense most immediately related to language—served as the major epistemic sense for Stephen. Here Stephen reverses the process: he uses language to block auditory sensory impressions that raise offending associations:

> The rainladen trees of the avenue evoked in him, as always, memories of the girls and women in the plays of Gerhart Hauptmann; and the memory of their pale sorrows and the fragrance falling from the wet branches mingled in a mood of quiet joy. His morning walk across the city had begun, and he foreknew that as he passed the sloblands of Fairview he would think of the cloistral silverveined prose of Newman, that as he walked along the North Strand Road, glancing idly at the windows of the provision shops, he would recall the dark humour of Guido Cavalcanti and smile, that as he went by Baird's stonecutting works in Talbot Place the spirit of Ibsen would blow through him like a keen wind a spirit of wayward boyish beauty.   (p. 176)

Literature for Stephen is not something to be merely enjoyed or trifled with; living in his present circumstances, he survives by escaping into aesthetic idealism. By the chapter's end, Stephen would probably embrace such experiences, but with a different kind of detachment.

As Stephen walks toward the university, his mind wandering freely among the literary fragments, allusions, and images embedded within it, he evokes an interesting self-image: he sees himself as a monk. The proximity of this image to the nun could suggest an association with the whole *religious/priest/retreat* motif; that association, however, is not supported. Instead, there is implied a dedication to some as-yet-undefined dogma not by a novitiate of a cloistered order but by a viewer, if not participant. of the rough reality of society. Images of Stephen as a religious personage external to any formal religious order are repeated a number of times throughout the chapter, emphasizing the degree of relevance his chosen vocation has for him.

As his walk continues, Stephen focuses his attention once again on the images and bits of language that enter through his senses:

> Every mean shop legend bound his mind like the words of a spell and his soul shirvelled up, sighing with age as he walked on in a lane among heaps of dead language. His own consciousness of language was ebbing from his brain and trickling into the very words themselves which set to band and disband themselves in wayward rhythms:
>
> > The ivy whines upon the wall
> > And whines and twines upon the wall
> > The ivy whines upon the wall
> > The yellow ivy on the wall
> > Ivy, ivy up the wall.
>
> Did any one ever hear such drivel? Lord Almighty! Who ever heard of ivy whining on a wall? Yellow ivy: that was all right. Yellow ivory also. And what about ivory ivy?   (pp. 178–79)

The disdain he feels for the frozen and dead slogans desecrating shop fronts is similar to that he he feels for his own mental processes. *Language* 'trickling" into words or combinations of words is especially deplorable because of the association with the trickling water in the square at Clongowes. Later, Stephen compares with disgust his own mental habits and functions with lice and vermin, the latter suggesting disgust similar to his earlier reaction to the rat in the boghole. A literary critic could find many things wrong with these lines of poetry, but Stephen's specific criticism is revealing. It is not the stretching of visual associations in "yellow ivy" or "yellow ivory" or even "ivory ivy" that displeases him; it is "ivy whining" that he cannot accept. The first three images could exist in the real world; the fourth cannot. As a child, Stephen toyed with the notion of a green rose. There, he merely passed over the question of its existence; here, his relation with the physical universe is far too important to be trivialized by such linkings. To join *whining* with *ivy* would be a synesthetic association of sense attributes. Similar fusions have been presented by Joyce and accepted by Stephen, but only at moments of epiphanic intensity, not in casual, everyday experiences or verse. Free associations of this sort may be permissible, but only so long as wordplay is not confused with reality: "The word now shone in his brain, clearer and brighter than an ivory sawn from the mottled tusks of elephants. *Ivory, ivoire, avorio, ebud*" (p. 179). Art must be faithful to realistic detail: the mode of thought that could produce such distorted verse is literally excremental in Sephen's mind. The paradoxical closeness of aesthetic ideal and excremental baseness first suggested by associative patterns of images becomes a thematic counterpoint in Stephen's conversation with Lynch that follows.

Language also influences Stephen's social experiences. Indeed, most of his relations with his school friends are affected by language. His initial impression of Davin is shaped by the latter's speech:

—Do you remember, he asked, when we knew each other first? The first morning we met you asked me to show you the way to the matriculation class, putting a very strong stress on the first syllable. You remember? Then you used to address the jesuits as father, you remember? I ask myself about you: *Is he as innocent as his speech?*   (p. 202)

Similarly, Stephen's relation with the prefect takes a decided turn for the worse when the cleric uses the word *funnel* instead of *tundish*:

> The little word seemed to have turned a rapier point of his sensitiveness against this courteous and vigilant foe. He felt with a smart dejection that the man to whom he was speaking was a countryman of Ben Jonson. He thought:
> —The language in which we are speaking is his before it is mine. How different are the words *home, Christ, ale, master* on his lips and on mine! I cannot speak or write these words without unrest of spirit. His language, so familiar and so foreign, will always be for me an acquired speech. I have not made or accepted its words. My voice holds them at bay. My soul frets in the shadow of his language. (p. 189)

In the diary Stephen indicates the impact the experience made on him:

> That tundish has been on my mind for a long time. I looked it up and find it English and good old blunt English too. Damn the dean of studies and his funnel. What did he come here for to teach us his own language or to learn it from us? Damn him one way or the other! (p. 251)

Often, the thrust of social intercourse is defined by language; for example, as Stephen stands outside his class with some schoolmates,

> a lean student with olive skin and lank black hair thrust his face between the two, glancing from one to the other at each phrase and seeming to try to catch each flying phrase in his open moist mouth.   (p. 196)

Later, Stephen refutes a point of argument with the remark: "Keep your icon. If we must have a Jesus, let us have a legitimate Jesus" (p. 198). Those present react to his statement not on the logical or semantic level, but the rhetorical: "By hell, that's a good one! said the gipsy student to those about him. That's a fine expression. I like that expression immensely" (p. 198).

The impact of language on Stephen's mind evokes a metaphor with interesting associations: "The heavy lumpish phrase sank slowly out of hearing like a stone through a quagmire. Stephen saw it sink as he had seen many another, feeling its heaviness depress his heart" (p. 195). The association between rude language and quagmire suggests a relation between such language and the bogwater of the ditch that epitomized Stephen's traumatic experiences at Clongowes. That *language* can carry the same impact now as the *cold water* did then is indicated in another verbal exchange between Cranly and Temple. When Temple calls Cranly a "ballocks," Stephen watches his attempt to laugh off the injury:

> The gross name had passed over it [Cranly's face] like foul water poured over an old stone image, patient of injuries: and, as he watched him, he saw him raise his hat in salute and uncover the black hair that stood up stiffly from his forehead like an iron crown.   (p. 232)

Trivial social intercourse as well as trivial habits of mind that produces images such as whining ivy are epitomized by language. The metaphoric link through language with earlier images suggesting fear and excrement indicates just how repugnant both are to him. It is from this mental and social quagmire that Stephen now attempts to raise himself. His goal is his vocation; his means is the aesthetic theory.

The emphasis on the psychological aspects of the theory is reflected in the number of images that suggest the mind or the perceptual process. In Chapter I, the context of experience from which the epiphanic experience arose and to which it returned was closely related to the *brimming bowl* image; the last two passages quoted above suggest a similar, although desecrated, image of mind. Both contain bodies of water into which sensory experiences enter and slowly disappear as they sink lower and lower. Before Stephen begins his walk with Lynch, "a tide began to surge beneath the calm surface of Stephen's friendliness" (p. 203); immediately after the discussion, Stephen's "mind, emptied of theory and courage, lapsed back into a listless peace" (p. 216).

As they walk along, one of Lynch's favorite figures of speech is to swear in *yellow*. To Stephen's taunting offer of a cigarette Lynch responds "damn your yellow insolence" (p. 204). When Stephen begins to talk about Aristotle and aesthetics, Lynch interrupts him: "Stop! I won't listen! I am sick! I was out last night on a yellow drunk with Horan and Goggins" (p. 204). Just before Stephen lists the three modes of perception, Lynch calls MacCann a "sulphuryellow liar." In their discussion, there are a total of five references to *yellow*, all metaphoric. The association between *yellow* and *excrement*, emphasized earlier in the section, forms an ironic base on which the aesthetic theory is developed. This link is further reinforced by other images from the excrement group present here:

> You also told me that when you were a boy in that charming carmelite school you ate pieces of dried cowdung.
> Lynch broke again into a whinny of laughter and again rubbed both his hands over his groins but without taking them from his pockets.
> —O I did! I did! he cried.   (p. 205)

As their walk continues, Lynch makes repeated references to *excrement;* to characterize another classmate, Lynch laments "To think that that yellow pancakeeating excrement can get a good job. . . and I have to smoke cheap cigarettes!" (p. 211). During the height of the discussion of aesthetics, Stephen asks:

Are you following?
—Of course, I am, said Lynch. If you think I have an excrementitious intelligence run after Donovan and ask him to listen to you. (p. 212)

The strong association among *Lynch, yellow,* and *excrement* is extended to include language (sulphur-yellow liar) and the mind itself in the image *excrementitious intelligence.* The distance in connotation between Lynch's talk and Stephen's statements of lofty, idealized art is great. Joyce perhaps intended to undercut Stephen's self-image through irony; there is no indication, however, that Stephen regards this difference in any way other than the realistic difference that separates their minds and personalities. From Stephen's point of view, any irony present would be cosmic: the irony that beautiful art (epiphany) is cast in the normal, the everyday, even the "excremental" realms of experience.

If we map the relations among the major images present, we see that this orientation of opposite values among images forms a balanced whole. See figure 7.1.

Figure 7.1

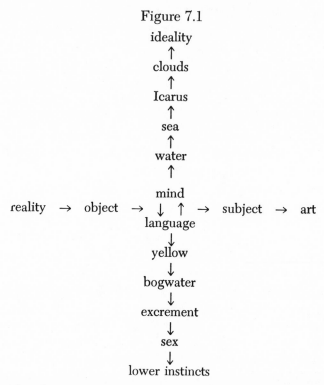

The theory itself seeks to resolve mind and language, both in the argument presented and in the imagery present. *Lynch's* language is associated with *yellow, bogwater,* and *sex,* all implying, for Stephen, the lower instincts. Mind is associated with images of water—especially the *brimming bowl* and the *sea*—and in turn with *Icarus, clouds,* and *ideality. Water* images appear on both sides of the diagram, but with widely different connotations. The total associative pattern, embodied in a single mind, contains contrary and opposite facets at the same time; at epiphanic moments the "ends" meet, the cycle is completed, and these contraries coalesce into an orientation of mind that is distinctly more mature and more complex. We have seen this pattern in the narrative of *Portrait;* here we see its theoretical development.

Before considering section 5.2, we should note an associative pattern that becomes important later. During the lecture on physics, the priest distinguishes between the words *ellipse* and *ellipsoidal.* Moynihan picks up the words and makes a joke, associating the latter with testicles: "What price ellipsoidal balls! Chase me, ladies, I'm in the cavalry!" (p. 192). This link between pure geometric form and the testicles appears again in section 5.2, when Stephen is composing the villanelle.

Section 5.2 has been ignored by most critics of *Portrait* or simply dismissed as the scene in which Stephen composes a bad poem. On one level the aesthetic quality of this idealized, romantic villanelle creates an irony that undercuts Stephen's aesthetic as a theory of art. (Should we seriously consider the abstract theories of someone who writes poetry of this sort?) On other levels, the poem and the section are interesting and important. We are given a sustained view of Stephen's thoughts as images float in and out of his consciousness before coalescing and precipitating into verse. The associative relations among these images are dramatically clear and comprehensive; we see links between this and virtually all previous epiphanic experiences. The experience, then, represents an epitome of Stephen's life brought into focus by the process of artistic creation; it is the culmination of the accumulative process operating since the beginning of the novel. Second, we are given a chance to verify the aesthetic theory in action. Since Stephen has just awakened, the images that furnish the substance of the poem are already in his mind and the initial stage of perception—

wholeness—is bypassed. Evident, however, are the analytic and recognition stages, characterized earlier as harmony and radiance.

The second stage, harmony, consists of breaking the image down into its componets, which later fuse in the third step, radiance. Thinking of Emma, Stephen sees her image break into images of a number of women:

> Rude brutal anger routed the last lingering instant of ecstasy from his soul. It broke up violently her fair image and flung the fragments on all sides. On all sides distorted reflections of her image started from his memory: the flower-girl in the ragged dress with damp coarse hair and a hoyden's face who had called herself his own girl and begged his handsel, the kitchengirl in the next house who sang over the clatter of her plates with the drawl of a country singer the first bars of *By Killarney's Lakes and Falls*, a girl who had laughed gaily to see him stumble when the iron grating in the footpath near Cork Hill had caught the broken sole of his shoe, a girl he had glanced at, attracted by her small ripe mouth as she passed out of Jacob's biscuit factory, who had cried to him over her shoulder:
> —Do you like what you seen of me, straight hair and curly eyebrows?   (p. 220)

This catalogue of associated image componets contains fragments of most of the women Stephen has known; here they coalesce in his mind to form a single, more realistic image of Emma. In her are traits of all women: "perhaps the secret of her race lay behind those dark eyes, upon which her long lashes flung a quick shadow" (p. 221). She is one part ideality and many parts flirt and hoyden. The resolution of these diverse characteristics—ranging from the ideal to the common—reminds Stephen of the eucharist and thereby produces an image for the poem—not of Emma, or any other woman, but a eucharistic hymn. The manner in which these components of women are synthesized into a religious image is quite abstract. The eucharist represents the fusion of spirit and matter, the ideal and the physical. The specif form, the auditory image of hymn, is a manifestation of this phenomenon in art. A similar process is involved in Stephen's realization of the diverse and contradictory associations with other women that shape his image of Emma. Similarly, they precipitate into an art form, the villanelle. Thus the image of the eucharistic hymn carries connotations much more personal and complex than those suggested by its religious denotation. Stephen's conscious realization of the complexity of this train of associations produces anger in him but also several lines of verse:

> The radiant image of eucharist united again in an instant his bitter and despairing thoughts, their cries arising unbroken in a hymn of thanksgiving.

> > Our broken cries and mournful lays
> > Rise in one eucharistic hymn.   (p. 221)

Earlier, with the *whining ivy image,* the increasing importance of language for Stephen was evident; the structure of images and ideas expressed in words must actually exist on some level. That level where these lines from the villanelle exist and on which they must be verified as "real" is the continuity of Stephen's personality. Verse that is subject to verification with regard to self as opposed to society or the physical universe Stephen termed *lyric* in the discussion with Lynch; the villanelle fits that definition. Because of the intensely personal dimensions of this experience, the lines of the next stanza—

> > While sacrificing hands upraise
> > The chalice flowing to the brim—

suggest that it is Stephen's self or mind—the brimming bowl earlier suggested mind or personality—that is being sacrificed to their love, their life, his art.

While the chalice suggests a link between this experience and the pandybat epiphany, other images establish ties with later epiphanies. As Stephen awakes from a dream:

> His soul was all dewy wet. Over his limbs in sleep pale cool waves of light had passed. He lay still, as if his soul lay amid cool waters, conscious of faint, sweet music.   (p. 217)

The images *dew, wet, cool waves, sweet music,* as well as the act of awakening from a dream suggest the epiphanic experience on the beach where the image of the girl fused with sea and bird in the image *seabird.* The train of associations is also linked with the aesthetic theory as Stephen remembers the phrase *an enchantment of the heart* (p. 217). The result here is an intensely emotional experience:

> The instant flashed forth like a point of light and now from cloud on cloud of vague circumstances confused form was veiling softly its afterglow. O! In the virgin womb of the imagination the word was made flesh. Gabriel the seraph had come to the virgin's chamber. An afterglow deepened within his spirit, whence the white flame had passed, deepening to a rose and ardent light. That rose and ardent light was her strange wilful heart, strange that no man had known or would know, wilful from before the beginning of the world: and lured by that ardent roselike glow the choirs of the seraphim were falling from heaven.   (p. 217)

The sequence is extended by *light* and *rose* images to the religious epiphany of Chapter III where these two images stood emblematically for the entire experience. The residue of all these experiences combine and coalsces with the phrase from Galvani in the lines of verse:

> Are you not weary of ardent ways
> Lure of the fallen seraphim?
> Tell no more of enchanted days.

Components of these experiences have been objectified, "made flesh" in the process of being transformed into art.

Images from the confessional epiphany remain strong, mixing with images from a different epiphany:

> The roselike glow sent forth its rays of rhyme; ways, days, blaze, praise, raise. Its rays burned up the world, consumed the hearts of men and angels: the rays from the rose that was her wilful heart.

> > Your eyes have set man's heart ablaze
> > And you have had your will of him.
> > Are you not weary of ardent ways?   (p. 218)

White hot rays that set hearts ablaze and consume the world suggest both the searing heat of the pandybat as well as the super-intense fires of hell. A link between these two groups of associations and the epiphany on the beach appears in the next stanza:

> Smoke, incense ascending from the altar of the world.

> > Above the flame the smoke of praise
> > Goes up from ocean rim to rim
> > Tell no more of enchanted days.

> Smoke went up from the whole earth, from the vapoury ocean, smoke of her praise. The earth was like a swinging swaying censer, a ball of incense, an ellipsoidal ball.   (p. 218)

Along with the discordant association with the pandybat experience suggested by the *fire* images, the image of the ellipsoidal ball carries rude sexual connotations suggested earlier by Moynihan's joke. Thus, the imagery keeps this seemingly rhapsodic and idealistic poem firmly linked in Stephen's imagination with experiences that cover every level of reality from the base to the ideal. All of these diverse associations in Stephen's mind coalesce and are embodied in this poem.

As Stephen is able to comprehend and come to terms with this complexity of associations that are part of his experience and his personality, his self-awareness grows. He is able to see the role that art plays in the perceptual process as well as the importance of perception for art. The section gives both an insight into the structural relations within Stephen's mind and verification of the second and third stages of apprehension as they relate directly to art and to epiphanic experience.

The graph of richness of imagery (2.7) indicates the level of intensity this particular experience has for Stephen. While radiance is inherent in all apprehension, only at moments where there are concentrations of images with strongly personal, diverse if not contradictory associations does the synthesis take place that produces the "enchantment of heart" that marks true epiphany. The composition of this poem is such an instance. The only scene in Chapter V with a higher concentration of imagery is that in which Stephen examines the lines about ivy, searching for the relation between physical reality and language or verse. After that, the level of in tensity diminishes before rising during the present section. It again decreases steadily in 5.3 and 5.4 until just before the conclusion of the novel.

Section 5.3 is the last scene in which the reader sees Stephen actually engaged in social intercourse; after this,

Stephen's interactions with others are revealed only through his journal. The matter of the section is Stephen's final conversation with Cranly. As they talk, Stephen's sense of the increasing importance of language as shaper of reality becomes apparent. This close germinal relation between language and thought and language and art prepares the reader for Stephen's final social withdrawal preparatory to the actual physical withdrawal from Ireland that Stephen alludes to but never makes.

As the section opens, Stephen is standing with friends on the steps of the library looking up at the birds flying in the evening sky:

> He watched their flight: bird after bird: a dark flash, a swerve, a flash again, a dart aside, a curve, a flutter of wings. He tried to count them before all their darting quivering bodies passed: six, ten, eleven: and wondered were they odd or even in number. Twelve, thirteen: for two came wheeling down from the upper sky. They were flying high and low but ever round and round in straight and curving lines and ever flying from left to right, circling about a temple of air. (p. 224)

Stephen sees structures in their flight as they circle about an imaginary temple.[1] The imposition of form over physical reality was most apparent in Chapter II; here Stephen attempts to deal with an area of experience of which he is unsure:

> And for ages men had gazed upward as he was gazing at birds in flight. The colonnade above him made him think vaguely of an ancient temple and the ashplant on which he leaned wearily of the curved stick of an augur. A sense of fear of the unknown moved in the heart of his weariness, a fear of symbols and portents, of the hawklike man whose name he bore soaring out of his captivity on osierwoven wings, of Thoth, the god of writers, writing with a reed upon a tablet

and bearing on his narrow ibis head the cusped moon.   (p. 225)

As in Chapter IV, Stephen identifies with the soaring birds through his name, Dedalus. There, in the flush of realization his feelings were of liberation, destiny, and sureness; here, he is less sure. The note of fear, reminiscent of the fear associated with birds in Chapters I and II, is here the abstract fear of the unknown. His determination is just as strong as it was in Chapter IV but it is tempered by a realistic sense of caution for what lies ahead. In the context of vocation, the temple at which Stephen sees himself a devotee is the temple of art. Stephen perceives his destiny, but his realization is not without uncertainty and apprehension.

In section 4.3 there was an interesting contrast between Stephen's earlier indecision, represented by linear *hither-and-thither* movement, and his epiphanic insight on the beach supported by images of circularity implying organic union and the fusion of opposites. The circular path of the birds, here associated with Stephen's own concept of art, offers a rather abstract contrast with other theories of perception :

> Why was he gazing upwards from the steps of the porch, hearing their shrill two fold cry, watching their flight? For an augury of good or evil? A phrase of Cornelius Agrippa flew through his mind and then there flew hither and thither shapeless thoughts from Swedenborg on the correspondence of birds to things of the intellect and of how the creatures of the air have their knowledge and know their times and seasons because they, unlike man, are in the order of their life and have not perverted that order by reason.   (p. 224–25)

Literal linear movement has been transformed into thoughts —Swedenborg's correspondence theories. His correspondences are linear, one-to-one, between entities in the physical world and their correspondent images in the ideal world; but there is no sense of resolution or coalescence between Swedenborg's two levels.[2] The sterility of such thought— suggested by linear motion between dialectical poles— stands in opposition to circular or helical images suggesting the organic resolution of opposite connotative strains so fundamental to Stephen's theory of epiphany and art.

The level of validation for Stephen's lyrical villanelle was his own past experiences and the configurations of images within his own mind. At a time when he is withdrawing from social intercourse, there is the danger that his art may become solipsistic; but this is not the case. As he and Cranly walk along, they hear a voice singing:

Behind a hedge of laurel a light glimmered in the window of a kitchen and the voice of a servant was heard singing as she sharpened knives. She sang, in short broken bars, *Rosie O'Grady*.

Cranly stopped to listen, saying:

—*Mulier cantat.*

The soft beauty of the Latin word touched with an enchanting touch the dark of the evening, with a touch fainter and more persuading than the touch of music or of a woman's hand. The strife of their minds was quelled. The figure of a woman as she appears in the liturgy of the church passed silently through the darkness: a whiterobed figure, small and slender as a boy and with a falling girdle. Her voice, frail and high as a boy's, was heard intoning from a distant choir the first words of a woman which pierced the gloom and clamour of the first chanting of the passion:

—*Et tu cum Jesu Galilaeo eras.*

And all hearts were touched and turned to her voice, shining like a young star, shining clearer as the voice intoned the preparoxyton and more faintly as the cadence died. (p. 244)

Stephen's reaction to the words and the experience, one of aesthetic pleasure, is different from Cranly's:

—There's real poetry for you, he said. There's real love. He glanced sideways at Stephen with a strange smile and said: —do you consider that poetry? Or do you know what the words mean?—I want to see Rosie first, said Stephen.   (pp. 244–45)

The experience has been moving for both. Cranly desires to objectify his experience by fiat—to declare the objective quality and validity of the song on the basis of his reactions to it. Stephen, too, has derived personal pleasure from the experience, but the question of aesthetic value must now be determined not just by his own reactions and associations. Poetry that transcends the level of lyric must hold up to verification against the physical world, the objective dimension of experience.

This necessity is extended to language in general. It is language that joins and resolves the dichotomy between subjective and objective experience. In this role, it is an important aspect of Stephen's identity and his relation with objective experience. As they walk along, Cranly urges Stephen to make a meaningless confession to please his mother:

—Your mother must have gone through a good deal of suffering, he said then. Would you not try to save her from suffering more even if . . . or would you?
—If I could, Stephen said. That would cost me very little.
—Then do so, Cranly said. Do as she wishes you to do. What is it for you? You disbelieve in it. It is a form: nothing else. And you will set her mind at rest.   (p. 241)

Stephen's reply is an icy silence. To make an insincere confession would be a violation of his integrity. Words—as was evident with the *whining ivy* image—are too closely related to identity to be used lightly and without meaning.

In sections 5.2 and 5.3, Stephen looks both inward toward the subjective continuum of experience and outward toward the objective world to verify the structural relations among language images. The subjective is emphasized in the villanelle, the objective in the song about Rosie O'Grady. *Language* functions broadly over the interface between both realms of experience, embodying the associative patterns among images that permeate the conscious and subconscious minds. It is *language* that unites and organizes this complex into an organic unity.

Section 5.4, composed of entries from Stephen's journal, represents the objectification of his subjective state—his thoughts and experiences rendered in language. This is Stephen's final step away from the meaningless talk of his school friends and the life in Dublin he finds impossible; alternately, he is willing to exist alone, without a single friend if necessary, to maintain his integrity and to preserve his vocation.

In the journal section, *language* plays a dual role. First it organizes and reflects Stephen's mental state, embodying the associative links among images within his mind. Although withdrawn from social interaction, Stephen's state is not solipsistic. The act of writing itself is an attempt to render his experiences in some external, objective form that can be verified. This rendering, however, is not art; it has no vitality of its own. The journal might appear to be dramatic art, according to Stephen's theory, in that the thoughts of the artist have solidified and the author is no longer visible within a social context. This is not the case; the section lacks a fictive world. It consists of impressions that

can "come alive" only in some specific mind that now, ironically, is withheld from the reader. For example: "22 March:
In company with Lynch followed a sizeable hospital nurse.
Lynch's idea. Dislike it. Two lean hungry greyhounds walk-
ing after a heifer" (p. 248). The tone of the passage is cold,
wooden, detached. The section may foreshadow the interior
monologue Joyce uses in the Molly Bloom soliloquy in
Ulysses; there Molly's thoughts wander through myriad
associations of past experiences but always return to the
present physical reality—she is lying in bed with Bloom.
Stephen's entries, however, lack that vitality; they appear to
be fashioned after some external, abstract form of what a
journal should be—comparable to Stephen's earlier unsuccessful attempts to imitate the running style Mike Flynn
advocated—rather than the free and accurate expression of
his own thoughts.

Stephen does not, however, view his present state of
social suspension as permanent:

> The spell of arms and voices: the white arms of roads,
> their promise of close embraces and the black arms of tall
> ships that stand against the moon, their tale of distant nations.
> They are held out to say: We are alone. Come. And the voices
> say with them: We are your kinsmen. And the air is thick
> with their compay as they call to me, their kinsman, making
> ready to go, shaking the wings of their exultant and terrible
> youth.   (p. 252)

He feels called to a new life. The image of arms is similar
to the bidding arms of the prostitute in Chapter II; the call
Stephen experiences now is just as strong as the call to his
sexual instincts was then. As before, the call has ambivalent
implications in Stephen's mind, indicated here by contrary
black and *white* images. He is withdrawing from the meaningless relationships that restrict and hold him back, not

from the vitality of life: "O life! I go to encounter for the millionth time the reality of experience and to forge in the smithy of my soul the uncreated conscience of my race" (pp. 252–53). The "reality of experience" is the epiphanic perception of experience described in the aesthetic theory; the consciousness of the race is a new archtypal mind formulated in either a new language or a language that has been restructured—one in which words carry fresh, new meanings and connotations. Stephen assumes the task of creating this mind/language. To do so, he seeks strength from his namesake: "Old father, old artificer, stand me now and ever in good stead" (p. 253). Stephen never completes this task; Joyce starts it in *Ulysses* and carries it to its logical conclusion in *Finnegans Wake*, where he literally takes the language apart syllable by syllable, before putting it back together to form a language of expanded and different associative relations. The detailed structure of this consciousness awaits a comprehensive examination.

If we look back at Chapter V, we see that the aesthetic theory of the first section develops in formal or abstract terms the matter of the final epiphany in Chapter IV, and, indeed, all such earlier experiences. This pattern of formalizing experience into habit or some abstract form has been present since the prostitute episodes of Chapters II/III. Following the statement of the theory, however, there is an interesting reversal of the pattern; in section 5.2 the theory leads to a meaningful personal experience, the villanelle, rather than the other way around.

Accompanying this increasing concern for art is a complex of images centering around language itself. Both theoretically and personally, language functions at the interface between thought and reality, self and art. In terms of the personal dimension, language embodies and organizes the components of experience buried in the subconscious by reflecting semanticlike relations among images. Because of the close dependency between language and personality, language is capable of producing blunt emotional responses as strong as those earlier produced by the cold water of the ditch. On the objective side, it is language that will furnish the medium for Stephen's art.

In the last three sections of the novel we see in Stephen's awareness of language the personal realization of the psychological state inherent in the three modes of poetry described in the aesthetic theory. In 5.2 the relations among images embodied in the villanelle are correlated against the personality of the artist, Stephen; in 5.3, Stephen, by refuting Cranly's claim that subjective judgment is sufficient to determine beauty, insists upon the objective verification necessary for epic art; in 5.4, Stephen has socially refined himself out of existence. While Stephen has progressed through these three different states experientially, ironically he has yet to produce any significant art. In fact, the language of the journal indicates personal regression. The content of the aesthetic theory and the patterns observed imply that only when Stephen can consolidate experience and reality will he be capable of transcending the lyrical and producing great art. *Ulysses,* in part, extends Stephen's quest for an integrated personality. It is debatable whether he achieves it, but whether he does or not, the work of art is not forthcoming. In the final analysis, we must look to Joyce for art and accept Stephen as character.

8
Conclusion

The aesthetic theory in Chapter V of *A Portrait* is developed in terms of the three stages of apprehension—wholeness, harmony, and radience—inherent in all acts of perception. At times, however, the *experience* of apprehension achieves a level of intensity that marks a clear transition from one level of personality development to another, from one organization of the data of experience to a different organization. This transition Stephen describes in Chapter V as a moment of "enchantment of heart"; he makes no clear distinction, however, between the level of emotional intensity associated with epiphanic experiences and that inherent in all acts of perception. In the introduction, I suggested that the problem could be resolved by a close scrutiny of the imagery of the novel. Images, when interpreted as any datum of sensory experience, constitute the matter of apprehension. There is reason to infer from Stephen's discussion with Lynch that at those moments of true radiance there will be large concentrations of sensory impressions. As the individual becomes increasingly aware of these impressions—his environment and his relation with it—his level of emotional or empathic involvement increases and he in turn becomes even more receptive. The result is a spiraling build-up of intensity that can, if sustained, result in epiphany or major redefinition of the basic personality in which patterns of association among the memory components of previous experiences are significantly altered. Thus, we would expect a quantitative relation between concentrations of important images in the text and the dramatic moments of epiphanic experience.

To test this suggestion a procedure was developed in Appendix A.44 that "measured" both the number of images present in a section of text and weighed them according to importance. It was assumed that images that occur more frequently in the novel are *generally* more important than images that occur less frequently. This assumption is true only on a statistical basis, not absolutely for all occurrences of all images. The application of this model, shown in chapter 2, indicates that the following scenes are the richest in imagery: the initial section ending with the frightening "pull out his eyes/apologise" refrain, Stephen's illness at Clongowes resulting from his fall into the ditch, the pandy-bat episode, the scene with the prostitute at the end of Chapter II, the sermons on death and hell and Stephen's reveries concerning Emma between them, his dream and subsequent confession, the experience of seeing the girl on the beach, and in the final chapter, the scenes concerning the "whining ivy," the composition of the villanelle, and the scene in which Stephen looks up at the circling birds before the symbolic dismissal of Cranly from his life. Clearly, these scenes are those which are most significant in Stephen's development.

Among them, some experiences are more important than

others. The pandybat episode, the scene with the prostitute, the confession, the scene on the beach, and Stephen's final walk with Cranly mark experiences where the most fundamental changes in his life occur. Each comes about as the result of a sustained build-up of both inner and outer forces, and each contributes to defining the habitual action in the succeeding chapter or section out of which the next sustained build-up emerges. In the introduction, I suggested that the image of sensory data and the Image of epiphanic experience marked the two extremes of a continuum; the differences in the degree of intensity among these five experiences (the reader will recall the qualified nature of the experience with the prostitute discussed in chapter 4) and the differences in intensity between this group and the other epiphanic experiences confirm that suggestion.

That these experiences are accompanied not just by dramatic "peaks" of image intensity but that they are coincident with a sustained build-up is apparent in the graphs for individual chapters. This pattern is especially apparent, for example, in the pandybat episode (2.3), the scene with the prostitute (2.4), the confessional scene (2.5), and the scene on the beach (2.6). Consequently, the first half of the original thesis—that epiphanic moments are coincident with increased awareness of the self in relation to the environment, indicated by large concentrations of important images—is substantiated.

The second part of the thesis is that the developments of Stephen's mind could be traced by noting the changing patterns of associations among images. It was assumed that "association" meant textual proximity: if two images are used close together a number of times in some portion of the novel, there exists some associative link between them within Stephen's mind. A number of independent computer procedures were used to trace these associative patterns. The frequency of occurrence of images was broken down by chapter and the list then sorted on that frequency. This material indicated new areas in Stephen's experience, increased and decreased prominence of various images, and other broad patterns of image associations and use. For example, these lists show vividly the relative importance of *fire* images in Chapter III and *water* images in the succeeding chapter. This does not imply that the careful reader would not notice these relative frequencies, but an interpretive point that makes use of this fact is strengthened if one can specify these frequencies exactly. Second, an image concordance was produced that listed each occurrence of each image with the five images surrounding it. This document facilitated checking the changing context or environment of an image over the course of the novel. Also useful in developing patterns of association was the factor anlysis program described in Appendix A.42. This program revealed clusters of images that frequently occur in the same context. It was run independently on each of the five chapters of *Portrait* so that the changing patterns of associations among these images could be analyzed. The factors or clusters that I found helpful are listed in Appendix D. Finally, a number of thematic groups of images were defined and their distributions over the novel computed. To reveal the inherent patterns of repetition within the raw distributions, the data for each of them were submitted to Fourier transformation. The resulting graphs and power spectra reveal the characteristic pattern for each theme (see Appendix E). Using these computer-produced aids, I was able to define the fundamental structure of associations among images and note the changes that take place during epiphanic experiences. Since the major body of this study is devoted to this analysis, a full summary here is impractical; the discussion that follows attempts to characterize the most important patterns found.

No attempt was made to explain why an association might have been formed between two images; it was assumed that these links build up from proximity within Stephen's experience. Essentially, such links are similar to semantic relations where there is no inherent reason for associating sign and meaning: they exist *de facto* or by tradition. These strong links often have a value dimension. In some instances groups of associated images exist in pairs connoting dialectical opposites: for example: *hot/cold, fire/water, black/white, red/green, hither-thither/circular form,* and so on. As Stephen's experiences grew, many of these contraries became resolved or fused into a complex unity embodying both extremes of associations. Such literal welding was seen in the images of *scalding tears* (uniting *fire* and *water*) and *seabird* (uniting *bird* and *sea*), to name two. The result of such fusions was a greater maturity of perception, a greater comprehensiveness of viewpoint, such that by the end of the novel Stephen's mind is a complex but integrated fabric of associative patterns.

In Chapter I, a number of themes emerge; among the most important are groups of images denoting *eyes, birds, fear, water/cold, fire/hot,* and *names.* These, in concert with slightly less important themes, develop into a clearly defined structure that forms the basis for the pandybat epiphany. From the beginning, *eye* images suggesting Stephen's sense of vulnerability were linked with *bird* images, connoting physical threat and fear. *Water* and *coldness,* too, functioned dialectically opposite another group, *fire* and *heat* images. The former were strongly associated with Stephen's fall into the ditch and, by implication, with a number of other unpleasant images including the *bloated rat, death, excrement,* and *guilt.* In contrast, *fire* imagery emblematically suggested the warmth and security of home, all that was opposite Clongowes. Permeating these relations was the theme of identity closely related to Stephen's name. Prior to the pandybat episode, a number of extensions among these groups were established. The pandybat was related both to *bird* imagery through the turkey and to a different *water* image, the sound of water dripping into a brimming bowl. The ditch became strongly associated with guilt through the smugging incident. Identity, in Stephen's mind, was closely linked to *face* and *eye* images. Consequently, when the prefect of studies unjustly punishes Stephen—reading in his face the character of an idle, lazy schemer—most of the important thematic patterns fuse into a new, more camplex structure in the searing pain of the bat that brings scalding tears to Stephen's eyes. Associations are no longer unidimensional; positive and negative facets join to produce in Stephen a distinctly more mature personality structure.

Chapter II, while relatively sparse in imagery, does expand and develop several themes. Dominant among these is the "metatheme" involving the dichotomy between the physical and the ideal, the objective and the subjective. Related to the unattainable ideal are the repeated references to *blue,* connoting that which is distant; the stylized running form Mike Flynn attempts to impose over Stephen's natural gait; and the variety of images from *The Count of Monte Cristo* that Stephen constructs to spur his escapes into fantasy. Images concerned with the most fundamental aspects of physical existence—*food, physical love,* and *procreation* —invariably appear in a pejorative context; all are linked in one way or another with the motif involving *filth, excrement,* and *death* first established with reference to the ditch. *Food*

Stephen associates with scum and slime, laughter and ridicule; the scene involving Stephen's first encounter with sexual intercourse is encompassed by slimy streets; the image *foetus* Stephen associated with death, not life. Most of the actions portrayed in this chapter involve Stephen's attempts to maintain the distance between these two extremes, to keep his concept of the ideal from crashing on the plane of objective experience where he is forced to contend. Often the results of his attempts are ironic in the extreme; for example, to defend his idealized image of Byron, Stephen repeats the *Confiteor* to distance himself from Heron's blows and demands to submit. Later, Stephen finally submits, but it is a submission to his own physical desires and the pull of the prostitute's arms. Thus, the thematic pattern concerning *submission* is reversed in Chapters I and II. In I, Stephen submitted to physical punishment but refused to submit to the implied guilt associated with it (in II, we see that triumph undercut by the derisive laughter of Father Dolan and Simon Dedalus); in II, while Stephen manages to withstand Heron's demands to submit, his submission to his own physical desires is complete on the psychological level but not the physical. He consciously seeks out the prostitute but is unable to actively embrace her; consequently, his self-image at this point is one of degeneracy and sinfulness, a self-image nearly opposite that at the end of the preceding chapter and that established in Chapter III.

In Chapter III, several major shifts in associations first suggested in earlier epiphanies become apparent. *Eye* images in Chapter I were strongly related to *bird* images, with an implied link of fear; *fire* images, primarily associated with the hearth fire of home, were highly positive in connotation. In III, *eyes* become closely associated with *light*, emblematic of God's grace and awareness. On the other hand, *fire* assumes the cultural association with *Hell* in the fundamentalist sermons of the retreat. The physical fear induced by these sermons leads to the literal catharsis that precedes Stephen's idealized confession. At the end, he is left exhausted but with a sense of sanctity.

The pair of themes, *bird* and *water,* opposite *eyes* and *fire* in Chapter I undergo a similar reversal in Chapter IV. The predominant form of *water* image, the *sea,* while physical and immediate, connotes the abstract concept of mind inherent in the aesthetic theory of Chapter V. Reflecting off the surface of the sea are cloud images, suggesting the distant, the idealized. Spanning the distance between *clouds* and *sea* in Stephen's imagination is the birdlike image of his namesake, Daedalus/Icarus. As the scene builds toward epiphany, Stephen grows increasingly aware of both the details of his physical surroundings and the mythic/abstract form of his perceptual experience. At the height of the experience the major thematic components fuse in the word *seabird,* indicating the function and power of language for epiphanic perception. Through language and literature Stephen will attempt to realize his identity as artist/creator, suggested by his name, and seek to reconcile the ideal with the physical.

The formal statement of this experiential insight occurs in Chapter V in the aesthetic theory. Through the perceptual process of the Image or epiphany, the artist derives the materials for his art; in turn, the Image or epiphany, when transcribed into art, joins him with his audience. Following the statement of the theory, we see Stephen's mind actively involved in the perceptual process just described. As he awakes, images rise and flow through his consciousness before precipitating into verse; within the creative act, experience and language fuse. The close dependencies among perception, language, and art realized abstractly by Stephen in the aesthetic theory, are realized experientially in the villanelle scene. The concluding scenes of *Portrait* reveal the consequences of that realization: Stephen's psychological preparation to assume the role of artist and shaper of his cultural environment. Ironically, Stephen feels that he must distance himself as much as possible, mentally and physically, from Ireland to accomplish his calling.

From earlier discussions and from this summary we can see that the associative relations among images grow and develop as Stephen grows and matures. Indeed, the associative structure of the components of experience—the imagery of the novel—defines the personality structure of Stephen just as the pattern of molecules in a crystal define that substance's crystalline structure. We have seen that Stephen's personality tends to be relatively stable within individual sections of the novel, but as the forces around him and his responses to them grow, the level of emotional intensity also grows until, characteristically, the experience culminates in epiphany. At that moment the major thematic developments of the section converge; after that time, the changes in Stephen's personality are reflected in the changes that have taken place in the associative relations among imagery. To a great extent, the changes in personality *are* the changes in associations and connotations among experiences. Thus, the second part of the original thesis, that the development of Stephen's mind can be traced by tracing the changing patterns of associations that take place at epiphanic moments, is confirmed.

To show that the major developments of the novel are reflected in, if not dependent on, the structural organization

of individual words in the linear sequence of the text, I was
forced to regard each and every occurrence of an image as
"meaningful" and "intentional"; at times, the proximity of
certain images may imply on some level of higher meaning
or intent an opposite or ironic connotation. For example, in
Section 4.1 Stephen's religious epiphany is manifest in concentrations of images with highly idealistic associations
(*flowers, whiteness, incense,* etc.); in the very middle of this
cluster occurs the image of a giant cash register in the sky
on which Stephen imagines his pious deeds are recorded.
An image so grotesque in the middle of numerous images
associated with Stephen's idealized confession completely
destroys any "serious" belief on the reader's part that
Stephen's present state of grace can be sustained. The effect
on the reader is an ironic distancing from the fictive world
of the novel: he sees that Stephen's self-concept at this
point is as unreal and grotesque as the image pattern in the
text. While this irony is carried in the imagery and while
the computer through its retrieval capabilities can facilitate
perceptions such as this, the realization must come from the
individual reader's interpretation of the text and the research
aids provided by the computer. At present we have no
model or formal definition of irony that the computer can
use to locate other instances similar to the scene in Chapter
IV. This may eventually be possible by assigning semantic
tags to words and then looking for passages dominated by
words within one particular range of a value spectrum but
containing words from another, distant point on that spectrum; the practicality and usefulness of such an approach
has yet to be demonstrated.

The materials employed in this analysis may be useful,
however, in dealing with irony on a larger scale. Repeated
readings of certain scenes in *Portrait* often produce in me

very different responses. When Stephen is waxing particularly rhapsodic—for example, in the villanelle scene—I, at
times, will "go along" with him; I will accept the level of
intensity of his epiphanic experience as real or valid within
his fictive universe. At other times, I want to say to him,
"Get off it! How can you possibly take yourself so seriously"?
This latter reaction represents, in effect, an ironic distancing
of my own responses and empathic projections from what is
presented as real or factual within the fictive world of the
novel. This irony, however, is quite different from the earlier
irony produced by the *cash register* image; here the irony is
pervasive, distancing me from the scene's entire portraiture
of Stephen. Because my response is not consistent, whatever
is distancing me from Stephen must be a function of my
own moods as well as of Joyce's narrative. The basis for this
particular kind of irony can be found in the aesthetic theory,
and the computer can, I believe, help locate such instances.

In the discussion of aesthetic theory, Stephen states that
the Image constitutes the material the artist portrays, but it
also is the element that joins the mind and senses of the
artist with the mind and senses of his reader. If taken literally, the relation described can be represented by the following diagram:

critical level	Reader's mind
intentional level	Joyce's mind
fictive level	Stephen's mind

While we cannot know Joyce's intentions, we must "go
through" that level if we are to project our responses into
Stephen's universe. The significance of this relation is most
important in the matter of ironic distance.

To digress for a moment, the primary difference between tragedy and melodrama is the viewer's different empathic involvement in the play's fictive world. The level of emotional intensity in tragedy usually rises slowly, carrying with it the viewer's empathic involvement; at the climax he is as transported as the character and he experiences an emotional release or purging similar to that of the tragic character. When the viewer's range of emotional responses is great, the effect is tragic catharsis. Melodrama lacks the slow, sustained build-up of emotional involvement that characterizes tragedy. Often the perils and falls of the melodramatic character are as bad as or worse than those of the tragic character, but the viewer is not on the same emotional level as the character; he has been left behind. Usually, the action proceeds from a relaxed normality to grave predicament so quickly that the viewer is unable or unwilling to follow empathically. Consequently, when the level of intensity is relaxed, the melodramatic character may claim catharsis or great relief, but the viewer is more likely to experience the comic relief that characterizes short, abrupt releases of emotional tension.

An analogous relation exists between epiphany and irony. The epiphanic scenes in *Portrait* are indicated by dramatic peaks in the concentrations of important images. Within the fictive world, there is no question of the intensity of Stephen's experience: the graphs of chapter 2 of this discussion make this apparent. If, however, we assume that the narrative should evoke in the reader an experience that at least approximates the experience depicted in the fictive world, the matter is not so simple. For example, the graphs indicate that Stephen's experience in creating the villanelle is epiphanic; mine is not. On the other hand, in experiences such as the pandybat episode and the epiphany on the beach, I am carried along by the narrative. As Stephen's involvement in his environment grows more intense, my involvement with the novel grows more intense. When he experiences the sudden clarification of thematic relations, I experience a sudden clarification where I see the major themes of the chapter converge, fuse, and redefine the relations among themselves. What, then, characterizes the difference in my responses to these portions of the narrative and to the villanelle scene?

The answer is embarrassingly simple. I have been "carried" through a build-up of emotional intensity in some instances and not in others. A close look at the graphs of Chapters I, IV, and V of *Portrait* indicates that the major epiphanies of I and IV are accompanied by a sustained build-up of image density and, hence, emotional intensity. These scenes move slowly, progressively toward climax. The villanelle, however, begins *in medias res* with the emotional intensity already very high when the scene opens. Stephen is highly aroused; I am not. This mode of presentation does not compromise the importance of the experience for Stephen, but it does compromise my reaction to his experience. Instead of sharing something of Stephen's epiphany, I experience an ironic distancing from him. When the reader is carried empathically through a wide range of emotional intensity with the fictive character, he is likely to share that character's epiphanic experiences just as the viewer, if carried slowly and deliberately through the progressions in emotional intensity of a tragedy, will share the tragic hero's catharsis. If the level of intensity jumps too abruptly in the fictive world, leaving the reader behind, he is likely to view the character as ironic, just as the viewer, if left behind, is likely to experience comedy under similar conditions in melodrama.

Translated into functional terms, this realization leads us to expect that scenes corresponding to peaks that top a sloping base are likely to produce strong responses in the reader; scenes whose peaks are very abrupt with little or no sloping base are likely candidates for extended irony. Consequently, the computer may be useful to the literary scholar in examining scenes he suspects are intended to be ironic as well as discovering leads to other scenes he may not have noticed that may also, upon close reading, be ironic.

The final question that remains is whether Joyce intended to portray scenes such as the villanelle section as ironic. We can't, of course, ever know what Joyce intended, but over the past few years, subjecting his work to the closest scrutiny I could give it, I have emerged with an overwhelming respect for his precision and craftsmanship. It is inconceivable to me that Joyce was not in control of every single feature of his work, that he did anything without some purpose. When I consider the effect of the irony of the villanelle on me, I am led to a different perspective on the novel. If the composition of a thoroughly mediocre poem accompanied by so much emotional energy is ironic, would not the grandiose aesthetic ideas of the character who wrote that poem also be ironic? The plot thickens and the irony grows deeper when we realize that although Stephen's statement of his theory may be highly ironic, the ideas expressed do describe the novel containing them; this assertion has been the basis for the entire study. The result is a realization of how completely Joyce controls our responses to his work. When he wants us to empathize with Stephen he takes us along; when he wants to jar us out of involvement with the plot and the fictive world, he leaves us behind. He constantly modulates our emotional responses through imagery; the basic pattern of this aesthetic orchestration corresponds with the rhythmic patterns that can be seen in the graphs of chapter 2. All writers do this to a degree; few do it as skillfully as Joyce.

In this study I have sought to demonstrate that the computer can be used to explore a work of literature by helping to evaluate a critical thesis derived much as any other critical thesis. In addition to demonstrating this thesis, I have also attempted to point out structural patterns that I feel augment the aesthetic aspects of the novel. Finally, I have attempted to show that the computer can potentially help in our consideration of the larger, conceptual aspects of literature, such as irony. If nothing else, I hope that this study indicates that the beast can be tamed, that the computer can aid us in the endeavor that our profession considers most important—the humanistic interpretation of literature.

Appendix A
Computer Techniques

1.10. In this Appendix the computational procedures used to process the text and analyze the imagery of *A Portrait of the Artist as a Young Man* are discussed. These procedures may be divided into three groups: general "housekeeping" programs that could be applied to any text, procedures that facilitate the selection of images and the building of tables making individual images readily accessible for examination, and, finally, programs that perform specific analytic functions. Each of these phases of processing will be described below. I shall attempt to define terms pertaining to computational procedures that might be unfamiliar to the general reader. Whenever possible, descriptions of mathematical procedures will be presented intuitively with references given for more rigorous treatments; models developed specifically in this work will be accompanied by formal definitions as well.

1.20. The text used for this study is the definitive edition of James Joyce's *A Portrait of the Artist as a Young Man,* corrected by Chester G. Anderson from the Dublin Holograph and edited by Richard Ellmann. The text was key-punched at the University of North Carolina Computation Center, conforming as closely as practical to the format of the printed page. Keypunching was done on I.B.M. 029 upper-case machines using the EBCDIC encoding scheme. Only two keypunching conventions were introduced. To help the computer recognize words and punctuation marks, the text was prepared in blank, delimited form : each individual unit to be recognized by the computer was separated by a space. Text words, of course, are routinely separated by blanks; this convention separates punctuation marks by blanks as well. Spacing would look like this : [look like this   :   ]. Second, a set of characters not expected to be found in the text was used to indicate a change in type font. Passages printed in italics were bounded on the left and right by the "less than" and "greater than" symbols (< and >). To facilitate proofreading, the text was punched with one line of printed text per standard eighty-character I.B.M. card. The total text constituted some ten thousand punched cards.

1.21. After the text was prepared in a computer-accessible form, the next step was to separate it into distinct entities (*i.e.*, words or punctuation marks) and to index them.[1] The text was introduced into the machine one card at a time, and the computer then scanned the card for a set of characters bounded by blanks. Each word or punctuation mark located by this procedure was placed in a "logical record" along with a number indicating where in the text it occurred; this record was then written onto magnetic tape[2] for additional processing and a printed version was made for manual reference. The particular format used was as follows :

2	6	3	7	18
LENGTH OF WORD	LINEAR SEQUENCE NUMBER	PAGE NUMBER	BLANK	WORD

A two-digit number indicating the length of the word was followed by a six-digit number indicating the relative sequence of the word or punctuation mark in the text. (The first word is numbered 1, the second 2, etc. until the end of the text.) The page number of the printed text on which the word appeared was included for manual reference. Finally, the word or punctuation mark was stored in an eighteen-character slot. (No word appearing in the text was longer.) As indexed by this scheme there were slightly more than 98,000 words and punctuation marks in the text.

1.22.   Next, the records were sorted primarily on word and secondarily on linear sequence number, using the standard system/360 sort package furnished by I.B.M. The sorted records would thus be in alphabetical order with repetitions of the same word-type appearing in text order. Again these records were stored on tape.

1.23.   The final program of the text preparation phase was a modified version of Sally Sedelow's SUFFIX program. This procedure groups words together by root or stem and discards all function words and punctuation marks. Each group of words with the same root but with different suffixes is identified by a five-digit number, called a MATCH-COUNT, which is attached to the logical record for each word. Thus each appearance of *complete, completely, completing*, etc. would be recognized as belonging to the same root group by the shared MATCHCOUNT. Also attached was a number indicating the total frequency for the particular word-type. Output records, again stored on tape, had the following format:

Length of Word	Linear Sequence Number	Page Number	Match Count	Frequency	Word
2	6	3	5	4	18

One record was created for each occurrence of each word; however, at this point function words and punctuation marks were discarded from the data set. This program marks the end of the basic data preparation steps.

1.30. The programs of phase two were designed to make individual images and the images around them readily available for examination. The first step was the selection of the words to be considered images. This was done manually and represents the only major task performed manually in the analysis, except, of course, the initial keypunching. It would have been desirable to have given the computer a definition of *image*, a text, and perhaps a dictionary, and to have allowed it to select the images using these criteria. Unfortunately, the state of the art does not make this approach feasible at the present time; recent work on thesauri and dictionaries, however, indicates that this may eventually be possible.

From an alphabetical listing those words were selected which I felt had sensory and thematic import. No systematic restrictions were placed on images: for example, no distinctions were made among *flame, flames, flamed, flaming, etc.* all were considered as variant forms of the single image *flame.* Several other persons have examined my selections; their fruitful suggestions often resulted in reconsiderations of individual words. Inevitably, some will disagree with my selections, but I have attempted to err on the side of over-inclusion rather than risk missing an important facet of the novel by leaving out some particular image. The final result is a list of some 1,312 images that is, I feel, a reasonable basis for the analysis. (A complete list of images is provided in Appendix B.)

1.32. The computer was furnished with a list of MATCHCOUNTS for those words considered to be images.

The list consisted of a series of cards, one image—or MATCHCOUNT—per card. To facilitate this process and to avoid keypunching 1,312 cards, I had the computer punch a card for each word-type in the text with its MATCH-COUNT. I then selected the cards for the image words and discarded the rest. These cards were read in ascending order of MATCHCOUNT; the data set from the suffix program was then passed against this list. Records with MATCH-COUNTS that also appeared on the list of image MATCH-COUNTS were selected and stored in a dictionary of images called IMG:

```
01 IMG
   02 MATCHCOUNT
   02 IMAGE
   02 FREQUENCY
   02 BEGIN
   02 FINISH
```

The index information for each occurrence of the image was separated and stored in a long list called LOC1. The starting position in this list of the index information (the linear number, page number, etc.) was placed in BEGIN, and the position of the last slot in the list where index information for an occurrence of the image group was placed, in FINISH. The process was repeated for all 1,312 images. Using the two lists, I could locate the textual information for all occurrences of any image by going to the slots in LOC1 between the particular BEGIN and FINISH numbers for that particular image. This organization is shown in Figure A.1 for the image *abyss*.

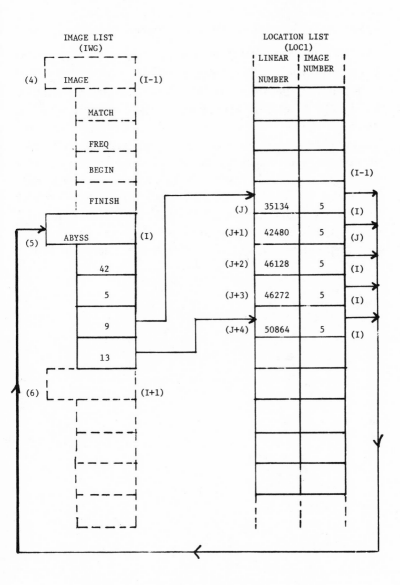

Figure A.1   Image and Location Tables

1.33. The list, LOC1, is in image order. A duplicate list of index information was created and sorted into linear text order; that is, the first entry would be the index information for the first image; the second entry, the information for the second image, etc. Using parts of all three lists I could now examine the environment of any image. Thus, I could look at, say, the five images before and after each occurrence of the image *fire*. To do this easily, however, I needed a number or pointer connecting the slot in LOC1 with the position in LOC2 for that particular image. When this number is attached, all three lists are connected logically by the numbers or pointers; the complete structure is shown in Figure A.2.

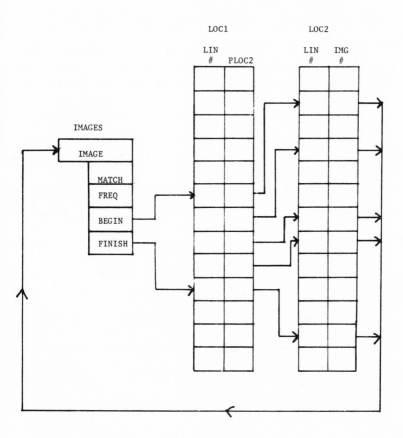

Figure A.2.   Complete Image Tables

1.34. These techniques, although written specifically for this analysis, could be applied to any study where one wished to store and examine a list of entities and their contexts. A generalized version of these programs has been written and described in *Computers and the Humanities*.[3] The completion of these steps marked the end of the "housekeeping" data processing chores; a discussion of programs used to analyze *Portrait* follows.

1.40. The first set of programs written specifically for this analysis produced image-frequency counts for each chapter of the novel. These frequency counts help determine for individual images broad patterns of distribution. If several images appear a large number of times in some chapters but not in others, we would suspect some sort of associative relation among them; such leads were pursued more thoroughly using analytic techniques to be discussed. (See Appendix B for a list of images and their frequencies of occurrence by chapter; the frequency listed is the cumulative frequency for all variant forms of images having the same stem indicated by similar MATCHCOUNTS.) The various counts were produced by checking each image position in LOC1 to see in which chapter that particular linear number fell, and counters for the five chapters were incremented accordingly. The computer produced a printed record of this information as well as a punched-card record, one image-type per card with its accompanying frequencies. These records were then sorted five different times, each time on the decreasing frequency of occurrence for a particular chapter, to produce lists of images in descending frequency order for each chapter. Helpful in themselves, these listings facilitated the selection of thematic groups of images used in subsequent programs.

1.41. The second major analytic program developed

groups or clusters of images that consistently occur close to one another within individual chapters. A rather elaborate model called factor analysis or, more precisely, principal component analysis, was used. If a group of images consistently appear within a hundred words of one another in a chapter, this would suggest that they are related in Stephen's experience. The principal component program reveals such tendencies. (See Appendix D for a list of factors developed.) The program was executed, with slightly varying lists of images, for each of *Portrait's* five chapters.[4] The major programming for this step was a procedure that computed the data used as input for the "canned" factor analysis procedure.

These programs were run for each chapter. Using the image frequency lists described above, I selected the individual images to be analyzed; the images chosen for each chapter were those that occurred more than a specified number of times in that chapter. (This number ranged from eight to five occurrences per chapter for the five different runs.) By this process some 90 to 120 images were examined for clustering tendencies in each chapter.

The text was divided into 100 word segments (words 1–100, 101–200, etc.). Using IMG and LOC2, the program then determined the frequency of occurrence for each selected image for each textual unit of the chapter. A set of counters, one for each image being considered, was established; the linear numbers and dictionary pointers in LOC2 were considered sequentially. So long as the linear number for the image was within the first 100 words of the novel, the appropriate counter was incremented by one. When the first linear number considered became greater than 100, a record of all the counter values was stored in auxiliary storage and the counters reset to zero. After all subsections of a chapter were thus examined, the data were then passed as input in the form of a list of numbers, or matrix, to the factor analysis program. Each row of the list or matrix represented the number of times that individual images appeared in a particular subsection of the text. There would be as many rows of numbers as subsections of text, and as many columns as images chosen for examination. Thus if one were interested in M different images and divided the text into N subsections, the list or matrix would be dimensioned MxN with MxN individual cells in it. See Figure A.3.

The principal component program itself looks at each pair of images in all text subsections and assigns the pair a value ranging from -1 to $+1$ (this value is called a correlation coefficient).[5] If the images consistently occur together in the same context, the correlation coefficient is near $+1$; if they never occur in the same environment, the correlation coefficient is near -1; a random distribution results in a correlation coefficient near 0. This process, then, reduces the NxM to a square (MxM) matrix called the correlation matrix. See Figure A.4.

	image 1	image 2	image 3	....	image M
section 1	f 11	f 12	f 13	....	f 1m
section 2	f 21	f 22	f 23	....	f 2m
section 3	f 31	f 32	f 33	....	f 3m
.	.	.	.		.
.	.	.	.		.
section N	f n1	f n2	f n3	....	f nm

Figure A.3

Subsequent steps in the process are probably easiest understood in terms of their geometric or vector analogue. We may regard each row of the correlation matrix as an ordered set of numbers $(a_{11}, a_{12}, \ldots, a_{1m})$, or as a point in a Euclidean space of dimension M, or as a vector. If one regards each row as a vector, then the set of all M vectors (one for each row) will generate a space of dimension D, such that D L M. For example,

	image 1	image 2	image 3	.... image m
image 1	a_{11}	a_{12}	a_{13}	.... a_{1m}
image 2	a_{21}	a_{22}	a_{23}	.... a_{2m}
image 3	a_{31}	a_{32}	a_{33}	.... a_{3m}
.	.	.	.	.
.	.	.	.	.
image m	a_{m1}	a_{m2}	a_{m3}	.... a_{mm}

Figure A.4

the three vectors given in Figure A.5 could be said to generate the usual three-dimensional Euclidean space since any point or any vector in the space could be generated by taking combinations of the three vectors

$$
\begin{pmatrix} 1 & 0 & 0 \\ 0 & 2 & 0 \\ 0 & 0 & 3 \end{pmatrix}
\begin{array}{c} a_1 \\ a_2 \\ a_3 \end{array}
$$

Figure A.5

given. For example b = (2,2,3) can be represented by $2a_1$ + a_2 + a_3 = 2(1,0,0) + (0,2,0) +(0,0,3) = (2,2,3). (See Figure A.6.) In general M vectors will generate a space of dimensionality less than or equal to M.

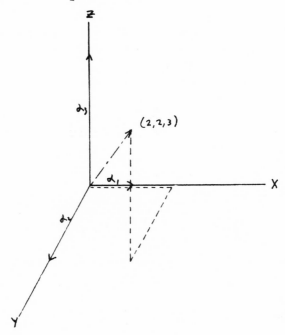

Figure A.6 Linear Sum of the Vectors

The factor-analysis model seeks a group of vectors, formed by various combinations of the original vectors, that comes nearest to generating the original space of the correlation matrix. This approximation is close when a number of the original vectors lie relatively near to one another. In 2-space, this process might be represented as shown in Figure A.7 where the original vectors, (a_1, a_2 . . . , a_8) might be approximated or reduced to β_1, β_2, with a_5 largely excluded.

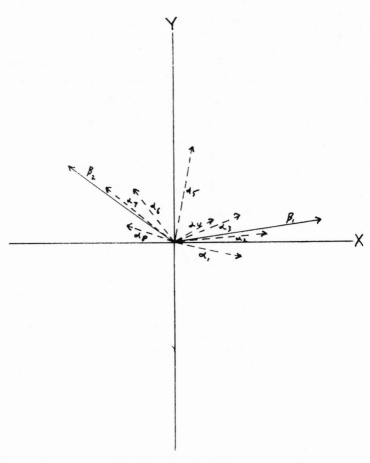

Figure A.7. Resolution of Vectors

What the program actually produces is a set of column vectors (or factor loadings) of the form shown in Figure A.8. Each element or weight of the factor represents the degree to which that particular variable (image, in our case) contributes to the factor. Thus individual factors can be thought to be most strongly characterized by those variables or images which contribute the largest weights. A negative weight implies the absence of that variable (or image) in the context of the variables

Figure A.8

word	a
1	11
word	a
2	21
word	a
3	31
.	.
.	.
.	.
word	a
n	n1

Figure A.9

word	
1	.05
2	.91
3	.63
4	.81
5	.53
6	.66
7	.32
8	.21
9	—.55
10	.11

or images that most strongly characterize the factor. See Figure A.9: this factor is best defined in conjunction with images 2, 4, 6, 3, 9, and 5: however, image 9 consistently *does not* appear in context with the others.

The set of factors developed for each chapter represents clusters of images that consistently appeared together. These groupings were verified by using an image concordance. Thus, by using the frequency lists, the set of factors indicating tendencies of images to occur close to one another consistently over a chapter, and a concordance listing each occurrence of each image with the five images on each side, I was able to infer the changing patterns of associations among images that develop over the novel and to verify these patterns by going back to the textual context for each occurrence.

1.42. The concordance program was virtually a trivial programming task once the data were put into the random accessible structure mentioned. This was done by having the computer look at each image, sequentially, in the dictionary. From there, it looked at each occurrence of each image in LOC1. From there, using the pointer to LOC2, it located the textual position of each occurrence, moved out five positions on each side of the particular image in LOC2, and then printed the sequence of images found. This process was repeated for each occurrence of each image.

1.43. To show that important moments in the development of Stephen's personality are accompanied by large concentrations of important images, a model was developed to quantify "richness" of imagery. Richness, in this context, is a function of both the total number of images present in a section of text as well as the relative "importance" of the individual images themselves. Since this model was developed for this project, it will be defined formally; a brief discussion of the computer implementation follows.

A grid was imposed over the text dividing it into units of 500 words, thus giving a resolution of just a little over a page of text per unit. The intent of the model was to represent the entire set of images as a space—or more precisely, as a geometric solid, embedded in a space, for which the volume could be computed. Consequently, the relative volumes of the images in a subset of the text could be computed and would indicate proportional richness of imagery. This was done in the following manner:

1. Let each image be represented as a point in some space such that each unique image adds a dimension to that space. Thus for N unique images, the space would be of dimensionality N.

2. Let the vectors associated with each point or image be orthogonal to one another and of the form $(O, O, \ldots, a_i, O, \ldots, O)$.

This configuration can be thought of as a mathematical extension of the familiar three-dimensional Euclidean space, where the vectors associated with each of the images would lie along one of the axes (see Figure A.10). Thus for N images, the space would be defined by N such axes and would be of dimension N.

3. The space generated will be such that each point in it will be represented by an ordered N-tuple $(a_1, a_2, a_3, \ldots, a_n))$.

4. This space is representative of the relative frequencies of the images of a_i = frequency of image (i) for some subset of the total text. Thus $O \leq a_i \leq f_1$ where f_i is the total text frequency of image (i).

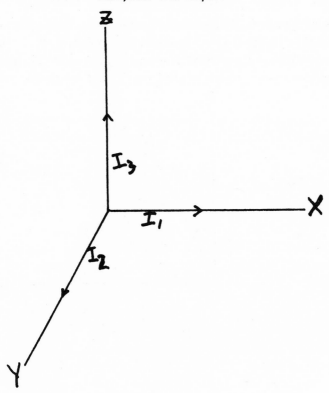

Figure A.10. Vector Representation of Images

Each point in this space, then, represents some collection of images. In our 3-space example, the point, (1, 0, 2), may be associated with some section of the text in which Image (1) appears once, image (2) not at all, and image (3) twice

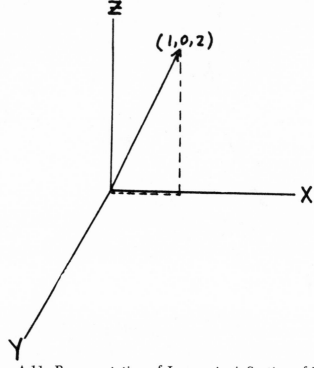

Figure A.11. Representation of Images in A Section of Text

(see Figure A.11). Thus we can associate each of the subsections of the text with a point in the relative frequency space defined by an ordered list of the frequencies of the 1,312 images of *Portrait* for that text subsection.

Not all images are equally "important" in the novel. Some that appear only one or two times carry relatively little weight as compared with images such as fire and water.

which are found throughout the novel in a variety of key passages. To make the model more sensitive to these images, a weighting scheme was imposed to make passages that contain a high concentration of frequently used images stand out from passages that might contain an equal number of images but images that merely represent a cross section of the total set of images.

5. Images were weighed using a function of their total text frequency This function may be represented as a mapping onto a weight-frequency space. Such a function is :

$$v(a_1 \ a_2 \ \ldots \ a_n) = (f_1^{a_1} \quad f_2^{a_2}, \ldots, f_n^{a_n})$$

This space has the additional feature that it is defined multiplicatively rather than additively, as was the relative frequency space, so that deviations from the norm are indicated more dramatically.

6. The "volume" associated with the set of images or any subset of them can be computed. For a given subset, defined by the point:

$$\alpha_1 = (a_{11} \ a_{12} \ \ldots \ a_{1n}),$$
$$v(a_1) = (f_1^{a_{11}} \ f_2^{a_{12}} \ , \ldots \ f_n^{a_{n1}})$$

This point can be projected onto the corresponding unit vectors and the volume of the parallelapiped formed computed. The volume for the first textual subset would be:

$$
B_1 = \begin{pmatrix}
\dfrac{a_{11}}{f_1} & 0 & 0 & \ldots & 0 \\[1em]
0 & \dfrac{a_{12}}{f_2} & 0 & \ldots & 0 \\[1em]
\vdots & & & & a_{1n} \\[1em]
0 & 0 & 0 & \ldots & f_n
\end{pmatrix}
$$

$$
\mathrm{VOL}(B_1) = \; \mid B_1 \cdot B_1' \mid
$$
$$
\text{But since } B_1 = \; B_1',
$$
$$
\mathrm{VOL}(B_1) = \; \mid B_1 \mid
$$

$$
= \; \frac{a_{11}}{f_1} \quad \frac{a_{12}}{f_2} \quad \frac{a_{13}}{f_3} \; \ldots \; \frac{a_{1n}}{f_n}
$$

Thus, for our familiar example, if each of the images occurred twice in the whole text: $(1,0,2) = (2^1, 2^0, 2^2) = (2,1,4,)$. The point $(2,1,4)$ is projected onto the axis. The volume of the parallelapiped, defined by the projections onto the axis, is then computed for each of the subsections of the text (see Figure A.12). This calculation is greatly simplified by using matrix algebra, as demonstrated above.

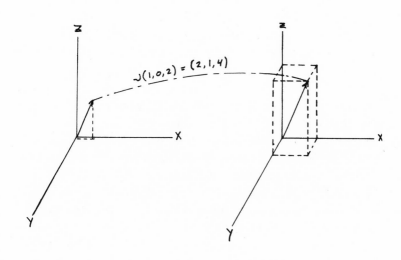

Figue A.12. The Mapping Function, U

7. By conceiving of a text as a linear sequence of words, we can impose a grid over the text that divides it into M equal subsections.

8. The volume associated with each of the subsections, computed in the B space, will reflect the relative richness of imagery in that subsection, where richness is related to both total number of images within a subsection and the relative "importance" of those images. Based upon these assumptions, the model produces a parameter for textual richness objectively derived within the terms of the model.

The model has several rather nice features. The additive identity, zero, maps onto the multiplicative identity, 1, as would be expected. Also, the model makes interpretation of points outside of the original set possible. For a given text, $T, 0 \leqslant a_i \leqslant f_i$. But if we hold the set of weights, F, constant, we may then apply them, through the mapping function, to any text. This would make comparisons for several works relative to some particular work possible. For example, it would be possible to measure the richness of the images of *Portrait* that also appears in *Ulysses*.

Actual omputation is far less complicated than the model. A set of accumulators, initiated at 1, is defined—one for each image in the text. Then a scan of either list of image locations is made. The linear number is divided by the unit (in this case, 500) and the corresponding accumulator, plus one, is multiplied by the total text frequency of the particular image. (For an image with linear number 2037, $2037/500 = 4$, accumulator 5 is multiplied by the frequency of that image.) The numbers developed are very large—in fact, a scaling procedure was used to avoid overflow—so that the value actually plotted on the graph is the logarithm of the number. The results of this procedure applied to *A Portrait of the Artist* can be found in chapter 2.

1.44.   Often images with the same denotative meaning carry similar connotative values. For example, *burn, burning, blaze,* and *flame* all function virtually alike in the associative structure of Stephen's mind. Some twenty-seven such thematic groups of images were defined and their respective collective distributions over the text computed, using units of 500 words per linear subsection.

To facilitate interpretation of the characteristic pattern inherent in the raw data for each theme, a technique known as Fourier analysis was used. Numerous discussions are available that include the equations for this model; a brief intuitive description follows. Any wave form, such as that produced by a voice spectrograph or an oscilloscope, that is made up of a finite number of points can be reproduced *exactly* by a combination of perfectly regular sine and cosine curves of different frequencies and amplitudes. That is, if a wave form is made up of some 1,000 points or observational values, that pattern, no matter how ocmplex or "ragged" it looks, can be duplicated exactly by no more than 1,000 sine and cosine curves with frequencies 1, 2, 3, ..., 1,000 cycles per unit and with approriate amplitudes. Accompanying the computer analysis of any given wave form—the graph of a thematic distribution over a text may be regarded as a complex wave form—are numerical values indicating the amplitude or power associated with each frequency. By picking the eight to twelve largest amplitudes and then plotting the associated sine and cosine curves for the respective frequencies, we can obtain a "smoothed" form of the wave that indicates its characteristic pattern. Appendix E contains graphs of thematic groups of images and their accompanying characteristic curves enabled me to determine patterns of interrelations and associations among not just single images but whole groups of images.

1.45. The lists of images with their frequencies in each chapter (1.41), the factor analytic procedure (1.42), and the concordance (1.43) are all used to examine the environments in which images occur, under the assumption that if images appear close together a number of times they are related in Stephen's experience. This analysis is done to trace the changing patterns of associations among images in Stephen's mind, thus revealing the structure of his personality. The analysis of richness of images (1.44) is used to test the hypothesis that major transitions in Stephen's development are accompanied by dramatic build-ups of important images. These procedures and the materials they produce are then used as tools by the critic to test and develop the ideas and hunches he has derived from his reading and contemplation of the novel.

Appendix B
Computer Listing of Images

#	IMAGE	FREQ: TOTAL	CH1	CH2	CH3	CH4	CH5
1	ABBEY	3	3	0	0	0	0
2	ABBOTS	2	2	0	0	0	0
3	ABLAZE	2	0	0	0	0	2
4	ABORO	1	0	0	0	1	0
5	ABYSS	5	0	1	4	0	0
6	ACCENT	10	0	3	1	2	4
7	ACHE	8	0	0	6	1	1
8	ACOLYTE	1	0	0	0	1	0
9	ADAM	6	0	0	6	0	0
10	AFLAME	2	0	0	0	2	0
11	AFRAID	17	7	6	1	0	3
12	AFTERGLOW	2	0	0	0	0	2
13	AGLOW	1	0	0	0	1	0
14	AGONY	11	1	1	9	0	0
15	AIR	87	25	10	11	18	23
16	AISLE	2	0	0	2	0	0
17	AJAR	1	0	0	0	0	1
18	ALMONDS	1	1	0	0	0	0
19	ALOUD	2	0	0	0	1	1
20	ALTAR	30	7	4	9	7	3
21	ALTARSTEPS	1	0	0	0	1	0
22	AMEN	7	1	0	5	0	1
23	ANGEL	28	2	0	18	6	2
24	ANGER	26	1	7	5	6	7
25	ANGRILY	19	4	3	2	1	9
26	ANGUISH	4	0	1	3	0	0
27	ANIMAL	8	2	0	2	0	4
28	ANNOYED	4	0	3	0	0	1
29	ANTELOPES	2	0	0	0	1	1
30	ANTLIKE	1	0	0	1	0	0
31	APE	5	0	0	1	0	4
32	APOLOGISE	6	5	0	0	0	1
33	APOSTLE	3	0	0	2	0	1
34	APPLAUSE	1	0	1	0	0	0
35	APPLE	7	4	1	1	1	0
36	APPLETREES	1	0	0	0	0	1
37	APRON	3	2	1	0	0	0
38	ARCHES	1	0	1	0	0	0
39	AROMATIC	1	0	1	0	0	0
40	ARROW	1	0	0	0	0	1
41	ARSE	1	0	0	0	0	1
42	ART	50	0	1	5	2	42
43	ASHES	4	1	0	2	0	1
44	ASHPLANT	4	0	0	0	0	4
45	ATBORO	1	0	0	0	1	0
46	AUBURN	1	0	0	0	0	1
47	AUDIBLE	1	0	0	0	0	1
48	AUTUMN	3	0	2	0	0	1
49	AZURE	1	0	0	0	1	0
50	BAAING	1	1	0	0	0	0
51	BABBLE	1	0	0	0	0	1
52	BABY	2	2	0	0	0	0

#	IMAGE	FREQ: TOTAL	CH1	CH2	CH3	CH4	CH5
53	BACON	4	1	0	0	0	3
54	BAG	1	0	1	0	0	0
55	BAH	1	0	0	0	0	1
56	BAIZE	1	1	0	0	0	0
57	BALCONIES	2	0	0	0	0	2
58	BALD	4	3	1	0	0	0
59	BALDHEAD	2	0	0	0	0	2
60	BALDWIN	3	0	0	0	0	3
61	BALDYHEAD	3	3	0	0	0	0
62	BALES	20	6	3	3	0	8
63	BALLAD	1	0	0	0	0	1
64	BALMY	1	0	1	0	0	0
65	BAND	8	2	4	0	1	1
66	BANG	2	1	1	0	0	0
67	BANTER	4	0	1	0	2	1
68	BAPTISED	5	0	0	4	0	1
69	BAPTISM	4	0	0	3	0	1
70	BARE	6	0	2	0	3	1
71	BAREFOOT	2	0	0	0	1	1
72	BAREHEADED	1	0	0	1	0	0
73	BARK	1	0	0	0	0	1
74	BARMAIDS	2	0	2	0	0	0
75	BARRACK	1	0	0	0	1	0
76	BARRELS	1	0	1	0	0	0
77	BARREN	2	0	1	1	0	0
78	BASE	6	0	1	1	0	4
79	BASIN	4	3	0	0	0	1
80	BASKET	8	0	1	1	0	6
81	BATH	6	4	0	0	1	1
82	BATLIKE	4	1	0	0	0	3
83	BAWL	3	3	0	0	0	0
84	BAY	1	0	0	0	0	1
85	BEACH	2	0	0	0	2	0
86	BEADS	4	0	1	1	2	0
87	BEAK	3	0	1	1	0	1
88	BEAR	7	0	0	5	0	2
89	BEARD	9	3	1	4	0	1
90	BEAST	11	0	1	10	0	0
91	BEAT	14	5	1	1	1	6
92	BECAUSEBORO	1	0	0	0	1	0
93	BED	35	23	1	4	2	5
94	BEER	1	1	0	0	0	0
95	BELL	29	14	4	3	2	6
96	BENCH	18	1	3	8	0	6
97	BENUMBED	1	0	0	1	0	0
98	BIBLE	1	0	0	0	0	1
99	BICYCLE	3	1	1	0	0	1
100	BIKE	1	0	0	1	0	0
101	BIRD	27	3	3	7	1	13
102	BIRDCALL	1	0	0	0	0	1
103	BISCUIT	1	0	0	0	0	1
104	BISHOP	6	5	0	1	0	0

#	IMAGE	FREQ: TOTAL	CH1	CH2	CH3	CH4	CH5
105	BITCH	4	1	0	0	0	3
106	BITTER	12	3	2	0	0	7
107	BLACK	28	10	7	1	1	9
108	BLACKLOOKING	1	1	0	0	0	0
109	BLACKROCK	5	0	5	0	0	0
110	BLANDLY	2	0	0	0	0	2
111	BLANK	2	0	1	0	0	1
112	BLANKET	5	1	1	2	0	1
113	BLASPHEMER	1	1	0	0	0	0
114	BLASPHEMIES	1	0	0	1	0	0
115	BLASPHEMOUS	3	0	0	1	0	2
116	BLAST	6	0	0	3	0	3
117	BLAZE	2	0	1	0	0	1
118	BLEAK	4	0	0	3	0	1
119	BLEATING	3	0	0	0	0	3
120	BLESS	34	10	1	14	8	1
121	BLEW	8	0	1	6	0	1
122	BLIND	14	5	2	6	1	0
123	BLINDCORD	1	0	0	0	1	0
124	BLINKING	1	0	0	0	0	1
125	BLOOD	34	2	6	8	2	16
126	BLOODRED	1	0	0	1	0	0
127	BLOOM	1	0	1	0	0	0
128	BLOSSOMS	2	2	0	0	0	0
129	BLOW	5	1	3	0	0	1
130	BLUE	19	5	7	1	1	5
131	BLUSH	3	1	0	0	0	2
132	BOAT	2	2	0	0	0	0
133	BODIES	13	0	0	4	4	5
134	BODILY	65	8	5	28	8	16
135	BOGHOLE	1	0	0	0	0	1
136	BOGS	1	0	0	0	0	1
137	BOGWATER	3	2	0	0	0	1
138	BOILING	2	0	0	2	0	0
139	BONE	7	2	2	1	1	1
140	BONNET	1	0	1	0	0	0
141	BOOING	1	1	0	0	0	0
142	BOOK	40	10	11	6	6	7
143	BOOTS	11	4	1	0	0	6
144	BOUS	4	0	0	0	4	0
145	BOWL	6	4	1	0	0	1
146	BOX	13	1	2	6	0	4
147	BRACKISH	1	0	0	0	1	0
148	BRANCH	5	2	0	0	0	3
149	BRASS	3	1	1	1	0	0
150	BRAY	1	0	1	0	0	0
151	BREAD	13	1	2	4	2	4
152	BREAKWATER	4	0	1	0	3	0
153	BREAST	12	1	2	3	2	4
154	BREATH	29	6	6	10	3	4
155	BREECHES	3	2	0	0	0	1
156	BREEZE	4	1	3	0	0	0

#	IMAGE	FREQ: TOTAL	CH1	CH2	CH3	CH4	CH5
157	BRICK	2	1	0	0	1	0
158	BRIDGE	10	0	1	0	6	3
159	BRIGHT	16	1	4	5	0	6
160	BRILLIANT	2	0	1	1	0	0
161	BRIM	6	2	1	0	0	3
162	BRIMSTONE	4	0	0	4	0	0
163	BRINE	1	0	0	0	1	0
164	BRONZE	1	0	1	0	0	0
165	BROTHER	56	22	6	10	7	11
166	BROW	5	0	0	3	0	2
167	BROWN	8	0	3	1	2	2
168	BRUSH	10	7	3	0	0	0
169	BUDDING	2	0	0	0	0	2
170	BUFF	1	0	0	0	0	1
171	BULL	4	0	0	0	2	2
172	BUM	1	1	0	0	0	0
173	BUMP	2	2	0	0	0	0
174	BURN	33	7	3	17	2	4
175	BURST	11	2	5	3	0	1
176	BUSH	3	1	1	0	0	1
177	BUTT	5	3	1	0	0	1
178	CABBAGE	3	1	1	0	1	0
179	CABIN	1	0	0	0	0	1
180	CACKLING	1	0	0	0	0	1
181	CADENCE	4	0	0	0	1	3
182	CAKE	2	0	0	0	0	2
183	CALF	3	0	3	0	0	0
184	CALICO	1	1	0	0	0	0
185	CALM	20	1	5	3	4	7
186	CALVARY	1	0	0	1	0	0
187	CANAL	2	0	0	0	0	2
188	CANCER	2	2	0	0	0	0
189	CANDLE	6	2	0	3	1	0
190	CANDLEBUTTS	3	0	0	0	0	3
191	CANDLESTICK	2	0	0	1	0	1
192	CANE	9	2	7	0	0	0
193	CANKER	2	2	0	0	0	0
194	CANON	3	1	0	0	1	1
195	CANOPY	1	0	0	1	0	0
196	CANVAS	2	0	1	0	1	0
197	CAP	19	8	2	0	0	9
198	CAPUCHIN	3	0	0	1	2	0
199	CAR	13	8	3	0	0	2
200	CARD	5	4	0	0	0	1
201	CARESS	5	0	1	0	2	2
202	CARMELITE	1	0	0	0	0	1
203	CARNIVAL	1	0	0	0	0	1
204	CARPET	3	2	0	0	1	0
205	CARRIAGE	3	0	3	0	0	0
206	CARROTS	1	0	0	1	0	0
207	CASK	1	0	0	0	0	1
208	CASTLE	13	12	1	0	0	0

#	IMAGE	FREQ: TOTAL	CH1	CH2	CH3	CH4	CH5
209	CAT	2	0	2	0	0	0
210	CATACOMBS	1	0	0	0	1	0
211	CATAFALQUE	2	2	0	0	0	0
212	CATCALLS	1	0	0	0	0	1
213	CATECHISM	5	0	0	4	1	0
214	CATTLE	3	0	1	1	0	1
215	CAVE	5	0	1	2	1	1
216	CAVERN	2	0	1	0	0	1
217	CELERY	1	1	0	0	0	0
218	CEMETERY	1	0	0	1	0	0
219	CENSER	3	2	0	0	0	1
220	CEREMENTS	3	0	0	0	3	0
221	CESSPOOL	1	0	0	0	0	1
222	CHAIN	5	2	0	1	0	2
223	CHAIR	11	7	2	0	0	2
224	CHALICE	2	0	0	0	0	2
225	CHAMBERPOT	1	0	0	0	0	1
226	CHAMPAGNE	1	1	0	0	0	0
227	CHANCES	4	0	0	0	1	3
228	CHANDELIER	2	2	0	0	0	0
229	CHANNEL	2	1	0	0	1	0
230	CHAP	9	2	5	1	0	1
231	CHAPEL	49	13	10	20	5	1
232	CHARCOAL	2	1	0	0	0	1
233	CHEEK	20	7	3	0	7	3
234	CHEER	15	9	2	0	0	4
235	CHESTNUT	2	2	0	0	0	0
236	CHEWED	4	1	0	0	0	3
237	CHILD	71	2	10	31	10	18
238	CHILL	13	3	3	3	3	1
239	CHIME	1	0	0	0	0	1
240	CHIN	4	0	0	0	1	3
241	CHOCOLATE	5	1	2	0	0	2
242	CHOIR	7	1	0	1	3	2
243	CHOKED	2	0	0	2	0	0
244	CHORD	3	0	0	0	1	2
245	CHRIST	30	6	2	14	2	6
246	CHRISTENDOM	2	0	0	0	1	1
247	CHRISTMAS	9	7	2	0	0	0
248	CHURCH	34	4	0	11	5	14
249	CIGAR	5	1	2	0	0	2
250	CIGARETTE	9	0	2	0	0	7
251	CINDERPATH	5	5	0	0	0	0
252	CINDERS	2	1	0	0	1	0
253	CINNAMOMUM	1	0	0	1	0	0
254	CIRCLE	10	0	3	4	2	1
255	CITIES	26	1	8	4	3	10
256	CLAPPED	5	3	1	0	0	1
257	CLASSROOM	3	1	0	1	0	1
258	CLATTER	2	0	1	0	0	1
259	CLAY	2	0	0	2	0	0
260	CLEAN	7	2	0	1	1	3

#	IMAGE	FREQ: TOTAL	CH1	CH2	CH3	CH4	CH5
261	CLEAR	26	0	4	6	3	13
262	CLERGY	2	0	0	0	0	2
263	CLERICAL	2	1	0	0	1	0
264	CLICK	7	4	0	1	1	1
265	CLIFFS	1	0	0	0	0	1
266	CLOAK	10	5	0	1	0	4
267	CLOCK	5	0	0	2	0	3
268	CLOISTER	5	0	0	0	2	3
269	CLOTH	17	4	5	2	3	3
270	CLOUD	24	5	1	3	8	7
271	CLOUDLETS	2	0	0	2	0	0
272	COAL	9	3	2	1	0	3
273	COAT	12	4	5	0	1	2
274	COBWEB	2	1	0	0	0	1
275	COCK	4	2	1	1	0	0
276	COCOA	1	1	0	0	0	0
277	COCOON	1	0	0	1	0	0
278	COD	6	5	0	0	0	1
279	COFFIN	2	2	0	0	0	0
280	COIL	9	0	1	1	0	7
281	COIN	2	0	2	0	0	0
282	COLD	68	37	5	9	9	8
283	COLLAR	5	1	1	0	2	1
284	COLLYWOBBLES	3	3	0	0	0	0
285	COLORLESS	1	0	0	0	1	0
286	COLOUR	21	10	2	1	5	3
287	COMMUNED	13	5	1	3	2	2
288	COMMUNICANT	4	0	0	2	1	1
289	CONFESS	43	2	1	25	9	6
290	CONFLAGRATION	1	0	0	1	0	0
291	CONSECRATED	2	0	0	2	0	0
292	CONVENT	1	1	0	0	0	0
293	COOL	11	6	1	0	1	3
294	COPPER	5	2	1	0	0	2
295	COPYBOOK	2	1	0	0	0	1
296	CORD	3	0	0	0	3	0
297	CORDUROY	3	3	0	0	0	0
298	CORK	14	0	13	0	0	1
299	CORPSE	5	0	0	5	0	0
300	CORPSEWHITE	1	0	0	0	1	0
301	CORRIDOR	18	14	0	2	0	2
302	CORRIGAN	6	6	0	0	0	0
303	COTTAGE	6	3	1	0	1	1
304	COUGH	9	3	1	0	0	5
305	COW	3	0	2	0	0	1
306	COWDUNG	2	0	0	0	0	2
307	COWHAIRS	1	0	1	0	0	0
308	COWHOUSE	1	0	0	1	0	0
309	COWL	5	0	3	0	0	2
310	COWYARD	2	0	2	0	0	0
311	CRACK	6	3	2	1	0	0
312	CRADLE	1	1	0	0	0	0

#	IMAGE	FREQ: TOTAL	CH1	CH2	CH3	CH4	CH5
313	CRASH	3	3	0	0	0	0
314	CREAKED	2	0	1	0	0	1
315	CREAM	5	5	0	0	0	0
316	CRICKET	3	2	1	0	0	0
317	CRICKETBATS	3	3	0	0	0	0
318	CRICKETCAP	2	0	1	0	1	0
319	CRIED	61	33	8	1	2	17
320	CROCODILE	4	0	0	0	0	4
321	CROSS	17	1	4	4	1	7
322	CROWD	8	2	3	0	0	3
323	CROWN	7	0	0	3	0	4
324	CRUCIFIED	2	0	0	1	0	1
325	CRUCIFIX	1	0	0	1	0	0
326	CRY	33	8	5	2	6	12
327	CUP	6	2	1	1	0	2
328	CURED	12	0	1	9	0	2
329	CURL	7	2	2	1	0	2
330	CURTAIN	6	2	2	0	0	2
331	CYCLE	5	0	1	1	2	1
332	DAIRY	4	0	1	1	0	2
333	DAMN	38	0	7	19	1	11
334	DAMP	12	7	0	2	0	3
335	DANCE	16	3	7	0	0	6
336	DANK	1	0	0	1	0	0
337	DAPPLED	2	0	0	0	2	0
338	DARK	145	35	24	38	8	40
339	DARKPLUMAGED	1	0	0	0	1	0
340	DART	4	0	0	0	0	4
341	DAWN	4	0	1	0	1	2
342	DAY	148	42	27	30	15	34
343	DAYLIGHT	4	1	0	1	2	0
344	DEAD	33	7	11	5	0	10
345	DEAF	1	0	0	0	0	1
346	DEATH	34	2	2	24	1	5
347	DEATHBED	1	0	0	1	0	0
348	DEATHCHILL	1	0	0	1	0	0
349	DEATHMASK	2	0	0	0	0	2
350	DEATHWOUND	3	3	0	0	0	0
351	DEDALUS	127	62	54	2	4	5
352	DESK	16	8	4	4	0	0
353	DEUS	1	0	0	0	0	1
354	DEVIL	21	2	0	14	1	4
355	DEW	6	0	1	0	0	5
356	DEWLAPS	1	1	0	0	0	0
357	DIAMONDS	1	0	0	0	0	1
358	DICE	1	0	0	0	0	1
359	DIE	38	11	5	12	1	9
360	DIEU	2	2	0	0	0	0
361	DIM	19	0	6	3	9	1
362	DIMPLES	1	0	1	0	0	0
363	DIN	25	8	9	3	2	3
364	DINGDONG	1	1	0	0	0	0

#	IMAGE	FREQ: TOTAL	CH1	CH2	CH3	CH4	CH5
365	DINNERTABLE	1	0	1	0	0	0
366	DIRTY	4	1	1	0	0	2
367	DISH	9	7	0	1	0	1
368	DITCH	5	4	0	1	0	0
369	DIZZILY	1	0	0	1	0	0
370	DOCKS	1	0	1	0	0	0
371	DOG	6	3	2	0	0	1
372	DOLL	4	0	2	0	0	2
373	DOLLYMOUNT	1	0	0	0	1	0
374	DOME	2	0	0	0	1	1
375	DOMINICAN	1	0	0	0	1	0
376	DOOR	64	32	7	7	6	12
377	DOORWAY	10	0	5	1	0	4
378	DORMITORY	3	3	0	0	0	0
379	DOVE	3	0	0	0	2	1
380	DRAIN	2	0	1	0	0	1
381	DRAWL	5	0	2	1	0	2
382	DREGS	1	0	0	0	0	1
383	DRENCHED	2	0	0	1	1	0
384	DRESS	25	11	8	1	2	3
385	DRINK	7	3	0	0	2	2
386	DRY	8	1	1	0	3	3
387	DUBLIN	13	1	6	1	0	5
388	DUNG	3	0	1	1	1	0
389	DUNGHILL	1	0	0	0	0	1
390	DUSK	14	0	3	4	1	6
391	DUST	2	0	0	0	0	2
392	DYING	6	0	0	3	1	2
393	EAGLE	2	1	0	0	1	0
394	EAR	37	4	5	8	5	15
395	EARSPLITTING	1	0	0	0	0	1
396	EARTH	44	4	3	21	8	8
397	EASYCHAIR	3	2	1	0	0	0
398	EBBING	2	0	0	1	0	1
399	EBONITE	1	0	0	0	0	1
400	ECHO	13	0	2	0	7	4
401	ECSTASY	8	0	0	0	4	4
402	EDDIED	3	0	1	0	0	2
403	EGGS	2	0	0	2	0	0
404	EGGSHELLS	1	0	0	0	0	1
405	EJACULATION	2	0	0	0	2	0
406	ELBOW	13	3	2	3	1	4
407	ELEPHANT	4	1	0	1	0	2
408	ELLIPSOID	4	0	0	0	0	4
409	ELLIPTICAL	2	0	0	0	0	2
410	EMBERS	1	0	0	1	0	0
411	EMERALD	3	0	1	0	2	0
412	ENAMEL	2	0	1	0	0	1
413	ENFLAMING	1	0	0	0	0	1
414	EUCHARIST	6	0	0	1	1	4
415	EVENING	47	10	14	6	7	10
416	EXCREMENT	3	0	0	1	0	2

#	IMAGE	FREQ: TOTAL	CH1	CH2	CH3	CH4	CH5
417	EXCREMENTITIOUS	1	0	0	0	0	1
418	EYE	193	50	26	30	21	66
419	EYEBROWS	2	0	1	0	0	1
420	EYEGLASS	2	1	1	0	0	0
421	EYELID	6	0	1	1	1	3
422	FACE	164	48	24	24	20	48
423	FADE	23	0	6	2	8	7
424	FAINT	48	3	6	13	14	12
425	FAIR	11	1	1	1	3	5
426	FARTED	1	0	0	0	0	1
427	FAT	7	2	1	1	0	3
428	FATE	4	3	1	0	0	0
429	FATENCIRCLED	1	0	0	0	0	1
430	FATHER	188	84	59	17	8	20
431	FEAR	50	8	1	12	5	24
432	FEAST	5	0	0	4	0	1
433	FEATHERINGS	4	0	0	2	1	1
434	FEED	34	8	3	5	10	8
435	FENCE	1	0	1	0	0	0
436	FESTERING	2	0	0	2	0	0
437	FEVER	7	0	3	1	2	1
438	FIELD	18	2	3	9	1	3
439	FIERY	2	0	1	1	0	0
440	FIG	11	0	0	1	0	10
441	FIGTREE	1	0	0	1	0	0
442	FIGURE	29	2	9	2	5	11
443	FILE	44	11	8	14	2	9
444	FILM	3	0	2	1	0	0
445	FILTHILY	5	0	2	3	0	0
446	FINGER	38	14	7	3	3	11
447	FINGERNAILS	1	0	0	0	0	1
448	FINGERTIPS	1	0	1	0	0	0
449	FIRE	67	13	7	30	4	13
450	FIRECONSUMED	1	0	0	0	0	1
451	FIRELIGHT	3	0	2	1	0	0
452	FIREPLACE	7	1	2	1	1	2
453	FIRM	14	3	2	4	1	4
454	FISH	8	1	0	6	1	0
455	FLABBY	2	0	2	0	0	0
456	FLAG	3	1	0	0	0	2
457	FLAME	37	3	1	12	9	12
458	FLASH	5	2	0	0	0	3
459	FLAT	10	2	0	0	0	8
460	FLECKED	2	0	0	0	1	1
461	FLEECE	1	0	0	0	1	0
462	FLESH	22	0	0	14	3	5
463	FLEW	10	1	3	0	1	5
464	FLEXIBLE	1	0	0	0	0	1
465	FLICKERED	3	0	2	1	0	0
466	FLIES	2	0	0	1	0	1
467	FLIGHT	10	0	1	0	3	6
468	FLITTING	1	0	0	0	0	1

#	IMAGE	FREQ: TOTAL	CH1	CH2	CH3	CH4	CH5
469	FLOG	12	12	0	0	0	0
470	FLORID	1	0	0	0	0	1
471	FLOWER	21	2	2	4	4	9
472	FLOWERBEDS	1	1	0	0	0	0
473	FLOWERGIRL	1	0	0	0	0	1
474	FLUSH	13	3	4	0	3	3
475	FLUTTER	9	5	0	1	1	2
476	FLY	14	2	0	0	3	9
477	FOAM	1	0	0	0	0	1
478	FOETUS	1	0	1	0	0	0
479	FOG	3	0	1	2	0	0
480	FOOD	4	1	0	2	1	0
481	FOOT	21	2	3	4	1	11
482	FOOTBALL	3	3	0	0	0	0
483	FOOTPATH	5	0	1	1	1	2
484	FOOTSTEPS	1	0	1	0	0	0
485	FOREFINGER	2	0	0	0	0	2
486	FOREHEAD	14	2	4	4	1	3
487	FOREST	4	0	0	2	0	2
488	FORGE	25	2	3	9	3	8
489	FORK	3	3	0	0	0	0
490	FOUL	25	0	3	19	1	2
491	FOULSMELLING	1	0	0	1	0	0
492	FOUNTAIN	3	2	0	1	0	0
493	FOWL	2	1	0	0	0	1
494	FOX	8	5	1	0	2	0
495	FRAGMENT	3	0	1	1	0	1
496	FRAGRANCE	7	0	0	4	0	3
497	FRAIL	11	0	2	3	3	3
498	FRANCISCAN	3	0	0	0	2	1
499	FRANKINCENSE	1	0	0	1	0	0
500	FRECKLED	4	0	1	0	0	3
501	FRIAR	2	0	0	0	0	2
502	FRIGHT	12	5	1	4	0	2
503	FRO	10	6	1	2	0	1
504	FROG	1	0	0	0	0	1
505	FROWN	8	2	3	0	1	2
506	FRUIT	7	0	2	4	1	0
507	FUME	4	0	1	2	0	1
508	FUNGUS	1	0	0	1	0	0
509	FUNNEL	6	0	0	0	0	6
510	FURNACE	1	0	0	1	0	0
511	GAMECOCKS	1	0	1	0	0	0
512	GARDEN	23	0	15	3	0	5
513	GAS	5	4	1	0	0	0
514	GASFLAMES	2	0	1	0	1	0
515	GASJETS	2	0	1	1	0	0
516	GATE	13	0	5	2	4	2
517	GAYCLAD	2	0	0	0	2	0
518	GEESE	2	0	1	0	0	1
519	GEMS	1	0	0	0	0	1
520	GENUFLECTING	1	0	0	0	1	0

#	IMAGE	FREQ: TOTAL	CH1	CH2	CH3	CH4	CH5
521	GINGERNUTS	1	0	1	0	0	0
522	GIRAFFE	1	0	0	0	0	1
523	GIRDLE	1	0	0	0	0	1
524	GIRL	30	1	6	3	6	14
525	GLARE	1	0	1	0	0	0
526	GLASS	24	14	6	0	0	4
527	GLASSJAPS	1	0	0	0	1	0
528	GLEAMED	7	0	0	2	3	2
529	GLIMMER	8	0	1	3	3	1
530	GLINT	1	0	0	0	0	1
531	GLISTENING	1	1	0	0	0	0
532	GLITTERED	1	0	0	1	0	0
533	GLOOM	11	2	2	3	2	2
534	GLOOMILY	9	0	4	2	0	3
535	GLOSSY	1	0	1	0	0	0
536	GLOW	28	5	3	6	8	6
537	GNAWED	3	0	0	3	0	0
538	GOD	228	37	13	134	18	26
539	GODFORSAKEN	2	1	0	0	0	1
540	GODHEAD	1	0	0	1	0	0
541	GOLD	15	6	4	1	3	1
542	GONEBORO	1	0	0	0	1	0
543	GOODBYE	6	5	0	0	0	1
544	GOODNIGHT	3	2	0	1	0	0
545	GOSPEL	4	0	1	1	1	1
546	GOWN	4	0	3	0	0	1
547	GRAIN	8	0	2	5	0	1
548	GRAPES	3	1	2	0	0	0
549	GRASS	8	1	2	2	2	1
550	GRASSPLOT	2	0	2	0	0	0
551	GRATE	8	2	2	2	0	2
552	GRAVE	19	1	2	5	5	6
553	GRAVECLOTHES	1	0	0	0	1	0
554	GRAVEL	14	2	3	1	3	5
555	GRAVEYARD	2	1	1	0	0	0
556	GREASE	6	2	1	1	1	1
557	GREEN	28	18	3	2	1	4
558	GREENWHITE	1	0	0	0	0	1
559	GREY	40	11	3	3	5	18
560	GREYBLUE	1	0	0	0	1	0
561	GREYFRINGED	1	0	0	0	1	0
562	GREYGREEN	1	0	0	1	0	0
563	GREYHOUNDS	2	1	0	0	0	1
564	GURGLING	1	0	0	1	0	0
565	GUST	2	0	0	0	0	2
566	HA	8	1	6	0	0	1
567	HAIR	32	4	6	6	2	14
568	HALE	51	7	15	2	2	25
569	HALLWAY	1	0	0	0	1	0
570	HAM	1	1	0	0	0	0
571	HAND	157	55	21	29	7	45
572	HANDKERCHIEF	2	0	2	0	0	0

#	IMAGE	FREQ: TOTAL	CH1	CH2	CH3	CH4	CH5
573	HARBOUR	3	1	0	0	2	0
574	HARD	23	7	3	4	3	6
575	HARES	5	1	1	0	3	0
576	HARMONIOUS	1	0	0	0	0	1
577	HARMONISED	1	0	0	0	1	0
578	HARMONY	2	0	0	0	0	2
579	HARSH	5	0	0	1	0	4
580	HASH	2	0	2	0	0	0
581	HAT	18	4	4	0	3	7
582	HAWK	3	0	0	0	2	1
583	HAZE	2	0	0	1	1	0
584	HAZEWRAPPED	1	0	0	0	1	0
585	HEAD	89	24	17	17	1	30
586	HEART	102	11	18	33	9	31
587	HEAT	3	0	0	3	0	0
588	HEAVEN	38	1	1	27	7	2
589	HEAVILY	31	7	5	3	3	13
590	HEDGE	2	0	0	1	0	1
591	HEEL	3	0	1	0	0	2
592	HELL	76	3	2	56	1	14
593	HELLFIRE	1	0	0	1	0	0
594	HERBS	1	0	1	0	0	0
595	HERON	36	0	33	3	0	0
596	HILL	8	2	2	1	1	2
597	HIPS	1	0	0	0	1	0
598	HISS	5	1	0	0	0	4
599	HOLE	4	2	0	1	0	1
600	HOLLOWSOUNDING	2	0	2	0	0	0
601	HOME	50	16	16	5	0	13
602	HONEY	1	0	0	0	0	1
603	HOODED	1	0	0	0	0	1
604	HOOFS	3	0	1	0	0	2
605	HORIZON	1	0	0	0	1	0
606	HORSE	9	0	6	0	1	2
607	HOSPITAL	4	0	1	0	0	3
608	HOT	20	16	1	0	0	3
609	HOTEL	9	2	3	0	0	4
610	HOUNDED	3	1	2	0	0	0
611	HOUSE	48	11	15	7	5	10
612	HOUSEBORO	1	0	0	0	1	0
613	HOWL	3	0	0	3	0	0
614	HUE	3	0	0	0	3	0
615	HUM	2	0	1	1	0	0
616	HUNGRILY	2	1	0	0	0	1
617	HURRAY	3	3	0	0	0	0
618	HURROO	4	4	0	0	0	0
619	HURT	4	1	1	2	0	0
620	HUSH	2	1	1	0	0	0
621	HYMN	7	0	0	0	0	7
622	ICON	1	0	0	0	0	1
623	ILLUMINATED	1	0	0	1	0	0
624	IMAGE	60	0	13	3	9	35

#	IMAGE	FREQ: TOTAL	CH1	CH2	CH3	CH4	CH5
625	INAUDIBLE	2	0	0	0	2	0
626	INCENSE	9	2	1	1	2	3
627	INFIRMARY	8	6	1	1	0	0
628	INJURED	1	0	1	0	0	0
629	INJURIES	1	0	0	0	0	1
630	INK	2	1	1	0	0	0
631	INSECT	1	0	0	1	0	0
632	IRON	6	0	0	0	0	6
633	ISLAND	6	0	1	1	3	1
634	ITCH	1	0	0	0	1	0
635	IVORY	13	7	0	0	2	4
636	IVY	13	5	0	0	0	8
637	JAR	3	2	0	0	0	1
638	JARGON	3	0	0	1	0	2
639	JAW	5	0	1	0	1	3
640	JEER	2	0	1	1	0	0
641	JELLYLIKE	1	0	0	1	0	0
642	JERKED	3	0	1	0	0	2
643	JERUSALEM	1	0	1	0	0	0
644	JESU	29	1	1	10	1	16
645	JESUIT	21	3	8	0	4	6
646	JEWEL	2	1	0	1	0	0
647	JEWELEYED	1	0	0	1	0	0
648	JINGLE	3	0	1	0	0	2
649	JUG	1	0	1	0	0	0
650	JUICE	2	2	0	0	0	0
651	KETTLE	1	1	0	0	0	0
652	KIDNEY	1	0	1	0	0	0
653	KISS	21	10	5	2	1	3
654	KNEE	11	4	3	0	3	1
655	KNEEL	14	5	0	6	1	2
656	KNELT	26	7	4	14	1	0
657	KNIFE	7	3	0	1	2	1
658	KNOCKED	6	3	0	0	0	3
659	LACE	5	1	3	0	1	0
660	LAKE	6	0	1	2	0	3
661	LALA	3	3	0	0	0	0
662	LAMB	4	0	0	2	0	2
663	LAMP	25	0	5	3	0	17
664	LANDBORO	1	0	0	0	1	0
665	LANE	7	0	2	0	1	4
666	LANTERN	7	1	5	0	1	0
667	LAP	8	4	0	0	1	3
668	LARK	1	0	1	0	0	0
669	LASHES	3	0	1	1	0	1
670	LAUGH	63	17	13	0	4	29
671	LAUGHTER	17·	3	5	1	0	8
672	LAUREL	1	0	0	0	0	1
673	LAVATORY	2	2	0	0	0	0
674	LAVENDER	3	2	0	0	0	1
675	LAWN	3	1	1	0	0	1
676	LEAF	42	5	9	5	7	16

#	IMAGE	FREQ: TOTAL	CH1	CH2	CH3	CH4	CH5
677	LEATHER	5	3	0	0	1	1
678	LEG	11	5	4	1	1	0
679	LEMON	1	1	0	0	0	0
680	LEND	8	1	4	2	0	1
681	LETTER	14	2	6	3	1	2
682	LICE	3	0	0	0	0	3
683	LICKING	3	1	0	2	0	0
684	LIGHT	100	15	16	23	8	38
685	LIGHTNINGS	2	0	0	0	0	2
686	LILY	1	0	1	0	0	0
687	LIMES	3	1	1	1	0	0
688	LIMP	3	1	0	0	0	2
689	LINEN	5	0	1	0	2	2
690	LIP	48	9	13	7	10	9
691	LIQUID	6	0	1	1	0	4
692	LIT	14	5	1	1	1	6
693	LITANY	1	1	0	0	0	0
694	LITURGY	1	0	0	0	0	1
695	LOAFFER	1	1	0	0	0	0
696	LOINS	2	0	0	0	0	2
697	LOOKBORO	1	0	0	0	1	0
698	LORD	23	8	4	5	2	4
699	LORDBORO	1	0	0	0	1	0
700	LOUD	31	15	4	1	0	11
701	LOUSEMARKS	1	0	0	0	0	1
702	LUCIFER	3	0	0	3	0	0
703	LUKEWARM	1	0	0	0	0	1
704	LULL	5	0	0	4	0	1
705	LUMINARY	1	0	0	1	0	0
706	LUMINOUS	4	0	0	1	0	3
707	LUMPISH	6	0	0	0	1	5
708	LUNGS	1	0	0	0	1	0
709	LUST	10	0	2	6	2	0
710	LUTELIKE	1	0	0	0	0	1
711	LYRICAL	4	0	0	0	0	4
712	MAHOGANY	1	1	0	0	0	0
713	MANYCOLOURED	1	0	0	0	1	0
714	MAPLE	1	0	0	0	0	1
715	MARBLES	2	1	0	1	0	0
716	MARE	3	1	2	0	0	0
717	MAROON	6	6	0	0	0	0
718	MARSHLIGHT	1	0	0	1	0	0
719	MASK	4	0	0	1	2	1
720	MASS	36	9	4	10	10	3
721	MASSBOOK	1	0	0	0	1	0
722	MELODY	3	0	0	0	3	0
723	MERRILY	2	1	1	0	0	0
724	MERRIMENT	1	0	1	0	0	0
725	MERRYMAKING	1	0	1	0	0	0
726	METAL	4	1	0	2	0	1
727	MICE	2	0	0	1	0	1
728	MILK	11	0	7	0	0	4

#	IMAGE	FREQ: TOTAL	CH1	CH2	CH3	CH4	CH5
729	MIRE	10	0	4	3	2	1
730	MIRROR	7	1	2	0	3	1
731	MOAN	3	2	1	0	0	0
732	MOCK	13	0	3	6	0	4
733	MOIST	8	3	0	0	3	2
734	MOLE	1	0	1	0	0	0
735	MONEY	11	3	4	1	0	3
736	MONK	3	0	0	0	0	3
737	MONKEY	6	0	1	1	0	4
738	MOOCOW	3	3	0	0	0	0
739	MOON	10	2	3	2	1	2
740	MOONLIT	2	0	2	0	0	0
741	MOORINGS	2	0	2	0	0	0
742	MORGUE	1	0	1	0	0	0
743	MOTTLED	1	0	0	0	0	1
744	MOULDERING	1	0	0	0	0	1
745	MOUNT	19	1	6	9	1	2
746	MOUSTACHE	6	3	3	0	0	0
747	MOUTH	29	11	5	3	2	8
748	MUD	5	1	2	0	0	2
749	MUDDIED	5	2	2	1	0	0
750	MUMBLED	1	0	1	0	0	0
751	MURDER	6	2	0	4	0	0
752	MURMUR	35	2	8	11	5	9
753	MUSIC	29	2	6	7	6	8
754	MUTE	5	0	0	3	0	2
755	MUTTERED	2	0	0	0	0	2
756	MYRRH	1	0	0	1	0	0
757	NAIL	6	4	0	1	0	1
758	NAKED	8	0	0	0	4	4
759	NAME	98	38	12	10	15	23
760	NASAL	2	1	1	0	0	0
761	NASTY	10	10	0	0	0	0
762	NAUSEOUS	1	0	0	1	0	0
763	NAVE	3	0	0	2	0	1
764	NECK	15	4	3	1	1	6
765	NEEDLE	1	0	0	0	0	1
766	NEST	1	0	0	0	0	1
767	NETS	3	0	0	1	0	2
768	NIGHT	96	22	18	7	5	34
769	NIGHTCLOUDS	1	0	0	0	1	0
770	NIGHTSHADE	1	0	0	0	0	1
771	NIGHTSHIRT	2	2	0	0	0	0
772	NOISE	41	17	4	6	7	7
773	NOISILY	5	1	3	0	0	1
774	NOSE	12	3	4	2	0	3
775	NOTEBOOKS	2	0	0	0	0	2
776	NOXIOUS	1	0	0	1	0	0
777	NUN	3	1	0	0	0	2
778	NURSE	2	0	0	0	0	2
779	NURSEMAIDS	1	0	1	0	0	0
780	NURSERY	1	1	0	0	0	0

250

#	IMAGE	FREQ: TOTAL	CH1	CH2	CH3	CH4	CH5
781	OAR	1	0	0	0	0	1
782	OCEAN	7	0	0	2	0	5
783	ODOROUS	2	0	0	0	0	2
784	ODOUR	20	0	4	4	7	5
785	OIL	4	0	1	0	1	2
786	OILSHEET	1	1	0	0	0	0
787	OLIVE	3	0	0	0	1	2
788	ONIONS	1	0	0	0	0	1
789	OOZED	4	0	1	3	0	0
790	ORB	1	1	0	0	0	0
791	ORCHARDS	1	0	0	0	1	0
792	ORCHESTRA	1	0	0	0	0	1
793	ORDER	35	2	8	4	13	8
794	OUTBORO	1	0	0	0	1	0
795	OUTHOUSE	5	0	5	0	0	0
796	OVERCOAT	5	0	2	1	0	2
797	OX	1	0	0	0	0	1
798	OZONE	1	1	0	0	0	0
799	PAGE	21	6	5	2	2	6
800	PAIN	57	16	9	21	8	3
801	PALATE	28	7	4	5	4	8
802	PALM	7	5	1	1	0	0
803	PANDIED	10	9	0	0	1	0
804	PANDYBAT	10	10	0	0	0	0
805	PANTING	4	1	1	0	0	2
806	PAPA	1	0	0	0	0	1
807	PAPER	24	8	6	1	0	9
808	PARACLETE	1	0	0	0	1	0
809	PASTORS	2	2	0	0	0	0
810	PATCHWORK	2	0	1	0	1	0
811	PATH	7	1	2	3	1	0
812	PATTED	1	0	0	0	0	1
813	PEAL	5	0	3	0	0	2
814	PEEL	4	2	1	0	1	0
815	PENCIL	8	2	1	0	0	5
816	PEPPER	2	0	0	1	0	1
817	PERFUME	5	0	2	2	1	0
818	PHRASE	31	0	2	5	5	19
819	PIANO	3	1	1	0	0	1
820	PICTURE	12	3	4	2	2	1
821	PIG	6	0	0	1	0	5
822	PIGEON	1	0	0	1	0	0
823	PINK	6	2	3	0	1	0
824	PISS	1	0	1	0	0	0
825	PLANT	28	13	3	6	1	5
826	PLUCKED	2	0	0	0	0	2
827	PLUMP	8	1	3	0	0	4
828	PLUMPUDDING	1	1	0	0	0	0
829	POCK	4	4	0	0	0	0
830	POCKET	18	4	4	1	3	6
831	POLISHED	1	0	0	0	0	1
832	POLLUTES	1	0	0	1	0	0

#	IMAGE	FREQ: TOTAL	CH1	CH2	CH3	CH4	CH5
833	PONY	1	0	1	0	0	0
834	POOL	3	0	0	0	1	2
835	POPE	2	1	0	1	0	0
836	PORCELAIN	1	0	0	1	0	0
837	PORCH	9	0	2	0	1	6
838	PORTRAIT	6	4	1	0	0	1
839	POT	2	0	1	0	0	1
840	POTATOES	2	1	0	1	0	0
841	PRAY	80	16	6	35	18	5
842	PRAYERBOOK	2	0	1	0	1	0
843	PREACH	10	1	0	8	0	1
844	PREFECT	58	48	3	2	3	2
845	PRESS	25	11	6	1	1	6
846	PRIEST	94	18	7	12	37	20
847	PRIESTCRAFT	1	0	0	0	0	1
848	PRIESTRIDDEN	3	3	0	0	0	0
849	PRISON	12	1	1	9	0	1
850	PRISONHOUSE	1	0	0	1	0	0
851	PROFESSOR	14	0	0	1	0	13
852	PROSE	4	0	2	0	1	1
853	PROTEST	10	6	0	0	0	4
854	PSALMS	2	0	0	2	0	0
855	PUCK	2	2	0	0	0	0
856	PUDDING	4	2	0	2	0	0
857	PUDDLES	1	0	1	0	0	0
858	PULL	11	8	0	0	0	3
859	PULPIT	3	1	0	0	1	1
860	PULSATION	2	0	0	0	1	1
861	PUNCH	1	1	0	0	0	0
862	PUNGENT	1	0	1	0	0	0
863	PUNISH	23	5	0	16	2	0
864	PUPPY	1	1	0	0	0	0
865	PURGATORIAL	4	0	1	1	2	0
866	PURPLE	2	2	0	0	0	0
867	PURRED	4	2	0	0	0	2
868	PUTBORO	1	0	0	0	1	0
869	PUTREFACTION	2	0	0	2	0	0
870	PUTRID	1	0	0	1	0	0
871	QUADRANGLE	5	0	2	0	0	3
872	QUAE	1	0	0	0	0	1
873	QUAGMIRE	1	0	0	0	0	1
874	QUEER	59	19	5	6	5	24
875	QUIET	55	17	8	10	6	14
876	QUIVERED	7	4	0	0	0	3
877	RABBITS	1	0	0	0	1	0
878	RABBITSKIN	1	1	0	0	0	0
879	RACKET	1	0	0	1	0	0
880	RAGE	8	2	0	5	1	0
881	RAIL	2	0	0	1	0	1
882	RAILWAY	5	2	3	0	0	0
883	RAIN	17	3	0	6	1	7
884	RAINDROPS	1	0	0	0	0	1

#	IMAGE	FREQ: TOTAL	CH1	CH2	CH3	CH4	CH5
885	RAINFRAGRANT	1	0	0	0	0	1
886	RAINLADEN	1	0	0	0	0	1
887	RAINSODDEN	1	0	0	0	0	1
888	RAKE	1	1	0	0	0	0
889	RAN	14	5	5	1	1	2
890	RANG	5	3	0	1	0	1
891	RAT	7	6	0	1	0	0
892	RATTLE	6	0	3	2	0	1
893	RECTOR	52	37	5	8	0	2
894	RED	31	18	5	2	3	3
895	REDBROWN	1	0	0	0	0	1
896	REDEYED	1	0	1	0	0	0
897	REDHOT	2	0	0	2	0	0
898	REDRIMMED	1	0	0	0	0	1
899	REEKING	5	0	1	4	0	0
900	REFECTORY	12	12	0	0	0	0
901	REFLECT	13	0	1	3	4	5
902	RELIGION	18	8	0	2	0	8
903	RELIGIOUS	5	0	0	2	2	1
904	REPENT	26	0	0	20	3	3
905	REPTILE	2	0	0	0	0	2
906	REVEREND	3	0	0	0	3	0
907	RHYME	1	0	0	0	0	1
908	RHYTHM	15	0	3	0	1	11
909	RIBS	1	0	0	1	0	0
910	RICE	2	0	0	0	0	2
911	RIDDLE	4	4	0	0	0	0
912	RING	11	1	1	2	2	5
913	RIOT	5	0	4	0	1	0
914	RITE	3	0	1	0	1	1
915	RITUAL	1	0	0	0	1	0
916	RIVER	7	1	3	0	3	0
917	RIVULET	2	0	0	0	2	0
918	ROAD	38	8	15	1	1	13
919	ROADWAY	2	0	1	0	0	1
920	ROAR	9	8	0	0	0	1
921	ROBE	3	0	0	0	1	2
922	ROCK	8	0	4	1	3	0
923	ROOF	4	0	2	0	2	0
924	ROOM	32	10	9	6	0	7
925	ROPE	2	1	1	0	0	0
926	ROSE	40	16	2	8	4	10
927	ROSEBUSHES	2	0	2	0	0	0
928	ROSELIGHT	1	0	0	0	0	1
929	ROSESOFT	1	0	0	0	1	0
930	ROSEWAY	1	0	0	0	0	1
931	ROSIE	5	0	1	0	0	4
932	ROT	5	0	1	3	1	0
933	ROTUNDA	1	0	0	0	0	1
934	ROUGED	1	0	1	0	0	0
935	ROUGH	5	2	0	0	0	3
936	ROUGHHEWN	1	0	0	0	1	0

253

#	IMAGE	FREQ: TOTAL	CH1	CH2	CH3	CH4	CH5
937	ROUND	67	20	9	5	5	29
938	ROUNDHEAD	2	0	0	0	0	2
939	RUMBLING	1	0	1	0	0	0
940	RUMP	1	1	0	0	0	0
941	RUN	30	14	7	4	3	2
942	RUSSET	2	0	0	0	2	0
943	RUSTLING	1	0	0	0	0	1
944	SABBATH	1	0	0	0	0	1
945	SACK	1	0	0	1	0	0
946	SACKCLOTH	1	0	0	1	0	0
947	SACRAMENT	17	0	2	5	8	2
948	SACRIFICE	8	0	0	2	3	3
949	SACRILEGE	2	0	0	0	0	2
950	SACRILEGIOUS	1	0	0	0	0	1
951	SACRISTAN	1	0	0	1	0	0
952	SACRISTY	3	3	0	0	0	0
953	SAILOR	2	2	0	0	0	0
954	SAINT	48	5	2	26	9	6
955	SALT	1	0	0	0	0	1
956	SALVATION	3	0	0	1	1	1
957	SANCTUARY	1	0	0	0	1	0
958	SAND	11	0	0	4	6	1
959	SASH	3	0	1	2	0	0
960	SATAN	2	0	0	1	0	1
961	SAUCE	5	3	1	1	0	0
962	SAUSAGES	2	0	0	2	0	0
963	SAVIOUR	1	0	0	1	0	0
964	SAVOUR	2	0	0	1	1	0
965	SCALDED	6	6	0	0	0	0
966	SCARLET	7	1	0	1	2	3
967	SCHOOL	16	0	8	2	1	5
968	SCREAM	4	3	0	1	0	0
969	SCREECH	2	0	0	0	0	2
970	SCUM	7	2	2	2	0	1
971	SEA	25	6	0	5	12	2
972	SEABIRD	1	0	0	0	1	0
973	SEABORNE	2	0	0	0	2	0
974	SEADUSK	1	0	0	0	0	1
975	SEAHARVEST	1	0	0	0	1	0
976	SEAPORT	1	0	0	0	0	1
977	SEASHORE	1	0	0	1	0	0
978	SEATANGLE	1	0	0	0	1	0
979	SEAWALL	1	1	0	0	0	0
980	SEAWATER	1	0	0	0	1	0
981	SEAWEED	2	0	0	0	2	0
982	SEAWRACK	2	0	1	0	1	0
983	SECULAR	1	0	0	0	0	1
984	SEDUCE	2	0	1	0	1	0
985	SEED	3	0	0	2	0	1
986	SELFBOUNDED	1	0	0	0	0	1
987	SELFCOMMUNION	1	0	0	0	1	0
988	SELFCONTAINED	1	0	0	0	0	1

#	IMAGE	FREQ: TOTAL	CH1	CH2	CH3	CH4	CH5
989	SELFEMBITTERED	1	0	0	0	0	1
990	SELFMISTRUST	1	0	0	0	0	1
991	SELFRESPECT	1	0	0	0	0	1
992	SELFRESTRAINT	1	0	0	0	1	0
993	SELFSURRENDER	1	0	0	0	1	0
994	SENTENCE	11	3	0	3	1	4
995	SEPULCHRE	2	0	0	1	0	1
996	SERAPH	2	0	0	0	0	2
997	SERAPHIM	5	0	0	1	0	4
998	SERPENT	3	0	0	3	0	0
999	SEWER	2	1	0	1	0	0
1000	SHADE	1	0	0	1	0	0
1001	SHADOW	18	1	0	3	5	9
1002	SHAME	35	4	3	18	7	3
1003	SHARP	9	1	1	0	2	5
1004	SHAWL	5	0	2	1	0	2
1005	SHED	16	4	5	2	2	3
1006	SHELL	3	0	1	1	1	0
1007	SHIMMER	3	0	0	1	0	2
1008	SHINE	11	2	0	3	0	6
1009	SHIP	5	4	0	0	0	1
1010	SHIPWRECKS	1	1	0	0	0	0
1011	SHIRT	1	1	0	0	0	0
1012	SHITE	1	0	0	1	0	0
1013	SHIVER	14	11	1	0	0	2
1014	SHOCK	7	0	3	0	2	2
1015	SHOE	11	1	4	3	2	1
1016	SHONE	5	0	3	1	0	1
1017	SHOOK	20	7	3	1	1	8
1018	SHOUTED	10	6	1	0	0	3
1019	SHOVED	3	1	0	0	0	2
1020	SHOWER	3	0	0	1	0	2
1021	SHRIEKING	1	0	0	1	0	0
1022	SHRILL	7	0	0	0	1	6
1023	SHRINE	1	0	0	0	1	0
1024	SHRIVELLED	3	0	0	0	0	3
1025	SHRUBS	3	0	0	2	0	1
1026	SHRUNK	3	0	0	0	0	3
1027	SICK	26	12	6	6	1	1
1028	SIDEALTAR	2	0	0	1	1	0
1029	SIENA	1	0	0	1	0	0
1030	SIGH	28	4	4	9	5	6
1031	SILENCE	105	21	18	16	17	33
1032	SILK	8	3	0	0	2	3
1033	SILVER	12	6	3	0	2	1
1034	SILVERCOATED	1	0	1	0	0	0
1035	SILVERPOINTED	1	0	0	0	0	1
1036	SILVERVEINED	1	0	0	0	0	1
1037	SILVERWRAPPED	1	0	0	0	0	1
1038	SIN	177	9	5	131	26	6
1039	SINCORRUPTED	1	0	0	1	0	0
1040	SINFULIMPENITENCE	1	0	0	1	0	0

#	IMAGE	FREQ: TOTAL	CH1	CH2	CH3	CH4	CH5
1041	SING	12	2	5	0	3	2
1042	SINLOVING	1	0	0	1	0	0
1043	SISTER	10	2	1	1	2	4
1044	SKIES	1	0	1	0	0	0
1045	SKIN	9	2	2	1	2	2
1046	SKIRTS	3	0	1	0	1	1
1047	SKULL	11	3	1	3	1	3
1048	SKY	22	3	3	3	6	7
1049	SKYHIGH	1	1	0	0	0	0
1050	SKYLIGHT	1	0	0	0	0	1
1051	SLATE	3	1	2	0	0	0
1052	SLATEBLUE	1	0	0	0	1	0
1053	SLEEK	2	1	0	0	0	1
1054	SLEEP	29	5	7	4	3	10
1055	SLEEVE	14	9	1	1	0	3
1056	SLENDER	8	0	0	0	4	4
1057	SLIME	9	6	1	1	0	1
1058	SLOBBERING	3	0	0	0	0	3
1059	SLOTH	7	0	0	4	0	3
1060	SLOW	62	14	9	11	11	17
1061	SLOWDRIFTING	1	0	0	0	1	0
1062	SLOWFLOWING	1	0	0	0	1	0
1063	SLUGGISH	8	2	0	2	3	1
1064	SMACKED	6	2	0	0	1	3
1065	SMART	3	0	2	0	0	1
1066	SMELL	41	26	1	2	3	9
1067	SMILE	66	7	19	2	6	32
1068	SMITHY	1	0	0	0	0	1
1069	SMOKE	26	2	11	2	0	11
1070	SMOOTH	1	0	0	1	0	0
1071	SMUGGING	2	2	0	0	0	0
1072	SNAKE	3	0	0	1	1	1
1073	SNAP	1	0	0	0	0	1
1074	SNEEZE	1	0	0	0	1	0
1075	SNORT	2	1	0	0	0	1
1076	SOARING	5	0	0	0	4	1
1077	SOB	9	3	3	1	1	1
1078	SOFT	68	15	9	12	6	26
1079	SOFTHUED	1	0	0	0	1	0
1080	SOFTLYLIGHTED	1	0	1	0	0	0
1081	SOFTWORDED	1	0	0	0	1	0
1082	SOLDIER	9	2	1	5	0	1
1083	SOLITARY	1	0	0	0	1	0
1084	SONG	20	7	5	0	1	7
1085	SOOTHED	7	0	1	2	0	4
1086	SORDID	2	0	1	1	0	0
1087	SOUL	202	1	7	106	48	40
1088	SOULFREE	1	0	0	0	0	1
1089	SOUND	33	12	7	3	3	8
1090	SOUR	3	1	0	0	1	1
1091	SOURSMELLING	1	0	0	0	0	1
1092	SOUTANE	11	4	2	1	1	3

#	IMAGE	FREQ: TOTAL	CH1	CH2	CH3	CH4	CH5
1093	SPACE	15	0	3	4	1	7
1094	SPADE	3	1	0	0	2	0
1095	SPECKLED	2	0	0	0	0	2
1096	SPECTACLES	4	3	0	0	0	1
1097	SPEECH	22	1	5	1	2	13
1098	SPIED	5	3	0	1	0	1
1099	SPIRIT	48	0	2	18	15	13
1100	SPITE	7	2	2	1	0	2
1101	SPITTLE	3	0	1	1	0	1
1102	SPRAY	4	0	1	0	0	3
1103	SQUALID	4	0	1	3	0	0
1104	SQUALL	6	0	3	0	2	1
1105	SQUARE	17	6	3	5	0	3
1106	SQUEAK	2	0	0	1	0	1
1107	STAGNATION	1	0	0	0	1	0
1108	STAIN	6	0	4	0	2	0
1109	STAIRCASE	17	10	0	1	0	6
1110	STAIRS	1	1	0	0	0	0
1111	STALE	6	1	1	2	1	1
1112	STAMMERING	1	0	0	0	0	1
1113	STANK	1	0	0	1	0	0
1114	STAR	6	0	0	3	1	2
1115	STASIS	8	0	0	0	0	8
1116	STENCH	5	0	0	5	0	0
1117	STEPHANEFOROS	4	0	0	0	4	0
1118	STEPHANOS	2	0	0	0	2	0
1119	STEPHANOUMENOS	2	0	0	0	2	0
1120	STEW	4	0	0	1	0	3
1121	STICK	12	2	2	1	1	6
1122	STIFF	5	0	0	2	1	2
1123	STING	10	1	0	8	1	0
1124	STINK	10	4	1	1	2	2
1125	STINKPOT	2	0	0	0	0	2
1126	STOCKED	7	3	2	0	2	0
1127	STOMACH	1	0	0	0	1	0
1128	STONE	13	2	1	0	2	8
1129	STORM	1	0	0	1	0	0
1130	STRAW	3	0	3	0	0	0
1131	STRAWCOLOURED	1	0	0	0	0	1
1132	STREAKS	1	0	0	0	0	1
1133	STREET	41	1	13	11	4	12
1134	STUNG	4	0	0	0	0	4
1135	SUCK	5	3	0	0	0	2
1136	SUFFOCATED	2	0	0	1	1	0
1137	SULPHUROUS	1	0	0	1	0	0
1138	SULPHURYELLOW	1	0	0	0	0	1
1139	SUN	18	3	6	2	3	4
1140	SUNG	1	0	1	0	0	0
1141	SUNLIGHT	10	4	3	1	2	0
1142	SUNRISE	1	0	0	0	1	0
1143	SUNWARMED	1	0	1	0	0	0
1144	SUP	6	2	0	1	0	3

#	IMAGE	FREQ: TOTAL	CH1	CH2	CH3	CH4	CH5
1145	SURPLICES	1	1	0	0	0	0
1146	SWALLOW	7	2	1	0	0	4
1147	SWAMP	2	0	0	2	0	0
1148	SWANS	2	0	0	0	0	2
1149	SWEAR	2	0	0	0	0	2
1150	SWEAT	8	0	1	3	0	4
1151	SWEET	17	3	1	4	0	9
1152	SWISH	6	3	0	2	1	0
1153	SWOLLEN	4	2	1	1	0	0
1154	SWORD	4	0	0	2	1	1
1155	SYLLABLE	1	0	0	0	0	1
1156	TABERNACLE	6	0	1	3	1	1
1157	TABLE	45	19	5	6	4	11
1158	TABLECLOTH	1	1	0	0	0	0
1159	TAIL	6	0	0	5	0	1
1160	TALLOW	2	0	0	0	0	2
1161	TAN	2	0	1	0	1	0
1162	TAPPED	8	2	2	0	0	4
1163	TAR	1	0	0	0	1	0
1164	TASTE	5	1	1	1	1	1
1165	TAWNY	1	0	0	1	0	0
1166	TEA	12	4	1	1	4	2
1167	TEACUPS	1	0	0	0	1	0
1168	TEAR	22	10	2	8	0	2
1169	TEETH	9	1	1	0	0	7
1170	TELEGRAPHPOLES	3	1	2	0	0	0
1171	TENOR	2	0	1	0	0	1
1172	TEPID	2	1	0	0	0	1
1173	TESTAMENT	3	0	0	0	1	2
1174	TESTIMONIAL	1	0	0	0	0	1
1175	THEBORO	1	0	0	0	1	0
1176	THIGH	6	4	1	0	1	0
1177	THIN	16	7	3	0	1	5
1178	THISTLES	1	0	0	1	0	0
1179	THORNS	1	0	0	1	0	0
1180	THRILL	6	2	0	0	1	3
1181	THROAT	17	5	4	3	3	2
1182	THROB	3	0	0	1	2	0
1183	THRUST	12	0	4	2	0	6
1184	THUD	3	1	0	0	0	2
1185	THUMB	2	0	0	0	0	2
1186	THUMBBLACKENED	1	0	1	0	0	0
1187	THUNDER	11	10	0	0	0	1
1188	TICKING	3	0	0	3	0	0
1189	TICKLING	1	0	0	0	0	1
1190	TIDE	12	0	5	0	6	1
1191	TINGES	1	0	0	0	1	0
1192	TINGLE	5	3	1	1	0	0
1193	TITTER	4	0	0	0	0	4
1194	TOAST	2	2	0	0	0	0
1195	TOBACCO	4	2	2	0	0	0
1196	TOBORO	1	0	0	0	1	0

#	IMAGE	FREQ: TOTAL	CH1	CH2	CH3	CH4	CH5
1197	TONE	22	1	1	2	2	16
1198	TONGUE	14	1	2	6	2	3
1199	TORTURE	13	0	0	13	0	0
1200	TOWELS	2	1	0	0	1	0
1201	TOWER	5	5	0	0	0	0
1202	TRAIN	20	10	7	0	0	3
1203	TRALALA	4	4	0	0	0	0
1204	TRALALADDY	1	1	0	0	0	0
1205	TRAM	11	0	9	0	0	2
1206	TREAT	25	2	5	5	1	12
1207	TREBLE	2	0	1	0	0	1
1208	TREMOR	3	1	1	1	0	0
1209	TREMULOUS	4	0	0	1	2	1
1210	TRINITY	6	0	0	1	3	2
1211	TROUSERS	5	2	2	0	1	0
1212	TRUMPET	2	0	0	2	0	0
1213	TRUMPETBLAST	1	0	0	1	0	0
1214	TUCKED	4	2	1	0	0	1
1215	TUCKOO	2	2	0	0	0	0
1216	TUNNEL	5	5	0	0	0	0
1217	TURF	4	4	0	0	0	0
1218	TURFCOLOURED	5	2	0	0	2	1
1219	TURKEY	5	5	0	0	0	0
1220	TURNIPS	4	1	0	1	0	2
1221	TURRET	2	0	0	0	1	1
1222	TWIG	2	0	0	0	2	0
1223	TWILIGHT	1	0	0	0	0	1
1224	TWINECOLOURED	1	0	0	0	0	1
1225	TWINKLED	2	1	1	0	0	0
1226	TWIRLING	1	0	1	0	0	0
1227	TWIST	7	4	1	0	0	2
1228	TWITCHING	1	0	0	0	1	0
1229	TWITTERED	1	0	0	0	0	1
1230	UMBRELLA	10	1	0	0	0	9
1231	UNDEFILED	1	0	0	1	0	0
1232	UNDRESS	6	5	0	0	0	1
1233	UNDRIED	1	0	0	0	1	0
1234	UNLIT	2	0	0	1	0	1
1235	URINAL	2	0	1	0	1	0
1236	USAGE	1	0	0	0	0	1
1237	USBORO	1	0	0	0	1	0
1238	VAPOUR	9	0	3	2	0	4
1239	VEIL	13	1	2	3	3	4
1240	VEINS	3	0	0	2	1	0
1241	VELVET	7	7	0	0	0	0
1242	VERMIN	4	0	0	1	0	3
1243	VESTRY	6	0	6	0	0	0
1244	VINEGAR	1	0	0	1	0	0
1245	VIOLETS	1	0	1	0	0	0
1246	VIPER	1	0	0	1	0	0
1247	VIRGIN	16	1	0	6	5	4
1248	VISION	14	0	8	3	0	3

#	IMAGE	FREQ: TOTAL	CH1	CH2	CH3	CH4	CH5
1249	VOICE	139	31	24	18	20	46
1250	VOMITED	1	0	0	1	0	0
1251	VOWEL	4	0	0	0	1	3
1252	WADED	2	0	0	0	2	0
1253	WAFER	1	0	0	0	0	1
1254	WAIL	3	1	2	0	0	0
1255	WAIST	3	0	0	0	1	2
1256	WALK	110	27	23	17	8	35
1257	WAN	1	0	0	1	0	0
1258	WAR	4	1	0	1	0	2
1259	WARM	35	14	8	0	7	6
1260	WASH	9	3	0	0	1	5
1261	WATER	57	17	5	8	11	16
1262	WATERJUG	1	0	1	0	0	0
1263	WATERLOGGED	1	0	0	0	0	1
1264	WATERPROOFS	1	0	0	1	0	0
1265	WATERY.	1	1	0	0	0	0
1266	WAVE	23	6	2	5	8	2
1267	WAVELET	2	0	0	0	2	0
1268	WAX	14	10	0	1	0	3
1269	WEB	1	0	0	0	0	1
1270	WEEDGROWN	1	0	1	0	0	0
1271	WEEDS	6	0	0	4	1	1
1272	WEEP	4	0	1	3	0	0
1273	WEPT	1	0	0	1	0	0
1274	WET	16	5	0	1	3	7
1275	WHEEL	4	0	1	0	0	3
1276	WHEEZING	2	0	0	0	0	2
1277	WHIMPERING	1	0	0	1	0	0
1278	WHINE	8	1	1	0	0	6
1279	WHIP	2	1	1	0	0	0
1280	WHIRL	1	1	0	0	0	0
1281	WHIRRING	2	0	0	0	0	2
1282	WHISPER	21	1	2	6	2	10
1283	WHISTLE	13	4	1	0	2	6
1284	WHITE	46	21	4	8	3	10
1285	WHITEBOY	1	1	0	0	0	0
1286	WHITEGREY	3	3	0	0	0	0
1287	WHITEROBED	1	0	0	0	0	1
1288	WHITEWASHED	1	0	1	0	0	0
1289	WHORES	1	0	0	1	0	0
1290	WIDE	7	1	0	3	1	2
1291	WIDENING	2	0	0	2	0	0
1292	WIDESPREAD	1	0	0	1	0	0
1293	WIDEWINGED	1	0	0	0	0	1
1294	WILLBORO	1	0	0	0	1	0
1295	WIND	16	0	3	5	2	6
1296	WINDOW	44	6	12	8	3	15
1297	WINDSWEPT	1	0	0	0	1	0
1298	WING	8	0	2	1	1	4
1299	WINKED	1	1	0	0	0	0
1300	WINTER	6	4	0	0	1	1

#	IMAGE	FREQ: TOTAL	CH1	CH2	CH3	CH4	CH5
1301	WIRE	3	0	1	0	0	2
1302	WOMAN	53	8	7	7	5	26
1303	WOMB	1	0	0	0	0	1
1304	WOOD	19	5	3	4	2	5
1305	WOOLLY	1	1	0	0	0	0
1306	WORD	122	12	18	30	9	53
1307	WORM	7	0	0	7	0	0
1308	WORSHIP	6	0	0	1	3	2
1309	WRINKLED	2	0	1	0	0	1
1310	WRISTS	2	1	1	0	0	0
1311	YELLOW	20	5	3	2	2	8
1312	YELLS	2	0	0	2	0	0

Appendix C
Distribution of First Occurrences of Images

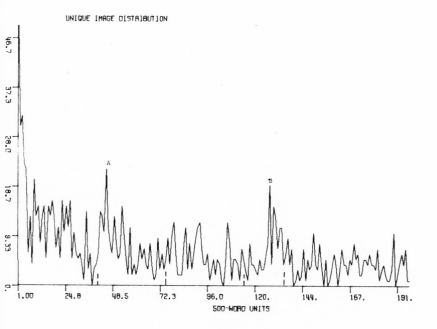

UNIQUE IMAGE DISTRIBUTION

500-WORD UNITS

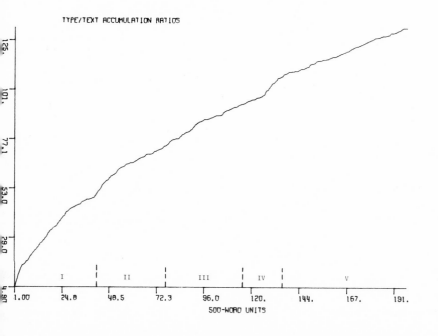

TYPE/TEXT ACCUMULATION RATIOS

500-WORD UNITS

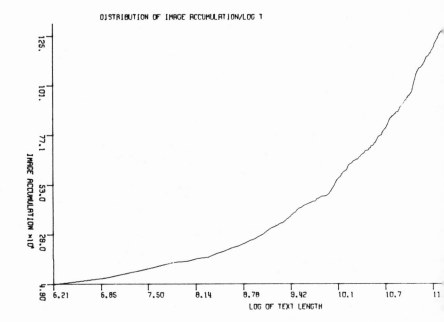

DISTRIBUTION OF IMAGE ACCUMULATION/LOG T

Appendix D
Factors for Individual Chapters of *Portrait*

FACTORS: CHAPTER I

#1	#2	#3
.884 warm	.850 pain	.849 soft
.799 chapel	.754 sound	.787 grey
.738 night	.716 sleeve	.632 air
.713 shiver	.643 tear	.538 evening
.701 sea	.597 pandybat	.351 quiet
.675 cold	.528 hand	
.607 dark	.455 loud	
.392 pray		

#5	#6	#9
.777 colour	.880 hat	.835 bless
.758 rose	.650 bed	.729 pray
.718 green	.566 noise	.566 finger
.570 cool	.353 cold	
.496 red	.329 water	
	.309 queer	

#10	#21	#25
.839 bird	.773 sin	.857 fire
.543 eye	.757 wax	.393 smell
		.384 water

#27	#30	#34
.774 white	.794 name	.829 brother
.355 house	.339 God	.681 queer
.327 cold	.301 quiet	.272 bed
		.239 grey

FACTORS: CHAPTER II

#3	#4	#6
.737 garden	.839 lip	.835 fire
.650 mountain	.680 press	.770 woman
.523 white	.558 soft	.477 dim
.471 soft	.478 eye	.343 sound
.392 road		.343 voice

#8	#9	#10
.821 chapel	.846 priest	.815 slow
.816 vestry	.619 smile	.628 hair
.412 white	.614 loud	.357 worm
	.361 jesuit	

#12	#13	#14
.819 name	.782 green	.839 fade
.623 cork	.534 sound	.808 sun
.449 city	.355 white	.360 dead
.403 dim		

#17	#18	#23
.838 afraid	.837 pain	.814 smoke
.759 cane	.475 school	.712 damn
.576 cried	.413 jesuit	.425 hair
.254 Heron	.352 blue	

#24	#28	#30
.873 ha	.717 light	.746 father
.722 laugh	.686 noise	.542 glass
.411 jesuit	.294 faint	.336 walk
.371 voice		
.366 dim		

FACTORS: CHAPTER III

#2	#6	#13
.854 bird	.697 flame	.806 noise
.791 mountain	.658 tongue	.777 rain
.701 fish	.449 flesh	.711 water
.417 air	.348 glow	.358 house
.394 hair	.309 church	

#15	#18	#24
.877 worm	.862 fire	.754 slow
.843 strong	.818 burn	.436 fear
.533 pain	.414 hell	.374 soul
.434 dead	.384 earth	.352 eye

#25	#38	#39
.835 spirit	.808 blind	.735 music
.463 flesh	.685 chapel	.459 light
.425 agony	.334 light	.354 Lord
.401 punish		
.322 murmur		

#41

.751 night
.565 hair
.388 house
.347 fear

FACTORS: CHAPTER IV

#1

.822 bless
.790 virgin
.573 sacrament
.523 angel
.419 saint
.392 altar

#2

.729 light
.693 wave
.674 leaf
.462 soft
.372 evening
.325 faint
.308 heaven

#3

.826 girl
.632 child
.587 grey
.457 sea

#4

.665 confess
.610 sin
.608 shame
.369 ear
.310 woman

#5

.739 air
.721 warm
.666 water
.385 grey

#7

.757 cheek
.738 flame
.476 faint

#8

.747 phrase
.665 woman
.516 body
.488 lip

#9

.818 sand
.725 tide
.412 warm

#10

.823 shadow
.488 smile
.454 priest
.426 face
.384 slow
.323 ear

#12	#16	#26
.843 door	.718 heaven	.734 fear
.803 chapel	.643 earth	.541 soul
.457 pain	.591 God	.469 body
.302 child		

#34

.753 murmur
.562 fire
.469 dark

FACTORS: CHAPTER V

#1	#2	#3
.781 bell	.861 smoke	.845 sweet
.674 cry	.743 die	.812 music
.542 bird	.706 earth	.420 smell
.523 white	.610 ball	.387 body
.384 lip		

#4	#5	#8
.708 speech	.880 ivy	.733 woman
.615 road	.683 yellow	.723 figure
.473 pray		.428 dark

#9	#12	#13
.778 flame	.756 order	.759 angry
.746 flat	.522 bird	.686 hand
.696 blood	.366 fly	
.415 laugh		

#14	#15	#16
.794 flower	.744 Jesus	.686 head
.645 warm	.623 hell	.570 green
.418 water		.491 shook

#22

.714 fire
.595 Lord

#24

.734 forge
.608 damn

#25

.782 speech
.408 name

#29

.765 Dedalus
.432 art
.424 queer

#31

.709 father
.641 girl

#32

.710 black
.672 hair
.358 grey

#33

.748 mouth
.689 fig
.384 phrase
.317 loud

#34

.809 rose
.545 heart
.405 spirit

#40

.781 stasis
.421 name
.420 rhythm

#41

.720 silence
.509 heavy
.487 faint

#43

.788 religion
.419 God

Appendix E
Smoothed Distributions of Thematic Groups of Images

THEMATIC GROUPS

1. Agression
2. Air/sky
3. Animals
4. Art
5. Auditory
6. Bird
7. Body
8. Buildings
9. Clothes
10. Colors
11. Death
12. Emotions (other than fear)
13. Excrement
14. Fear
15. Fire/heat
16. Food/taste
17. Human reference
18. Language
19. Light/dark
20. Objects (physical)
21. Places (physical)
22. Plants
23. Religion
24. Sight (quality)
25. Smell
26. Tactile
27. Water/cold

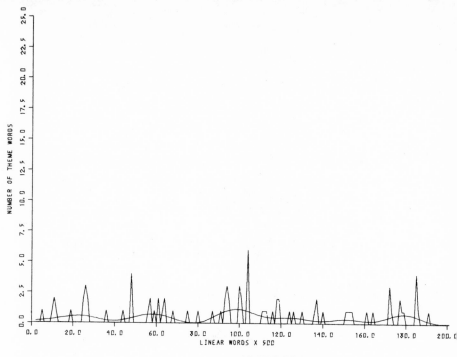

AGGRESSION

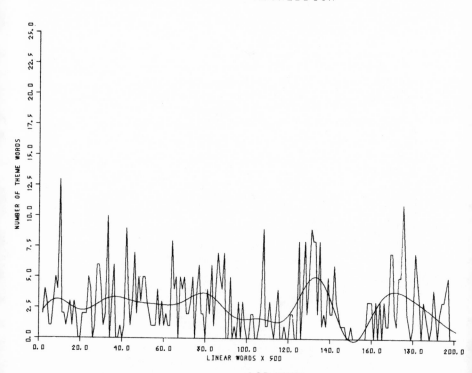

AIR/SKY

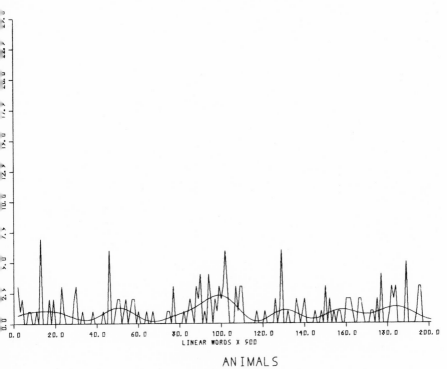

ANIMALS

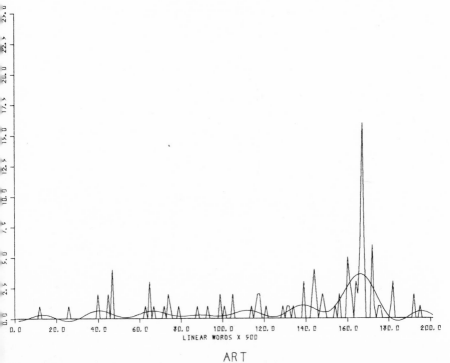

ART

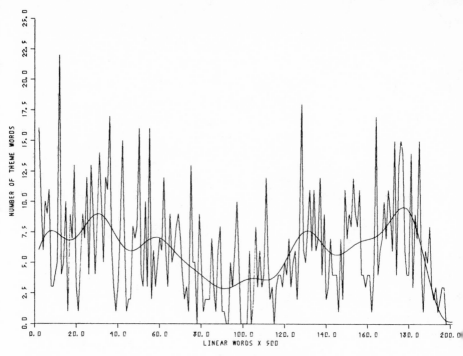

AUDITORY

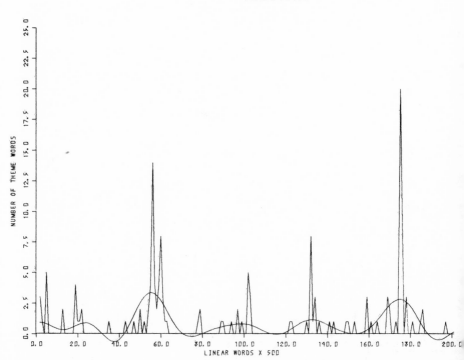

BIRD

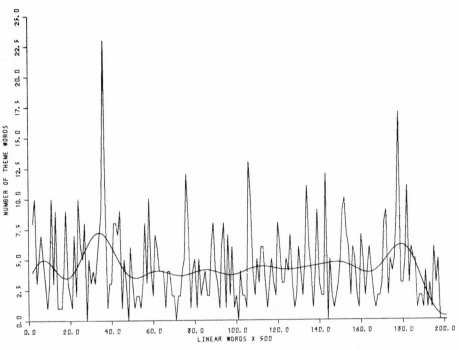

PARTS OF THE BODY

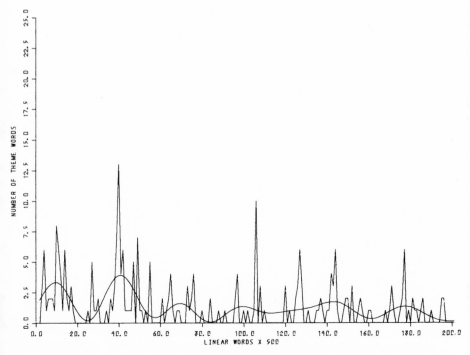

BUILDING

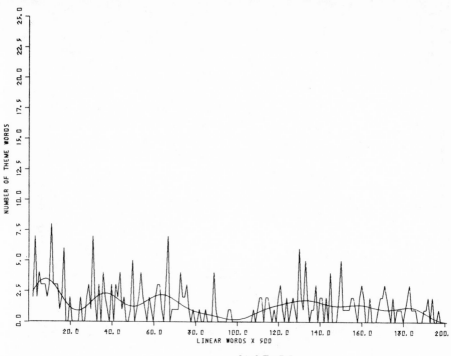

CLOTHES

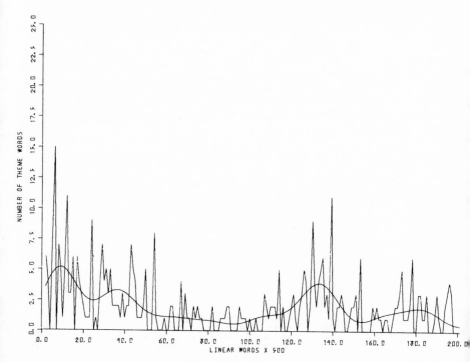

COLOR

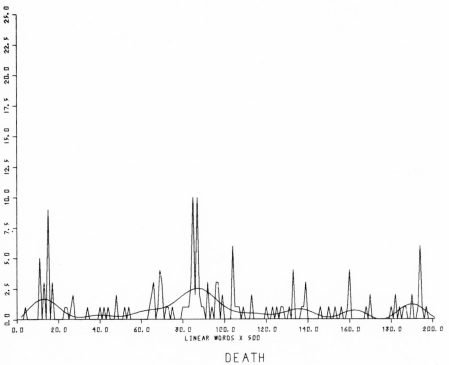

DEATH

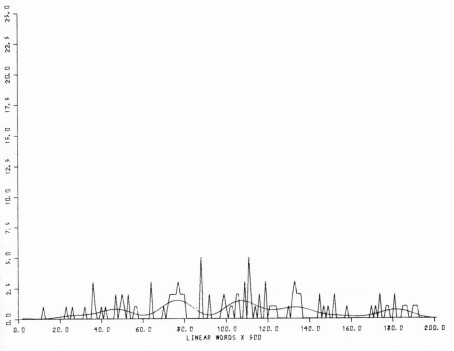

EMOTIONS OTHER THAN FEAR

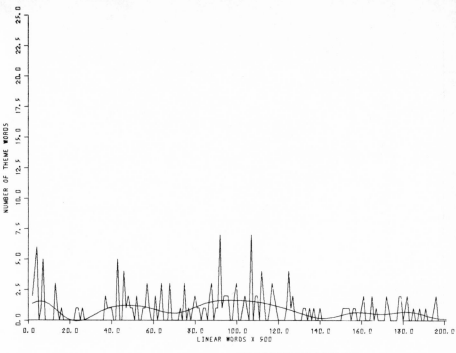

EXCREMENT/FILTH

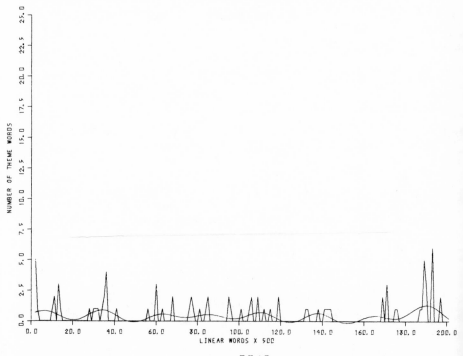

FEAR

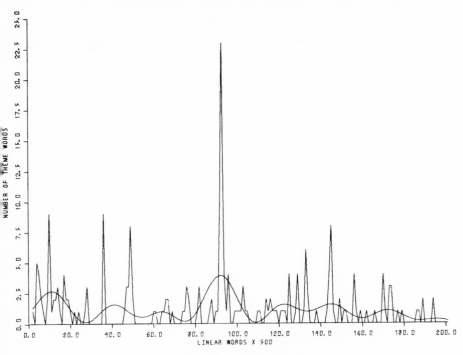

FIRE/HEAT

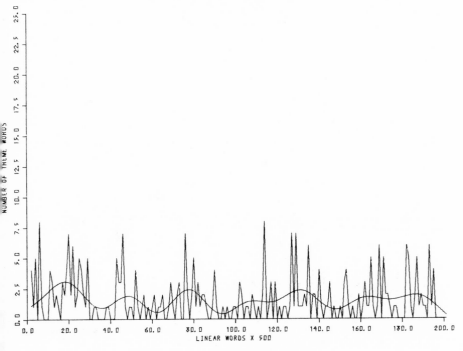

TASTE/FOOD

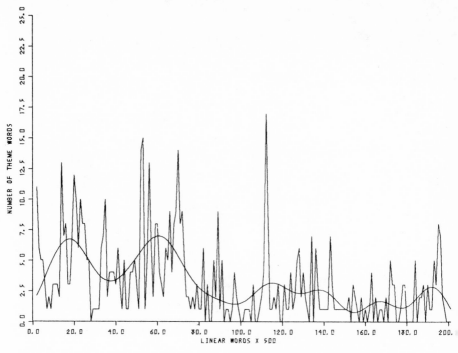

HUMAN REFERENCE

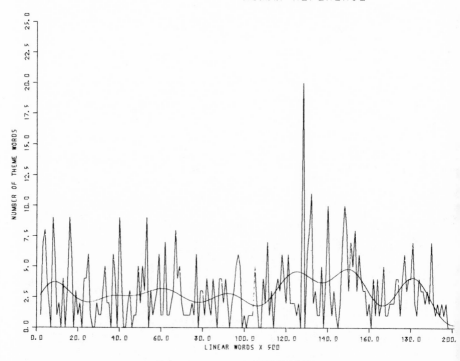

LANGUAGE

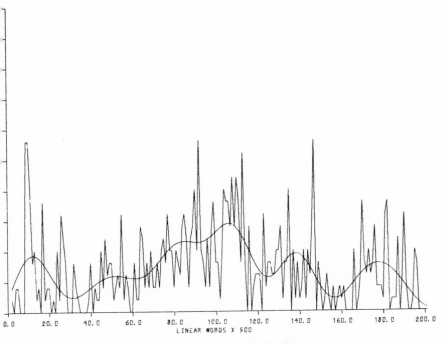

LIGHT/DARK

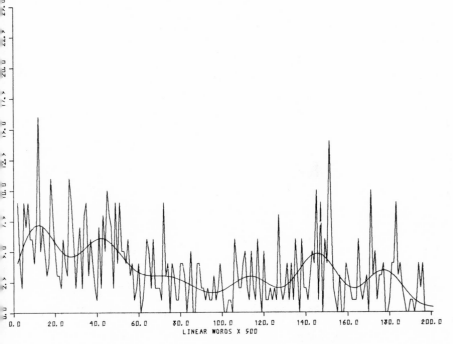

PHYSICAL OBJECTS

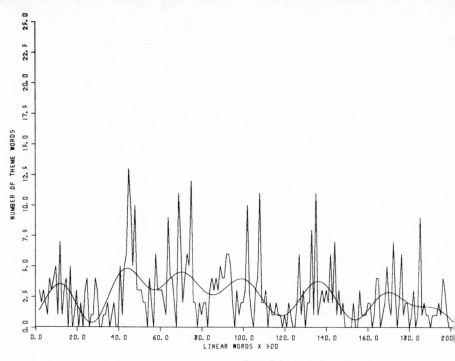

PHYSICAL PLACE

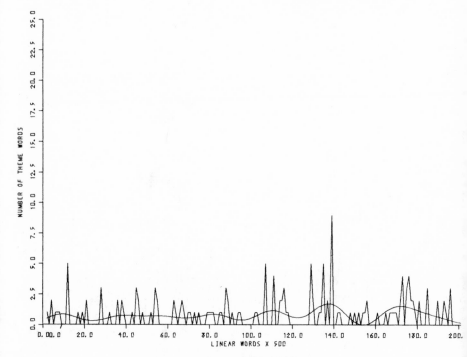

PLANTS

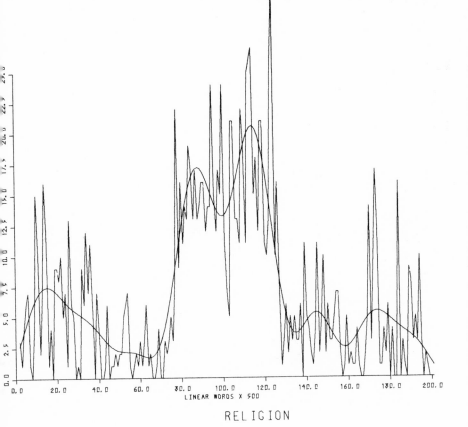

RELIGION

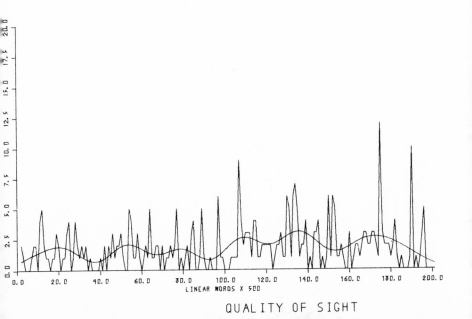

QUALITY OF SIGHT

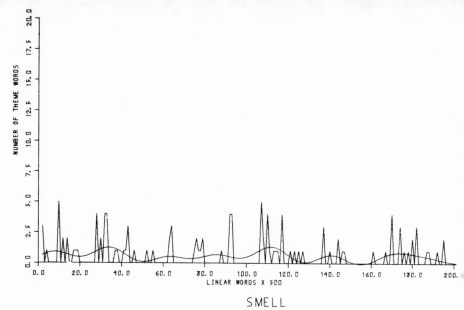

SMELL

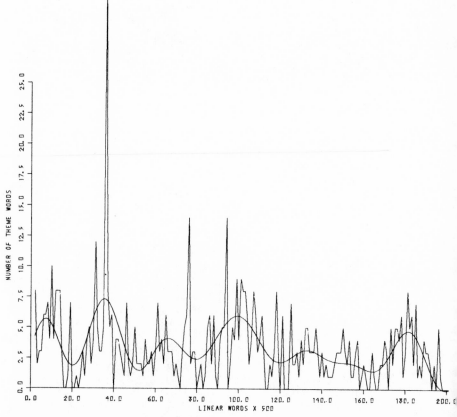

TACTILE

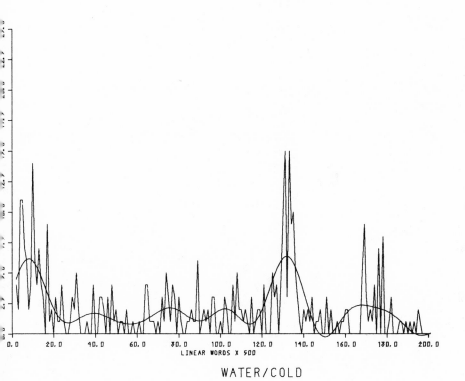

WATER/COLD

Notes

NOTES TO CHAPTER 1

1. Typical is Barabara Seward's discussion of the group of images associated with rose. She successfully draws our attention to the number of Dantesque parallels found in *Portrait;* however, her allegorical approach forces her into overly restrictive generalization. For example, she states that the young Stephen's childhood prattling, "the green wothe botheth," indicates his

> incipient creativity, and by positing a green rose he is creating in imagination that which does not exist elsewhere. As a flower whose colour is that of Ireland and whose creation is dependent upon Stephen's imagination, the green rose of the child's initial artistic effort acts as a symbolic foreshadowing of the young man's final determination "to forge in the smithy of my soul the uncreated conscience of my race" ("The Artist and the Rose," *University of Toronto Quarterly,* reprinted by Thomas E. Connolly, *Joyce's Portrait: Criticisms and Critiques* [New York: Appleton-Century-Croft, 1962], pp. 167–82).

She observes further:

> Green is suggestive of fertility and therefore of potentiality, but at the same time implies present unripeness or immaturity (*ibid.*).

The association between green and unripeness, while strong in the early chapters, diminishes and is replaced by a different link later in *Portrait.*

2. William York Tindall, *A Reader's Guide to James Joyce* (New York: The Noonday Press, 1962), pp. 85–86.

3. "The Portrait in Perspective," *James Joyce: Two Decades of Criticism,* ed. Seon Givens (New York: Vanguard Press, 1948). Reprinted by Connolly, p. 39.

4. *Ibid.*, p. 38.

5. James Joyce, *A Portrait of the Artist as a Young Man* (New York:

The Viking Press, 1968), p. 212. All future references to *Portrait* are from this edition, and page numbers will be given in the text.

6. Frank Kermode, *The Romantic Image* (New York: Vintage Books, 1964), p. 1.

7. *Ibid.*, p. 2.

8. *Ibid.*

9. Arthur Symons, *The Symbolist Movement in Literature* (New York: E. P. Dutton & Co., 1958), p. 2.

10. *Ibid.*, pp. 2–3.

11. Walter Pater, *The Renaissance* (London: Macmillan and Co., 1914) p. 236.

12. *Ibid.*, p. 237.

13. We can, of course, note sources and influences in Joyce's writings, but we cannot view this aesthetic as coming from any single tradition. This point has been emphasized by Maurice Beebe in discussing the importance of the liberties Joyce takes with his Thomistic materials. See "Joyce and Aquinas: The Theory of Aesthetics," *Philological Quarterly* (January 1957). Reprinted by Connolly, pp. 272–89.

14. James Joyce, *Stephen Hero* (New York: New Directions Press, 1963), p. 213.

15. A. D. Hope, "The Esthetic Theory of James Joyce," *Australasian Journal of Psychology and Philosophy* 21 (December 1943). Reprinted in Connally, pp. 200–201.

16. Alfred North Whitehead, "Objects and Subjects," *Adventure of Ideas* (New York: The New American Library, 1933), p. 178.

17. *Ibid.*, p. 180.

18. *Ibid.*, p. 179.

19. *Ibid.*, p. 181.

20. It should be noted that there is considerable difference in opinion concerning the term *epiphany*. Robert Scholes has argued that the term should be reserved for the specific genre of which there are forty extant epiphanies out of the seventy-one Joyce is known to have written. Sidney Feshbach, however, points out that the definition given by Joyce emphasizes the process of aesthetic apprehension (*PMLA* 87 (March 1972): 304–6). To limit the term today to only the genre would seem overly restrictive, for Joyce himself modified the epiphanies of the notebooks when he included them in his formal writings; second, to exclude from consideration passages not among the epiphanies of the notebook ignores the fact that almost half of those written by Joyce have been lost. Consequently, I have used the term to refer to passages in the text and the resulting phenomenological experiences for Stephen that conform to the definition given in chapter 5—not to only those passages identified as epiphanies in the notebooks.

21. Caroline Spurgeon, *Shakespeare's Imagery and What It Tells Us*

(Boston: Beacon Press, 1961), p. 5. I do not agree with Spurgeon's biographical interpolations, but her definition of image and her subsequent analytic techniques unquestionably open up the work of literature for close textual examination.

22. This definition of *image* is similar to Caroline Spurgeon's. Since Stephen substitutes *image* in *Portrait* for *epiphany* in *Stephen Hero,* I shall distinguish between sensory image and epiphanic Image by capitalizing the latter. Whenever possible, I have simply reverted to the earlier term, *epiphany,* when indicating this concept.

NOTES TO CHAPTER 3

1. Care must be taken not to overemphasize the importance of statistical measures such as frenquency of occurrence. Low-frequency images or even images that appear only once during the novel will be seen to be particularly important at the epiphanic moments in *Portrait;* however, if we consider tendencies over a broad spectrum of images, those which occur more frequently generally seem to play more important, substantive roles than those which appear less frequently.

2. Figure 3.4 does not represent a formally defined mapping of images. The purpose of the graph is to show the pattern of transitions between major clusters of images; therefore, points on the graph usually represent clusters, not individual images. Also, the vertical ordering is arbitrary and large vertical displacements have no formal meaning. The horizontal axis represents the text considered linearly from the beginning of 1.2 to its end.

3. This cluster is developed by the principal component analysis program, described in Appendix A.41. So strong, in fact, is this grouping that it ranked third among factors developed after the hot/cold factor and a highly significant factor concerning the pandybat episode, yet to be discussed. See Appendix D.1 for a specific listing of this factor.

4. The process of fusion is further emphasized by another aspect of the imagery of this experience. One of the strongest factors developed by the principal component analysis procedure was the following cluster of images associated with the panybat episode:

> .850 pain
> .754 sound
> .716 sleeve
> .643 tear
> .597 pandybat
> .528 hand
> .455 loud

Apparent in this grouping is the very strong link between images of pain, associated with hand and the pandybat, and the loud sound that the bat makes. There is virtually synesthetic fusion of the tactile and auditory senses—just as there has been a fusion of the thematic associations of images.

NOTES TO CHAPTER 5

1. See Appendix E for distribution of this group.

NOTES TO CHAPTER 6

1. The dominance of religious imagery in this section is evident in Appendix E. The level of intensity of these images, constant through Chapter III, is maintained through section 4.1.

2. This pattern of creation has been operative since the first page of the novel. There, Stephen took the words of a song and rearranged them in terms of their sounds. This act is trivial until the "creation" is examined for meaning or formalized into action.

3. The importance of the auditory as the fundamental epistemic sense for Stephen—and perhaps Joyce—is strongly suggested by the references to Stephen's weak eyesight, implying increased awareness of the auditory dimension of experience.

NOTES TO CHAPTER 7

1. The images of priest, temple, and the staff that Stephen carries, and the fact that Stephen is looking up at the patterns of the birds' flight all suggest a parallel between Stephen's search for vocation and the ancient Roman Augurs' method of prognostication based on signs read from birds.

2. Emanuel Swedenborg, *Heaven and Hell,* trans. Samuel Noble (New York: American Swedenborg Printing and Publishing Society, 1872), p. 43. See there and following for a detailed discussion of Swedenborg's correspondence theories.

NOTES TO APPENDIX A

1. For most of the programs used in Phase One, I am endebted to Sally Yeates Sedelow for allowing me to modify and use her Automated Language Analysis Package.

2. A tape storage unit for the computer is much like the familiar sound tape recorder. Information is stored on the tape in the form of magnetic impulses that are "written" and "read" with heads similar to those on a tape recorder. To read any portion of a tape, however, the computer must begin at the beginning and read until it finds the desired information.

3. John B. Smith, "RATS; A Middle-Level Text Utility System," *Computers and the Humanities* 6, no. 5 (May 1972): 277–83.

4. The specific program I used is one from a catalogue of procedures maintained by Elliot Cramer and the U.N.C. Psychometric Laboratory; there are numerous factor analytic programs available and most computation centers provide them with documentation explaining their use.

5. The discussion of principal component analysis is intuitive and is intended for the reader with limited mathematical background. For a rigorous development of the model, see Harry H. Harman, *Modern Factor Analysis* (Chicago: The University of Chicago Press, 1967).

SELECTED BIBLIOGRAPHY

Beebe, Maurice. "Joyce and Aquinas: The Theory of Aesthetics." *Philogical Quarterly* 36 (January 1957): 20–35. Reprinted in Connolly, pp. 272–89.

Connolly, Thomas E. *Joyce's Portrait: Criticisms and Critiques.* New York: Appleton-Century-Crofts, 1962.

Feshbach, Sidney. "Hunting Epiphany-Hunters." *PMLA* 87 (March 1972): 304–5.

Harman, Harry H. *Modern Factor Analysis.* Chicago: The University of Chicago Press, 1967.

Hope, A. D. "The Esthetic Theory of James Joyce." *Australasian Journal of Psychology and Philosophy* 21 (December 1943): 93–114. Reprinted in Connolly, pp. 183–203.

Joyce, James. *A Portrait of the Artist as a Young Man.* New York: The Viking Press, 1968.

———. *Stephen Hero.* New York: New Directions Press, 1963.

Kenner, Hugh. "The *Portrait* in Perspective." *James Joyce: Two Decades of Criticism,* edited by Sean Givens. New York: Vanguard Press, 1948, pp. 132–74. Reprinted in Connolly, pp. 25–60.

Kermode, Frank. *The Romantic Image.* New York: Vintage Books, 1964.

Pater, Walter, *The Renaissance: Studies in Art and Poetry.* London: MacMillan and Co., 1914.

Seward, Barbara. "The Artist and the Rose." *University of Toronto Quarterly* 26 (January 1957): 180–90. Reprinted in Connolly, pp. 167–80.

Smith, John B. "RATS: A Middle-Level Text Utility System." *Computers and the Humanities* 6 (May 1972): 277–83.

Spurgeon, Caroline. *Shakespeare's Imagery and What It Tells Us.* Boston: Beacon Press, 1961.

Swedenborg, Emanuel. *Heaven and Hell.* Translated by Samuel Noble. New York: American Swedenborg Printing and Publishing Society, 1872.

Symons, Arthur. *The Symbolist Movement in Literature.* New York: E. P. Dutton & Co., 1958.

Tindall, William York. *A Readers Guide to James Joyce.* New York: The Noonday Press, 1962.

Whitehead, Alfred North. *The Adventure of Ideas.* New York: The New American Library, 1933.

Index